Above *the* Pigsty

by Peter Van Essen

Von Essen 2016

 FriesenPress

Suite 300 - 990 Fort St
Victoria, BC, Canada, V8V 3K2
www.friesenpress.com

Library and Archives Canada Cataloguing in Publication

Van Essen, Peter, 1922-, author
      Above the pigsty / Peter Van Essen.

Issued in print and electronic formats.
ISBN 978-1-4602-6777-6 (bound).--ISBN 978-1-4602-6778-3 (paperback).--
ISBN 978-1-4602-6779-0 (ebook)

      1. Van Essen, Peter, 1922-. 2. World War, 1939-1945--Personal narratives, Dutch. 3. Netherlands--History--
German occupation, 1940-1945. 4. World War, 1939-1945--Netherlands. 5. Aalten (Netherlands)--Biography.
I. Title.

D811.5.V34 2015   940.54'81492   C2015-903522-8
                                                     C2015-903523-6

ISBN
978-1-4602-6777-6 (Hardcover)
978-1-4602-6778-3 (Paperback)
978-1-4602-6779-0 (eBook)

1. Biography & Autobiography, Personal Memoirs

Distributed to the trade by The Ingram Book Company

CONTENTS

DEDICATION

Dedicated to the memory of the Dutch citizens who supported the resistance movement from 1940 to 1945 and to the memory of the Canadians who came with the Allied troops to liberate the Netherlands in 1944 and 1945. Thank you for my freedom.

ACKNOWLEDGEMENT

I would like to thank my family members who helped make this book possible in so many ways: Dela Wilkins for taking the original typed pages to create computer documents, then editing it all down to a manageable book, Miranda Van Essen for her thoughtful illustrations to highlight the diary entries, Robin Cook for editing and proof reading, and other family members who shared photos and documents to enhance the book contents, who shared technical expertise for long distance collaboration, and who supported the process in so many ways.

INTRODUCTION

When I went into hiding during World War II, I had no idea what I would experience. I envisioned sitting in a semi-dark attic at an isolated farm. It turned out to be very different, and I was able to move about quite freely and work my heart out!

The people I met were unbelievable. Unselfish, helpful, courageous and God-fearing. I am thankful to all of them: farmer Oom Herman ter Horst who took me in, his family, relatives, and neighbours. The farm *de Koekoek* was a safe shelter, both physically and emotionally.

This book tells my own story, one *onderduiker* of an estimated 330,000 people in hiding in the Netherlands during the war. No two stories will be the same. Each person experiences and deals with the difficulties facing them in their own way. Going into hiding was considered an act of resistance to the enemy. The town of Aalten, with a population of 13,000, sheltered more than 2,500 *onderduikers*, perhaps the highest per capita in the country.

Keeping a diary during the occupation by the Nazis was illegal, punishable by death or being sent to a concentration camp. So was listening to the radio, or even owning a radio. We did it anyway.

When I translated my diaries into English, it was difficult to translate some words and phrases, as there is no English equivalent for some common Dutch words such as *gezellig*. At the back of the book there is a list of Dutch words and abbreviations which are used in the book.

Every farm had a name, but it was not the same as the last name of the farmer. Farmer Houwers lived on farm *Neerhof.* Farmer Neerhof lived at farm *Nooitgedacht.* There were some farms with the same name; farmer Eppink also lived on a farm called *Nooitgedacht* which was in a different section of the area called Dale. There is an illustration at the back of the book showing the location of the farms around *de Koekoek*.

During the war there was a great need for secrecy in order to protect other people. One example of this was an *onderduiker's* name: the name he was known by might be his real first name, a short form of his name (Lies' name was actually Cornelis), or a nickname. We would not always know his real last name, his place of origin or where he was in hiding. Even today, seventy years after liberation, I do not know where my friend Frans de Vries was hiding in Aalten, even though we visited each other often after the war.

It might seem that the distances we had to travel during the war were longer than the map shows today. A trip between Aalten and Driebergen today is about 107 kilometres. During the war the trip could be 150 kilometres or more, depending on the safety of the route and the access to bridges across the rivers. Travelling by bicycle added to the duration of the trip, with the need to plan overnight stops to sleep at a safe place.

Living under wartime conditions continued for a long time after the war ended. There were still travel restrictions, railway tracks in disrepair, rations, shortages of food and clothing, and homes unsuitable for living because of damage by bombs and fires.

I originally intended this story as a family record for my grandchildren and great grandchildren. What I did not expect was the interest that this story generated beyond the circle of family and friends. Many have told me that reading these words have given them a better understanding of both the suffering of the Dutch people in war time and also the overwhelming thankfulness of the Dutch to the Canadians who liberated them.

Peter Van Essen
2015

GROWING UP IN APELDOORN

Imagine growing up across from the beautiful park and gardens of the royal palace and then having to spend two years hiding in a pig barn during the 1940s. The direction of my life was influenced strongly by my family relationships, a strong personal faith, and deep loyalty to the Queen of the Netherlands.

Our family van Essen originally comes from the hamlet Elspeet in the Veluwe, in the province of Gelderland. Van Essen is a common name in the Netherlands; it means from the low area. Not all van Essens are related to each other. My family is known for being short in stature, but not as short as the *kleine* van Essens, who were even shorter than us.

My paternal grandfather, Hendrik van Essen, married Nenna Teunissen in 1884. My father was the oldest of the seven boys and one girl in the family. Following in their father Hendrik's footsteps, the brothers Gerrit, Teun, Dirk and Frits all worked for the *Paleis Het Loo*, the palace in Apeldoorn, in different areas: the gardens and greenhouses, the forest, parkland and wildlife area, the farms, masonry and brickwork. Dirk later became head of the silver room. Teun's wife, Dina, worked in the linen chamber at the palace. Most of our van Essen relatives lived on the same street, the Wieselseweg, or on one of the side roads adjacent to the park area of *Paleis Het Loo*.

As parents aged and needed assistance in daily living, it was the custom for the parents to move in with the eldest son. *Opa and Opoe* lived with our family for a number of years.

One of the Queen's customs was to pay an occasional visit to her retired personnel. These visits were arranged by a security staff person a few days ahead of time. Since the Queen came by car, the security person would sit beside the chauffeur and wait with him in the front seat.

One time when we were quite small, my older brother Gerrit and I decided to experience part of such a visit. It was during the holidays. The two of us hid under the table and pulled the big tablecloth further down on one side. When mother got up out of her chair at one point, she spotted us, grabbed us by our ears, and ordered us outside. I am not sure what the Queen thought about that!

Before the Queen left she would hand Opa a royal gift. Usually it was two rijksdaalders, each worth two and one-half guilders. That was more than half a week's wages in those days. Opoe would get a tin with Deventer *koek* or a package of Douwe Egberts coffee. Both companies had the right to advertise they were *hofleverancier*, provider of food and supplies to the royal family.

Often my grandparents would get something the Queen herself had knit. Queen Wilhelmina had two hobbies - painting and knitting. She knit often and turned out a lot of items. Once she gave Opoe a scarf made from 6-ply wool. It was big and it was heavy. My brother Gerrit could wind it around his neck twice and both ends would still drag over the floor. The scarf ended up in the textile box in our attic. We put things into this box that were not intended for immediate use, but that would come in handy later.

My maternal grandfather, Peter Peppelenbos married Janna Koldenhof in 1883 and they had three children. My mother, born in 1884, was the oldest. Her brother Teunis (Wout) died at a young age and younger sister Jansje never married. After Peter died, Janna married Harmen Gerritsen and had two more sons, Hendrik and Willem. Harmen Gerritsen also worked at the palace, in the gardens and the woods.

Gerrit van Essen and Hermina (Mina) Hendrika Peppelenbos, my parents, were both born in November 1884 *achter in Wiesel*. We called it the back of Wiesel. Wiesel is about 4 kilometres from the centre of Apeldoorn. Young Gerrit and Mina often met for conversations on a small wooden bridge near the Wieselseweg. Mina was coming home from her night shift work at the children's hospital, and Gerrit was going to his day job at the palace. After they were married in 1907, they built their home on the vacant land beside *de*

Plankenbrugge. Gerrit and Mina had nine children: Nenna, Jannie, Henk, twins Teun and Bep, Miep, Gerrit, Peter and Nen.

Gerrit and Mina, 1905.

During his lifetime, my father Gerrit worked at the palace *Het Loo* for over 50 years, serving three queens: Queen Emma (regent), Queen Wilhelmina and Queen Julianna (regent). Our home was on the Wieselseweg, directly across from the palace forest.

As family members of employees of the palace, we were allowed to take walks in the royal gardens and parks. The swimming pond was open for boys only (no change rooms) from seven to eight o'clock every evening in the summer, and there was a large rink for ice skating in the winter.

Apeldoorn, Paleis 't Loo (The Palace)

The palace was a popular illustration for writing paper in Apeldoorn.

We loved to listen to my father tell stories about his youth and his work at the palace.

My father was the oldest of eight children. In 1889, when he was about 5 years old, he started to help with some chores, mostly feeding the chickens, the pigs, and the goats. At age six, Gerrit was old enough to go with his family to work in the *Meibos*, a wooded area with hundreds and hundreds of young oak trees ready for harvest. The adults used sharp axes to create row after row of felled trees. The younger folks hacked off all the branches so the only thing left were trunks. Piled up into neat heaps, these trunks awaited a severe beating with a big stick all around the bark, from top to bottom. This loosened the bark so it could be easily removed and transported to the tanneries. The acid in the bark was used to treat all kinds of leather products.

The family practically lived in the woods during this harvest time. Living off the land was still the most honourable way to provide for a family. Opa and Opoe would take all the children and load up the wheelbarrow with bags of flour and other long-lasting ingredients. Several goats were taken in tow and some families would also carry a few baskets with chickens. Out in the woods each family would dig a hole for a living space. They covered the hole with tree-trunks and sod. That would do for the summer.

When the harvest was finished the family moved back home. My father Gerrit attended the Koningsschool in Apeldoorn. This school was built in 1851 and opened on May 3, 1852 under the assignment of King Willem the Third, husband of Queen Emma. The students who attended this boys-only school were all sons of the employees of the palace *Het Loo*.

Gerrit's father, Hendrik van Essen, worked at *Het Loo* for many years in the forestry division. In 1896 Gerrit, at age 12, began his first job at the big farm at *Het Loo* in the milk chamber. One of his duties was to deliver milk products to the palace kitchen. Milk, cream, butter and buttermilk were neatly packed in a silver box that was securely locked with a key. After Gerrit had carefully hung the strap of the box around his neck, he took it to the kitchen area at the palace. There the box was received by the man in charge, who opened it with his own key to empty it. Gerrit then brought the empty box back to the farm. He loved nature and enjoyed these walks. He learned a lot about trees and shrubs and this knowledge came in handy later in his life.

Around that time a hunting party found six motherless foxes in very bad shape. Princess Wilhelmina heard about it and wanted to save the baby foxes. Gerrit was asked to assist the Princess by helping to feed the six orphans. After a few months of feeding, the foxes were released back into the woods. I think this time together created a certain bond between the Princess and young Gerrit. Gerrit was a strong supporter of the Dutch royal family, and would continue to work for the palace for over 50 years, until he retired in 1949.

One of Gerrit's next jobs was looking after the ponies of the Princess. Horses and carriages were kept in perfect shape and ready at any time for a drive through the beautiful woods. The horses were cleaned and brushed upon return; the wagons were washed and polished in their own building annex. When a horse or favourite dog died, it was buried in a special cemetery, one for horses, and another for dogs. Each grave has a stone with the name, date of birth and date of death of the animal.

Some of the lower-ranked employees were occasionally assigned to take their turn as security guards. After the regular work day they were hastily dressed into their uniform, a blue coverall to cover their daily working clothes. They kept their own caps and wooden shoes on, but were given a rifle to carry. Their duty was to patrol the area around all the buildings. Gerrit was then about 25 years old.

My father was also an *imker*. He looked after the beehives at the palace and also kept hives at home. Once my brother and I saw what looked like a pineapple hanging from a tree and ran to tell our dad. Father managed to find hives for this swarm as they were looking for a new home.

Wieselseweg 54, De Plankenbrugge, in 2010.

I, Peter van Essen, am the second youngest child in this family of five girls and four boys. I was born at the house on the Wieselseweg on 15 January 1922. My oldest sister Nenna died in 1921 at age 12, before I was born. My mother died in 1939 of cancer, but my father and most of my siblings lived to be 90 or older.

Some memories from my childhood and youth 1922 to 1939:

Having my picture taken for the first time, 1924.

Sitting under the living room table during a hurricane, August 1925. The nearby town Borculo was severely damaged.

Receiving books for my birthday, 1927. I still have these first books, a story book and a drawing book.

Turning the handle on the grindstone while my father sharpened our home-made skates.

I was enrolled at the Koningsschool in May 1928. Age 6 years, student #1457.

Peter, second from left.

Learning to play the harmonica, 1928.

Receiving a book called *Peerke en zijn kameraden* at Sunday school, 1929.

In 1930, we had to start writing at the very top line of our school exercise book to save money on paper.

Winning a book, *De Gekantelde Karos*, as a prize in an essay contest, 1935.

Picking *bosbessen* in July to earn money for my bicycle licence. Cost of the licence: two and a half guilders. Blueberries sold for 4 or 5 cents a Dutch *pond*. It took 10 to 12 days to earn enough for the licence.

Helping with the wash. We had a wheelbarrow with a wooden tub and I often turned the hand wringer. Clothes were rinsed in the creek across the road and then hung on a clothesline in the side yard.

My grade seven soccer team won the silver medal when I was captain in 1935. A picture of our team is in the 2002 Koningsschool commemorative book. I wore my older brother Henk's hand-me-down soccer shoes, which were so big that I had to wear two pairs of socks in them so they would not fly off my feet.

Visiting Schiphol on a school trip and having our picture taken beside the plane called *Ekster*.

Having a tinplate photo taken on a visit to Amsterdam. It was the mid-nineteen thirties, depression time. Everything was cheap, but nobody had any money.

Princess Julianna visiting our geography class, 1935.

In grade seven and eight we had to study the French language. This was a leftover custom from the French occupation of the Netherlands during the eighteenth century.

Starting my first job at age 14, in 1936. I earned one guilder per week (about 40 cents Canadian).

Playing in a harmonica orchestra as a teenager, 1937.

Getting my first new suit, 1939. The cost was 16 guilders; I paid 10 guilders down and the balance in monthly installments. Before this I only wore hand-me-downs.

Visiting our neighbours at New Year's to eat *oliebollen* and *appelflappen*. These deep-fried pastries were a once-a-year treat. We knew exactly which neighbour had the nicest *oliebollen* and Tante Dina made delicious *appelflappen*.

Before 1940 there was no electricity at our house, therefore we had no vacuum cleaner, electric kettle, toaster, washing machine, tape recorder, record player, C.D. player, computer, or television. We had no running water and therefore no bathtub or shower. Only a few homes had a telephone. We did not own a camera. What we did have was gas for lights and for cooking, a pump outside for cold water, brooms for cleaning floors and a *teil* to take a bath, on Saturday only. The bath water had to be heated over a fire.

Competition for business was strong in the 1930s. Stores would do almost anything to keep their customers. Many businesses came door-to-door to make deliveries or pick up items for repairs. Not just groceries, milk, bread, fruits and vegetables, but also umbrellas, shoe repair and even chair repairs were part of this service.

A few special people came by our house almost weekly; the one I remember best is Zwartje, the fish-man. He had a white horse, and a red wagon with a big white tarp, like a covered wagon. We called him *Zwartje* because of his white horse. He travelled the 30 kilometres overnight from Harderwijk on the shore of the Zuider Zee with a load of fish that had just arrived. The local fishermen would return to the harbour by Friday afternoon and Zwartje would be in Apeldoorn on Saturday morning. Mother would usually buy one or two pails of herring. Sometimes three or four pails if my aunt Eef, who lived on the Houtentorenweg, wanted some. The back of our house had a dark green trapdoor in the upper part of the house and we would hang a large white cloth against this trapdoor to indicate to my aunt that fish had arrived. One of their children would come down to pick up their portion. When Zwartje came back from his vending mission into town, he was often invited to stop for a coffee. If he had any fish left over, mother was welcome to take what she wanted. The herring was baked or fried in oil and tasted delicious. Any leftover baked fish was put on a large platter and generously sprinkled with vinegar. These leftovers tasted even better the next day.

The ice cream man, Joop de Lange, was another vendor that came by once in a while. Not every week like Zwartje; we could not afford to buy ice cream that often. But on occasion we were allowed to stop Joop as he came by. We were lucky if we received enough money to buy one ice cream each. Most times we had to share one between the two or three of us. After all they were not cheap, four or five cents each.

POLITICS AND WAR 1931-1943

The Dutch Nazi Party, *Nationaal-Socialistische Beweging in Nederland (NSB)*, was formed in 1931 as a political party. In 1939 Germany invaded Poland. The Netherlands wanted to stay neutral as they had been in the first World War. Hitler gave a radio message on May 9, 1940 that Germany would respect our neutrality. However, his troops were already positioned at our border. The next day, on May 10, German soldiers crossed the border into the Netherlands, the movement supported by many airplanes. Our army was not prepared, but fought fearlessly for five days, then surrendered. Dutch soldiers became prisoners of war (POWs). They were shipped to Germany by train and later released. After about one year, they were recalled back to Germany to become POWs again. When this happened, many did not report back, went into hiding, or simply stayed at home hoping for the best. Hiding at that time meant going to stay with a relative in another town. Others escaped to England and worked with the Allies.

Prior to 1940 many Jews fled out of Germany into the Netherlands to escape an uncertain future in Germany. Now we started hearing stories of Jews drowning themselves in the canals of Amsterdam and others taking their own lives by other means. Apparently they knew what awaited them when Germany occupied the Netherlands.

Although things were not too bad in the beginning, it gradually became worse. Everything was rationed, from soup to nuts. Trucks and cars were converted to run on wood. A burner was attached to the vehicle; this was filled with small chunks of wood that created a gas to run the vehicle. For the driver and a helper, this meant getting up very early every morning to stoke the car.

The Netherland's borders were now closed too, and there was no import of many of the most necessary items. Factories closed for lack of raw materials, which in turn caused massive layoffs.

1941: Jews were given a curfew and were forced to wear a special identification mark, a yellow Star of David with the word *Jood*. Many places posted signs saying: *Verboden voor Jooden*. At first Christian Jews were left alone, but not for long. They too were forced to wear the Star of David. No Jew was allowed to have a radio, a bicycle, or a watch. In the church where I helped as an usher, a Christian Jew, Mr. Blaauw, attended the evening services. His curfew was 8 p.m. Church started at seven in the evening. Whenever he was in church, he asked me to warn him when it was quarter to eight so that he could leave and make it home in time for his curfew. I learned later that this man died in a concentration camp.

1942: Jews were shipped out to Auschwitz in Poland and other concentration camps in Germany. Some were also sent to a newly created camp in Westerbork, the Netherlands.

1943: In Apeldoorn there was a large Jewish Psychiatric Hospital called the *Jodenbosch*. All of the patients, physicians, nurses and staff were shipped to Germany and Poland in railroad cattle cars in January 1943.

Dominee Frits Slomp was a preacher who was very outspoken about the atrocities committed by the Germans. He got into trouble for some of his activities. He had been helping some men go into hiding. He was arrested by the Germans, but escaped and went into hiding himself. He became known throughout the country as Frits *de Zwerver*. He travelled to the *Achterhoek* where he contacted a Mrs. Kuipers in Winterswijk. She urged him to become a travelling preacher, visiting different churches and arranging meetings to inform and encourage people to get involved in helping the Jewish people and the *onderduikers*. She became known as Tante Riek. Mr. Hendrik Jan Wikkerink from Aalten was also an early contact and became known as Ome Jan, leader of the Resistance movement in the *Achterhoek*.

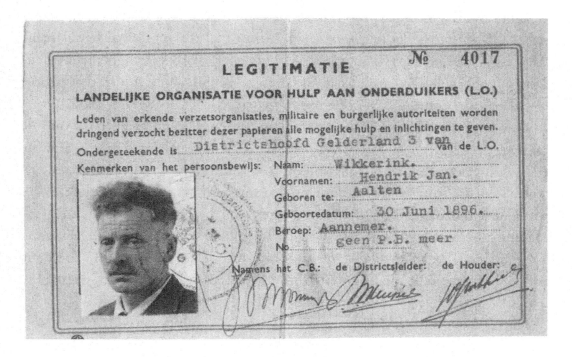

LEGITIMATIE № 4017

LANDELIJKE ORGANISATIE VOOR HULP AAN ONDERDUIKERS (L.O.)

Leden van erkende verzetsorganisaties, militaire en burgerlijke autoriteiten worden dringend verzocht bezitter dezer papieren alle mogelijke hulp en inlichtingen te geven.

Ondergeteekende is Districtshoofd Gelderland 3 van de L.O.

Kenmerken van het persoonsbewijs:

Naam: Wikkerink.
Voornamen: Hendrik Jan.
Geboren te: Aalten
Geboortedatum: 30 Juni 1896.
Beroep: Aannemer.
No geen P.B. meer

Namens het C.B.: de Districtsleider: de Houder:

L.O. permit of Ome Jan Wikkerink.

About this time, January 1943, the L.O. organization was born. L.O. stands for *Landelijke Organisatie voor hulp aan Onderduikers*. However, it was nearly April when we heard the first rumours about its existence.

During this time, I still lived at home with my father, my younger sister Nen (born in 1924), and my next older brother Gerrit (born in 1920). The older siblings were married or working elsewhere. Nen took care of the housekeeping, cooking, and laundry. Brother Gerrit and I, together with Dad, looked after the financial end of things. The mortgage on the house was one of these commitments, and I made the regular payments at the *Boerenleenbank*. Gerrit was employed by a local barber. In early 1943, Gerrit was forced to report for work in Germany.

The German occupation effectively stopped all imports into our country. The two to three month inventory of raw materials in factories was soon used up, resulting in many lay-offs. Because I worked in the shipping department at Heijmeijer, I was kept on at work until the fall of 1940.

From the beginning of the war we had a complete blackout after dark. No street lights; homes had black paper in front of all the windows. It was really dark especially on starless and moonless nights. Our bicycle lights had blackout paper as well; only a small slit to let enough light shine out so that people could see you coming, but not enough to see where you were going.

One night, as I left the office, I had an accident. It was very dark outside and my eyes had not adjusted yet from light to dark. I started biking anyway. I knew my way. Suddenly I smashed into something. An old cargo truck was parked on the side of the road directly in my path. My bike was stuck under the truck, the handlebars and steering column bent out of shape. I hit the loading platform of the truck with my face, and was bleeding. It hurt and I was dizzy. A store owner came running outside to help me. He took me inside and gave me some first aid. Others helped to free the bike out of the grip of the truck.

How I came home is still unknown to me. We did not have a phone, so I assume that I walked the approximately 40-minute distance home. The bike got fixed and I healed.

Some empty buildings near the railroad station were converted into office space and workshops for unemployed people. The *Arbeidsbureau* supplied instructors and teachers. I signed up for a course in bookkeeping, free of charge. A former colleague from Heijmeijer, Henk Slijkhuis, and I decided to make a real effort with our studies.

The classroom was noisy and often outright wild. Many of the young men were quite immature. You had to protect your belongings from being ripped-up, stolen or damaged. Sponges drenched in water or ink flew in all directions. We complained to Mr. Rood, the Director, and were given another small room where we could work quietly.

One morning Mr. Rood came in to talk to us. He had a request from the *Arbeidsbureau* for an office worker and wanted to give Henk and me first chance for an interview. Although it was only temporary, I got the job. Later City Hall needed additional help and I got an interview there.

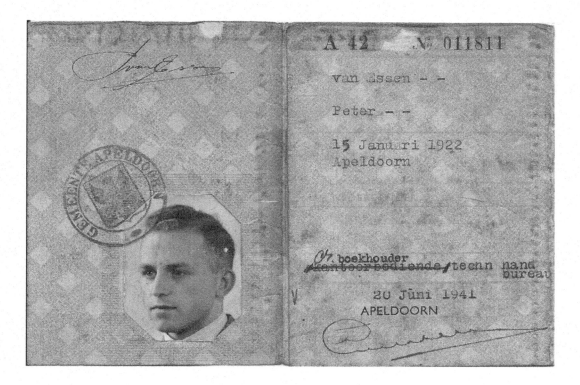

Peter van Essen identity card.

My temporary job at City Hall was mainly issuing personal identity cards. I noticed an ad in the local newspaper about van Reekum Handelsmaatschappij. They were looking for an assistant bookkeeper. When I was hired, I was assured of a steady job. Unknown to me, the owner of this company was a member of the National Socialist Movement in the Netherlands, the NSB. He sympathized with the Germans.

In March 1943, at the age of 21, I received the first request to register at the *Arbeidsbureau* in Apeldoorn, now under German control. Germany needed all available manpower to work in their factories, shops, and farms. Their own men were needed by their army and were sent off to fight the war. The only way to replace these labour forces was to order the available men in occupied countries to register and then ship them off to Germany.

Since I did not want to go to work for the enemy, I did not register. A second request did not help me change my mind and neither did a third. Now it became more difficult to stay at home. However, where was I to go?

Through the grapevine I heard that there was a secret organization trying to help young men to go into hiding. Of course nobody could give you the name or names of the people involved. Towards the end of May 1943, I came home from the office and found that another letter had arrived from manpower. This time it was more serious: **Register within a week or we will pick you up and put you in a concentration camp.** I was glad for the warning, but also worried about what to do next.

After supper I went to my bedroom to pray about this terrible dilemma and to ask the Lord for guidance. Remembering the Bible story about Hezekiah in II Kings 19, who took the letter he received to the temple and spread it out before the Lord, I was encouraged to do the same. I put the letter on my bed while I prayed for an answer.

That same evening we had our weekly pre-confession class at church, from 7 to 8 p.m. A second group of young people had their class right after ours. As I came out of my class, two of the young men who were waiting outside called me over and said that their boss wanted to talk to me. I knew this gentleman, Henk Wolf, an accountant and a member of our church.

On my way home I dropped by to see him. His wife opened the door and showed me into the office. Moments later Mr. Wolf came in, looked me straight in the eyes and said, "If you have an opportunity to hide from the Germans, would you accept that?"

With tears in my eyes, I said, "Yes, I will." Then I told him that not even two hours ago I was praying for an answer. You can imagine my feelings of joy and gratitude. I biked home, thanking the Lord for His answer.

The next few days were kind of hectic. I registered at the *Arbeidsbureau*, did some shopping, finalized things here and there. I told Dad and my sister that I had registered but was not going to Germany. They did not understand this but were happy for me. I said they would hear later where I was and how I was doing.

The day I registered at the *Arbeidsbureau*, I did something that was probably not very nice. I knew the office layout inside out since I had worked there a few years earlier. It was very busy; many men were waiting to be registered. I wanted to use the bathroom, and since I knew where to go, I walked through the hallway. As I passed by the kitchen, I smelled some delicious food. On the stove was a large pot of stew. Nearby on the counter was a large container of soap. Now at that time there was no normal soap available. It looked like a mixture of sand, ashes, and some other strong-smelling ingredient. I took a large handful of this goo and dumped it into the pot on the stove. The stew started to change colour and a funny kind of suds appeared on the top. For me it was time to continue my trip to the bathroom. I presume that later in the day many others had to go in the same direction.

It was now only a matter of days and I would be shipped off to Germany. However, things were neatly organized to prevent this and to send me off in another direction. I was told by Mr. Wolf that my destination was the town of Aalten, in the *Achterhoek* district in the province of Gelderland. This is 65 kilometres from where I lived in Wiesel, but about 4 kilometres from the German border. I arranged to have my bike shipped in advance by train to Aalten so that I would have transportation on arrival.

ABOVE THE PIGSTY

JUNE 1943

Friday, June 25

Today I am supposed to leave for deportation to Germany with the D-train that leaves Apeldoorn at 8:37 a.m. As previously arranged, I have to be sure to miss this train. I will now go on the next train to Deventer that leaves at 9:30 a.m. and goes to Enschede. There the train for Germany will take us to our final destination.

At eight o'clock in the morning, I am waiting in an obscure hall close to the train station awaiting the arrival of the train. I can observe the platform and all the activities. Many men stand, grouped together, watched by three or four guards from the *Arbeidsbureau* who are there to make sure that all the men get on the train when it arrives. As the train leaves the station, I spring into action. I grab my suitcase and run to the station where I apologize for being too late. I missed the train! The guards from the *Arbeidsbureau* discuss how to solve this problem. I know the outcome already. Finally, it is agreed that one man will stay with me, wait for the next train, and put me on it with the instruction to get off in Enschede where the other men will be waiting to be transferred to a train heading for Germany. I will then have caught up with them and their list with names is complete. You should know that this man, who volunteered to stay with me, is also the one who suggested this plan of action and is one of the good guys. The others leave us alone and after about 15 or 20 minutes, the remaining guard says, "I think I explained well enough what you should do, and I see no need for me to wait any longer. Make sure you catch the next train." Then he hands me the train ticket to Germany. I assure him I will not miss the next train. We part company.

Trains in those days had three classes. Almost everyone travelled third class. In order to be alone, or at least not run the risk of finding myself in a car with another transport to Germany, I have taken the precaution of purchasing a second class ticket to Deventer. However, when I get into the second class car for this 20 minute trip, I end up sitting across from a lady officer of the *Jeugddienst*, an organization sympathetic to the Germans and organized for training young people in the principles of the National Socialistic movement of the Deutsche Reich. She is friendly and eager to talk. She is about my age and good looking. I do not agree with her politics and somehow I try to convey this to her, very carefully of course. Just before we stop in Deventer, I make it very clear what I think about her organization.

From Deventer I go to Zutphen on a train that leaves at 10:30 a.m. When I arrive in Zutphen I learn that there is no train to Aalten until 4:00 p.m. This is too long a wait, so I buy a ticket to Arnhem, and there I board the 1:00 p.m. train for Aalten.

Suddenly, the whole railcar fills with German soldiers. I feel very strange sitting here with my suitcase on my lap, the only civilian in this section. What have I done? How will this end?

The soldiers do not seem to notice me or pay any attention to me. It seems they are concerned about getting to their destination. Perhaps they are not even aware of the threats to me as a Dutchman if I try to evade deportation to Germany as instructed in my letter.

When I arrive at the train station in Aalten at three o'clock, I weigh myself. Big upright scales are located in stores and other public locations to help you keep an eye on your weight. Since I don't know how long I will be here and what the food will be like, I think it would be interesting to weigh myself now and again later when I go home. Just as a matter of curiosity. About 140 pounds or 127 Dutch *pond*.

I leave my suitcases at the station in Aalten and show my voucher for my bike that was shipped ahead and had arrived the day before. Unfortunately, the rear tire is flat. The reason I leave my suitcases at the station is that it would look very suspicious if all young men arriving in Aalten went biking through town with their suitcases, going to the same address. The secrecy would not be maintained very long.

The instructions I received were to go to Patrimoniumstraat 12. Follow the tracks and it will bring you right to this street. From the train station, tracks lead through various parts of the town. A small freight train delivers goods to the industrial area and the warehouses. Following the tracks makes it unnecessary for any *onderduiker* to ask for Ome Jan or for Patrimoniumstraat 12. That would raise suspicions again. The whole trip by bike takes about six minutes, not counting the four times that I have to stop to pump up the flat tire. The last time I could have skipped, because I am only four houses away from my destination. If only I had known.

I ring the doorbell and a young girl opens the door. She is mopping the floor in the hall. She looks cute, but her hair is a mess. Her hair sticks out in all directions because she has to bend over to mop the floor on her hands and knees. I say that I would like to speak to Ome Jan. She invites me in and directs me to the office. Shortly after, Mr. Jan Wikkerink, known as Ome

Jan, comes in to the office and I introduce myself, telling him that Mr. Henk Wolf has sent me. He then asks me a number of questions: where do you live, how old are you, what does your father do, and what church do you belong to. Of course, he already knows all these things about me, but just wants to make sure that I am the right person. He invites me into the front room and assures me that he will find a place for me to stay. It might take a few days, but don't worry.

When I enter the front room, I am surprised to see six other young men sitting there. I thought I would be the only one. Apparently this activity goes on day after day. After a little while all six of them leave, and only now do I dare to introduce myself to the two young ladies in the room, both daughters of Ome Jan. The oldest girl is Jo and the other is Henny, who is the one I saw in the hall. We have a conversation and a cup of tea. My stomach makes a little noise for I have not eaten all day. No problem, I have a few sandwiches in my travel bag and I start to eat one. Halfway through my sandwich we are called to the supper table, which is quite a relief. After supper I feel normal again. While here, I write a letter home to let them know that I have arrived safely.

When the dishes are done, Oom Johan, the butcher from the Dijkstraat, comes to pick me up. I will sleep at his place tonight. I meet his family and we talk until 11:45 in the evening. Then we hurry to bed.

Saturday, June 26

After a good hour of sleep they wake me up. The Tommies are coming. A Tommy is an Allied airplane on its way to bomb Germany. These planes only fly at night. Because Aalten is so close to the German border there is more danger here than there was in Apeldoorn. German fighter planes come to meet the Allied planes just before the Tommies enter into Germany. Spotlights search the sky and one plane is shot down. We find out later that the crew of five died. We spend the rest of the night in the shelter until about one hour before sunrise.

After breakfast I go back to Patrimoniumstraat. One of the Wikkerink sons, Gerrit, is going to one of the farms to get milk. He asks me if I want to come along. We get on our bikes and head for the farm called *Boerderij de Koekoek*.

I meet the farmer and his wife and they invite me to stay there for the day. "Because," says the farmer, "at the Wikker they are busy enough with all those *onderduikers*." Gerrit has to bike back home alone.

De Koekoek in 1943.

I am attracted to this place and its surroundings, it is very serene. I offer to help with whatever is to be done and so my first job is cleaning *druufkes bezen*. After this we pull up the tobacco plants. I notice that the garden needs weeding and I take care of that.

I pick up my suitcases at the train station and in the evening return to Oom Johan for a night's sleep.

Sunday, June 27

I had a very good sleep. At 3:00 p.m. I am back at *de Koekoek*; they want me to sleep there tonight. This family consists of Father, Mother, daughter and four sons. The daughter and the three oldest sons have jobs, while the youngest is still in high school. The farmer has six cows and a few pigs. There are some chickens running around but he has no horse. Most of the farm work is done manually, and for certain jobs he can borrow the neighbour's horse. The neighbour lives in the same house, a duplex farm, which is very rare. Thus, here are two farms under the same roof at *de Koekoek*. The neighbor is known as *den Eume*. Living quarters are in the front; behind this is a communal threshing floor, then, on either side, a very primitive bathroom. I would have called it an indoor outhouse. Behind this, also on either side, is the stable for the cows. Later, when we occasionally have a church service on the threshing floor, it is comical to hear the comments that come from the stable. Sometimes very fitting; a loud burp or moo.

This family has also given hospitality to Wim, a medical student from a university where students have revolted and strongly protested against the Nazi occupation. He offers me his bed to sleep in and he will sleep in the hay loft above the cow barn. I find time to write a letter to Mr. Wolf to thank him for his involvement.

Monday, June 28
Today I have to do some household chores. They find it too dangerous for me to work outside.

Tuesday, June 29
This morning we eat pancakes with bacon. Wow, is this ever nice. I receive an invitation from Henny Wikkerink to come to their home tomorrow night for her father's birthday party. Her sister Lien is the fiancée of Johan, one of the sons of farmer ter Horst. I decide not to go, for I hear they are very busy already.

Wednesday, June 30
We eat pancakes with bacon again. Today is Ome Jan's birthday. I learn that Mr. and Mrs. Wikkerink are called either Father and Mother Wikkerink or Ome Jan and Tante Dela.

Today is the first time ever that I milk a cow. Oom Herman, the farmer, says that Emma is the easiest cow to milk. She is 20 years old and all the farmer's children learned the art of milking by pulling Emma's strings. It works fairly well, only I cannot milk her clean yet. Oom Herman takes care of that.

JULY 1943

Thursday, July 1

I write two letters today, one to Mr. Wolf, the other home. The food here is really good; I eat like a horse.

Friday, July 2

I decide to let my moustache grow. Work around and in the house. All this unusual work makes me hungry. At supper time I eat four small plates of bean soup and two plates of oatmeal porridge. I have gained one and half Dutch *pond*.

Saturday, July 3

Spend the day cleaning around the house, and in the evening, cleaning myself.

Sunday, July 4

To church with the whole family, the *Westerkerk*.

Monday, July 5

Haying in 't Hof, the field behind the farmer's house.

I now have an address where my relatives can send mail. It is the farmer Jansen who lives two farms from here at *te Hennepe*. I write home to tell them they can send letters to Maria Jansen so the Jansens will know it is for me.

Tuesday, July 6

Work in the hayfield.

The crew of five that died in the plane crash is buried today in the *Nieuwe Kerkhof*.

Wednesday, July 7

One of the Resistance workers comes to talk to Oom Herman as we are working in the field. He is Willem Wikkerink, a distant relative of Ome Jan.

After a while Oom Herman comes back and Willem disappears on his bike. "He came for you," says Oom Herman. "He had a place for you to stay."

"Then why did he leave without me?" I asked.

"I told him you could stay here with us, if you would like to?" I assure him that I really like it here and am very grateful to him and his family for taking me in.

In the evening we attempt to do something very different. We want to catch a *torenvalk*. The five of us, Herman, son of the farmer, Wim, a student, Gerrit Wikkerink, Gerrit Driessen, grandson of a neighbour, and I set out for 't Goor. This is a piece of land claimed from a marshland and made into workable land. On our way there, Gerrit W. does not watch where he is going and rams his bike against a post along the bicycle path. He has no choice but to walk home. Gerrit D. is a terrific climber and goes high into a tree with a hawk's nest in it. He comes back with two young birds in his cap.

We keep one of the young hawks at our farm. In the *schoppe* we build a suitable cage where it can stay for a while. But now we have to feed it. We catch some mice and cut them up into small portions, hoping the hawk will eat them. No problem, the bird seems to be hungry. We get some more and more and more. We cannot keep up with this appetite and don't always have the mice to feed it. We start catching frogs and throw one into the cage. Does the hawk know how to handle this one? You bet! First, she picks out the eyes of the frog, and then starts on the insides.

We call the bird Ghandi. Don't ask me why.

After a few days we let her out of the cage and she comes running after us. It seems she is always hungry. When we offer her food, we first call to her, "Ghandi", and she comes hopping and running to get her treat. Later she comes flying toward us. It does not take long before she perches on the roof top of the barn or the house. Now some town's people get involved, especially old Mr. Wiggers from the bakery shop. They have heard about Ghandi and bring some mice. Children also come as enthusiastic spectators. It is amazing what Ghandi can do. I take a mouse in my hand and call Ghandi who is sitting on the house top. She sees me standing there, way below, swoops down and grabs the mouse out of my hand and is now sitting on the barn roof. I have not felt as much as a touch from her. Now I want to play a trick on her.

I take a mouse and hold it by the tail between my thumb and index finger, tightly. Stretching out my arm, I call Ghandi. I figure she will not be able to get this one. She gives a good shriek, swoops down and in no time is on top of the barn roof... with the mouse. I see now that I am hanging on to the mouse tail and skin only. In mid-air under my hand Ghandi swung upside down to grab her treat. This happened time and again.

Eventually Ghandi disappeared, first for a few days, then for good.

Thursday, July 8
Today is my brother Gerrit's birthday. He is in Germany. He is almost two years older than I and was forced to go to work there before I came into hiding.

Friday, July 9

During the night there are many Allied planes which we call Tommies. The farmer learns that the Germans are searching for *onderduikers* and he wakes us up to go and hide someplace else. From midnight until 6 a.m. we stay in an old shed about five minutes walking distance from the farm.

The warning system seems to be highly organized. Often the German *Schutzstaffel* (S.S.) raids the towns. The S.S. is stationed in Arnhem. Somehow word comes from these headquarters that the S.S. is fanning out in a certain direction, say, easterly, that's where we are. The first person receiving the warning informs two or three others, who in turn do the same thing. If possible, by telephone, otherwise on foot or by bike. We have received warnings at our farms within ten minutes of the S.S. leaving Arnhem. Once we received a warning half an hour before they left. The message was: "Watch out, S.S. leaving within the next half hour in an easterly direction." That is pretty efficient, I think.

Saturday, July 10

As usual I do some cleaning up to make it look neat around the house and barn.

Tuesday, July 13

The farm consists of several small parcels of land in different locations; we have to move the cows from one field to another. The cows do not always co-operate. Herman, the youngest son, and I walk to 't Engeland to move the cows from there to 't Vree. The old cow gets away from Herman. He hollers and screams to control the situation and is finally, after a couple of falls and much running, able to get hold of her again.

Wednesday, July 14

At noon hour I swim in the creek with Herman.

NEWS: Invasion of Sicily.

Thursday, July 15

Wim needs a haircut and so do I. We go to the barber in the next town, Lichtenvoorde. On our way back we stop for tea in Hotel *de Koppelpaarden*.

Gerrit ter Horst lives in Eindhoven with his parents and sisters. His father is a brother of Oom Herman. Gerrit occasionally comes for a visit to the farm with his sisters Annie (age 11) and Toos (age 9). They are here now. The three of us (Wim Papiermole, Herman ter Horst and I) like to tease the girls in a big way. With the help of Wim, who is, after all, studying to be a medical doctor, we work out a plan and hope it will succeed.

Friday, July 16

I am just finished shaving when the girls come down for breakfast. I am cleaning up my shaving tools but remove the blade from my razor.

We talk about shaving, and growing a beard. Wim asks, "Did you ever ask yourself why men always have to shave but not ladies?"

"No, why is that?"

"Well, women can prevent it by shaving themselves at an early age. Just once. The best time is about 12 or 13 years of age."

Since Annie is the oldest I ask her if she is ready for it. "The brush is still standing here, full of soap."

Instantly she is on the chair ready for a bit of fun.

No problem applying the soap. She thinks that is all. "No, hold it; we have to shave you clean yet."

She thinks this is too crazy and wants to run away, but is promptly (by Wim and Herman) put back on the chair.

I am ready for her with the safety razor without the blade. But she does not know that.

First she does not want to cooperate but with the razor close to her face she becomes as still as a mouse.

It does not take long now and the soap is gone.

Delighted she jumps from the chair, thinking this is it. However, we tell her there is one (only one) more thing to make it a great success. She has to cover her face, and especially under her nose, with some fresh goose poop. There is plenty to be found behind the little barn.

Unfortunately Tante hears this last part of the conversation. She puts a stop to it and says: "*Das neet waor heur, geleuf't maor neet.*" "That is not true; don't believe a word of it."

We think this is the end of the story. Too bad.

Saturday, July 17

For lunch we have pancakes with bacon. My weight climbs and is now 130 Dutch *pond*. My tummy is expanding too.

Danger is lurking again and we leave the house at 11 p.m. I meet up with some other men and we stay hidden in the bushes, alongside a pasture, eleven of us. We try to sleep a bit but we wake up often because of the cold weather. When it gets light, about 6:30 a.m. we go back to the farm. I am very cold and stiff as a board.

Peter Van Essen

Sunday, July 18
The cow belonging to *den Eume* gives birth to a calf.

Monday, July 19
The barley has to be harvested. This is done by hand with a sickle. I want to try it, but it does not work too well. My arms swing around wildly, and I do not cut much barley. At one time I hit the ground and pull everything up, roots and all. The next time, I hit so high, the stubble is so long, that you have to keep your eyes closed when you bend down. The farmer thinks it is better that I bind the sheaves and put them together.

Wednesday, July 21
Yesterday we finished harvesting the barley. Today we start with the rye that grows in den Es. I will try my luck again and it goes a lot better. I like it, but for now I go back to binding up the sheaves. We find a phosphorus bomb that is buried partly in the ground. We dig it out to see what it looks like. It is not large, but heavy enough to go through a roof and spontaneously start a fire.

Thursday, and Friday, July 22 and 23
Back to den Es until 9 p.m. It is very warm and when we go home, I feel very, very tired.

So far, I have been working every day and sometimes pretty hard. I don't mind. It's better than doing nothing.

Today I am in for a special trial. Unknown to me the farmer and his sons are going to try to tire me out.

My job is the same as yesterday, binding up the sheaves. Oom Herman and son Gerrit are cutting, one behind the other. I am binding. When the cutters get to the other end of the field they turn around and start the next two rows. I have to keep up with them. But they want to see how much it takes to get me tired out. Since I am doing pretty good with keeping up, they increase their tempo and this goes on several times. Eventually things slow down considerably, to my relief. When we go home at supper and milking time we are all tired. I am very tired. At the supper table we talk about our work and how much we accomplished. Then they tell me that the whole thing was set up to get me to quit. Oom Herman confessed that he really hoped I would take a much needed rest so he could do the same. When that did not happen, they started to slow things down on their own.

Saturday, July 24
We finish the rye and it is early enough to go for a nice swim in the *Slingebeek*.

Sunday, July 25
During the night, we hear many Tommies. The NEWS says that there was heavy bombardment of Essen, Hamburg and Keulen. We see many bright flares hanging in the sky, burning phosphor, and fighter planes attacking each other.

A letter for home will be delivered by te Paske; he is studying at the police academy in Apeldoorn.

Monday, July 26
NEWS: Mussolini resigns according to BBC Radio.

We also listen to some nice music on the radio.

Tuesday, July 27
Warm weather. We dig potatoes. The potatoes are very poor quality and really small. I bet you could put 12 of these in your mouth and still whistle the national anthem.

Our hawk, Ghandi, disappears.

Wednesday, July 28
Driessen, the neighbor we call *den Eume*, is picking up the harvested rye to stack it behind the barn. He is not going to stack it on the land, as usual, for that will obstruct the view. The Germans don't allow it. Ghandi came back this morning, but by evening she is gone again.

Thursday, July 29

This afternoon at two o'clock we witness a severe fight between a German plane and an English plane.

Friday, July 30

Today we pick up our rye. Oom Herman is really good at making a nice *viemhoop* which is then covered with a tarp. Each corner of the tarp is weighted down with a brick tied to a rope attached to the tarp, to keep it from blowing away. While we are busy doing this, Wim accidentally throws his pitchfork into my knee.

Saturday, July 31

This morning I have trouble getting out of bed. My leg is very stiff. I look like an imitation of *Zes en een kwart,* our nickname for Seyss-Inquart, the Nazi-appointed figurehead in Holland, who has a stiff leg.

AUGUST 1943

Sunday, August 1

Many airplanes fly over during the night.

NEWS: Remscheid is bombed and on Hamburg they dropped 1,300 tons of bombs in 45 minutes. In Milan, political prisoners are being released.

Monday, August 2

We harvest oats at Wubbelskamp, one of the parcels of land.

Tuesday, August 3

Same. With Gerrit and Herman.

Behind the farm, across the lane is a little *Zondagschool* building. The farmer has agreed to keep it clean and tidy. Herman, the youngest son, and I will do some cleaning today. In the attic there are many sparrows' nests with young birds. They make a real mess inside and we decide to clean them out. In order to get into the attic, we put a table under the trap door, a chair on top of the table. Herman hoists himself up. He leaves his wooden shoes on the table. I suggest that he throw the nests down to me so that I can throw them outside. The odd nest still has a few baby birds in it. One of these I put into Herman's wooden shoe. When we finally finish this messy job, he comes down, steps into his wooden shoes and jumps up and out in a hurry. "What in the world...?" Since we don't wear socks in the summer you can imagine what his toes look like. The little bird is as flat as a pancake.

Thursday, August 5
We have to move the cows again, this time to 't Goor.

Today we help the neighbour, Papenborg, harvest his oats. Papenborg is a lovely older man and his wife is a saint. He is very sick, suffering from arthritis, cannot come out of bed, and has much pain. So much that sometimes he cries because of the pain. But as soon as you step inside his house he is quiet, composed and greets you with a smile.

His field of oats is on a piece of land called 't Sledevoort. A young lady comes by to warn us about danger. We leave the oat field and go to work close by Papenborg's house in an open field where we have a clear view of the surroundings.

In a neighbouring district called Barlo, the Germans have arrested four young men and one nurse. Another boy of 18 escapes and starts to warn the neighbourhood.

NEWS: Orell and Catania are in Allied hands. Around Orell 120,000 German soldiers are killed and 12,400 are taken prisoner.

Friday, August 6
NEWS: Bjelgorod is liberated.

Two boys from Barlo are to be transported by train to Amersfoort to the concentration camp. One of the boys jumps off the train and escapes. Other people get in the way of a policeman who starts running after him. They hold the policeman up, even take his revolver, and then these people take off as well.

Saturday, August 7

I decide to clean things up around the house so it will look tidy for the weekend. For the night I go to Papiermole, Wim's parents, who live in Aalten.

Sunday, August 8

10:30 a.m. church. Dominee Drost from den Hague preaches. Spend the day with Papiermole and also sleep there again.

Monday, August 9

Harvest oats in 't Goor with Gerrit, Herman and Wim.

Tuesday, August 10

Same as yesterday. We receive word that more danger is lurking. Keep your eyes open for the next few days.

Wednesday, August 11

At 2:30 in the morning we get a warning that something is going on in the neighbourhood.

We get dressed in a hurry and go out into the fields and meadows. Walk around until four o'clock when we start approaching the farm. Standing by the *viemhoop* we hear a whistle that seems to come from the farm *Nonhof*, one of the neighbours. That farmer is a member of the NSB, sympathizing with the Germans. We hear two shots fired and shortly after, another whistle, this time by the *Zondagschool* building. We hide in the bean patch to await things.

After about half an hour, we hear a car door slam close by, direction *Neerhof*, who is our other neighbour. A car is being driven away. At 6:30 a.m. we come out of hiding and by seven o'clock we hear what has been going on. Fourteen members of the NSB were looking for the farm *Nonhof*. They asked for directions at farmer Bouwhuis, who wasted no time warning the immediate area of danger. At *Nonhof* the NSB picked up one young man, we don't know why.

Thursday to Monday, August 12 to 16

I have a chance to go home to Apeldoorn for a couple of days. Oom Herman and I make the trip by bike.

We leave at 8 a.m. and arrive at 12:30 p.m. I stay at my Oom Teun during the daytime and go home at 9:30 p.m. when it is dark. I visit a few people but only in the evening after dark.

On Monday, I bike back to Aalten in just over three hours. It is hot summer weather and when I arrive back at the farm I have to hang out my pants and vest to dry. The rest of my clothes go into the wash.

The afternoon is spent harvesting buckwheat in 't Goor.

Tuesday, August 17

Fix bicycle tires, almost all day. What a job. Since you cannot buy a new tube, the old ones have to be fixed time and again. Outer tires are made of car tires cut in strips and stapled together to fit the rim. It provides a terrible ride, very bumpy. One of our neighbours, the *Peerdeboer* goes out early in the morning to milk his cows. Milk cans hang on the handlebars of his bike. Because of these terrible tires, the cans bang against his bike and many a morning we wake up from the noise it makes.

Wednesday, August 18

Together with Gerrit ter Horst and Gerrit Driessen we build an oat stack.

Thursday, August 19

Today is my nephew's birthday. Gerrit Weeda is 2 years old.

Friday, August 20

We are going to pick up the oats and buckwheat from 't Goor and tomorrow we will stack it at the farm.

Sunday, August 22

NEWS: heavy bombardment of Duisburg and Dortmund. We can see the skies lit up and hear clearly the rumble of explosions.

Monday, August 23

The farmer is going to teach me how to thresh barley with a flail. This is neat. Barley is spread out on the threshing floor and with four of us, two on each side, we swing the flail. It has to be done in rhythmic order 1 – 2 – 3 – 4, 1 – 2 – 3 – 4. At first it is hard to get into the swing of things, but after hitting myself a few times, I get the hang of it and I surprise myself, and the others too I guess.

NEWS: Berlin receives 2,000 tons of bombs from 700 bombers.

Tuesday, August 24

NEWS: end of conference at Quebec (Roosevelt and Churchill).

Two Russian prisoners of war escape from Bocholt, Germany. Police and German soldiers are searching for them. They expect that they came across the border into Holland. They check our farm to see if the escapees are here.

Wednesday, August 25

The radio mentions much sabotage in Denmark.

Thursday, August 26

NEWS: during the night three airfields in France are bombed. Also an Italian cruiser. Unrest in Bulgaria; political activity in the Balkan.

Friday, August 27

Work in the field 't Engeland. We pull thistles and spread out the cow manure. If left on a heap it will create spots the cows would not touch when grazing. We catch two wood pigeons. In the evening we go to *Oosterkerk* to hear an organ recital by Feike Asma. We enjoy the first piece "The Cuckoo and the Nightingale" to the end. The next piece is "Largo". It has just started when someone announces that the Germans are raiding the town looking for young men to be sent to Germany as labourers. I don't think twice, but leave immediately, carefully choosing my way back to the farm. I am not the only one. Many men sneak out to head back to their hiding places.

Saturday, August 28

To prepare it for use, we have to winnow the barley. We also need to clean the rabbit cages today.

Monday, August 30

Thresh buckwheat with the flail. NEWS: The radio announces that Taganrog is now clear of German troops.

Tuesday, August 31

Queen Wilhelmina's birthday. The Commander-in-Chief of the Dutch Navy is confident that the Queen will be back in the Netherlands on her birthday in August 1944. In fact, she did not return until May 1945.

We spend the day digging potatoes in den Es.

The neighbour's sow has 12 piglets. Oom Herman has to cut their teeth.

Peter Van Essen

At 7:45 p.m. the Queen will address the nation via BBC radio. We are not allowed to have a radio with short wave to listen to the BBC. Germans have confiscated all the radios, but of course not everyone obeyed this order. We go upstairs, where the radio is hidden and listen to the Queen's message. During this time a neighbour comes in with a message for us and waits in the little kitchen downstairs. When we come down, he says that he heard everything but kept an eye out for intruders. We are lucky it was him and not someone else.

NEWS: Northern France has been bombed.

SEPTEMBER 1943

Wednesday, September 1

Four years ago today Poland was invaded by Germany.

NEWS: The Russian army has captured three cities or towns. One is Yelnia by Smolensk. Smolensk itself is involved in heavy fighting. In four days the Russian army has liberated 170 towns and villages. Berlin is being bombed again overnight.

Friday, September 3

NEWS: At 4:30 a.m. allied troops land in Italy. The Russian army moves ahead very speedily and breaks through rail line Briansk–Smolensk. The floodgate at Hansweert (Netherlands) has been bombed.

This is another day of digging potatoes.

Saturday, September 4

NEWS: Yesterday Allied planes bombed an airplane factory in Paris, also airports in Belgium. 24 hours after landing in Italy, the troops started to move inland. Heavy fighting in southern Italy. In August 16,000 tons of bombs fell on Germany, Italy received 3,000 tons.

The past night Berlin was bombed again. My sister's fiancé, Berend Gerrits, is there and I wonder how he is managing.

NEWS: Yesterday the Russian army recaptured 450 places; advanced 20 kilometres in 24 hours. In England they observed a national day of prayer. Reggio recaptured.

Monday, September 6
Amid the digging of potatoes, we hear NEWS that the Russian Army is now 15 kilometres from Stalino.

Wednesday, September 8
NEWS: Stalino recaptured. Italian Army capitulated. Russian Army still advancing.

Sunday, September 12
The entire family ter Horst is going to visit Westerveld from the Welink in IJzerloo.

We arrive there with 11 of us. We have a beautiful evening and loads of fun. After we come home in the evening we gather around the table and share a big pot of oat porridge.

Monday, September 13
A heavy day, digging potatoes, potatoes, potatoes. Wow!

When I come home there is a letter from my family and also one from my brother Gerrit who is in Germany. What a treat!

Tuesday, September 14
NEWS: Briansk (Russia) recaptured. In Italy Bari in Corenza fell into Allied hands. A strike in Malta.

The cows have to be transferred again to another pasture. This time it is from 't Vree to the Hagendiek. Wim and I are asked to take care of this important chore. I am supposed to lead the herd of three cows and two young men, with the good old and quiet Emma up front. Wim will follow with the other two.

However, Wim's duo seems to be in a hurry and with a good speed they shoot past me. I try to stop them by steering Emma in front of them, but to no avail. Wim is hanging on to the ropes of both his cows but cannot keep it up and has to let go. To watch him running after these cows is priceless and makes me laugh. He yells and screams. "Hu... huuu, huuuuuuu!" Nothing can stop them. Every time he starts running, they run. Finally he gives up and comes back for his bike. He asks me to wait for him until he comes back. I wait for a while, but this is ridiculous and I decide to go and walk on with my lonely Emma.

Via 't Villekesderp we safely reach the Hagendiek. It is an enjoyable hour long walk.

But where is Wim? I don't see him anywhere. I go back on my bike to find him. When I finally come to the Boterdiek I see something that resembles the trio. The cows seem very quiet and walk leisurely ahead of Wim. Without any further trouble they reach their new destination. Wim and I start to walk back to where he left his bike at Nerus from the *Stegge* farm. We bike home and tell the story. The result is a good laugh.

Wednesday, and Thursday, September 15 and 16
Potatoes, potatoes. NEWS: Njezjin recaptured.

Friday, September 17
We harvest tobacco.

NEWS: Pomny, Nowgorod, Sjewersk and Noworosyjsk recaptured.

Receive a letter from my sister who needs a place for two young men to hide.

Sunday, September 19
Today we have our first church service for the *onderduikers*.

It is becoming too dangerous to go to the regular church. The service is held on the threshing floor by Arendsen. Hendrik and Daatje are relatives of the Wikkerinks. Mr. Fukkink reads the sermon. Hard to understand. Of all things, he is reading an Easter sermon in September. The pigs in the pen at the end of the threshing floor make an awful noise and jump up to peek over the edge. Also the cows join in with a loud moo when we are trying to listen to the sermon and sing our songs.

Tuesday, September 21
(This section was not written in my diary at the time for the protection of the baby and his family.)

> Ome Jan has hidden many Jews, some from town, others from out of town. Besides an *onderduiker*, they also have Margo, a Jewish nurse, living at the Wikkerink home. Later they made a special hiding place for a Russian soldier escaped from a POW camp in Germany.

Peter Van Essen

The Rabbi of Aalten and his wife, Mr. and Mrs. J, had been placed in hiding with an older farm couple. Mrs. J was in the early stages of pregnancy when she was placed. As the due date came closer Mrs. J. became increasingly nervous and kept asking Ome Jan what they would do when the baby arrived. Ome Jan replied, "Don't worry, we will work things out."

Very early on September 21, a doctor and a nurse go to the farm to assist in the delivery of a healthy baby boy. The baby cannot stay at the farm with the older couple, because it would lead to suspicion about who else might be in the home. The doctor and the nurse dress the baby and place him in a cardboard box. They drive to Aalten by car where the baby will be delivered as a foundling on the steps of the Wikkerink home. They stop the car two blocks away from the house. The doctor puts on a pair of wooden shoes and walks to the house with the cardboard box. After ringing the doorbell, he runs away. By running away, any one of the neighbours who might hear something would mention that the person was wearing wooden shoes. A doctor did not wear wooden shoes.

When the family answers the doorbell, they see a cardboard box. A faint noise comes from the box. The younger children hope it is a kitten. What a surprise when they see a baby in the box.

Now comes the problem. The baby has to be registered and named. Later that morning the family contacts City Hall. The Mayor comes, accompanied by the Police and the city Secretary. Also, a doctor and a nurse come. What do you know? Ome Jan just happened to call the same doctor and nurse who attended the birth. But the authorities have no idea. The doctor has to declare the baby healthy and also that it is not of the Jewish race. Now the baby needs a name. I think it is amazing what they come up with. First name *Jan*, after Ome Jan. Second name *Willem*, after the Queen, secretly. Last name *Herfstink*. September 21, his birth date, is the first day of fall. *Herfst* is fall, in Dutch. The addition *ink* means son of.

After a few weeks the parents are put in hiding with a family closer to town. Then, when Mother Wikkerink takes Wimke for a stroll, she drops in occasionally at these friends and Wimke has a little visit with his real parents who live in the small attic of the house.

On January 1, 1978, Yad Vashem recognized Hendrik Jan Wikkerink and his wife, Dela Gesina Wikkerink-Eppink, as Righteous Among the Nations.

(Back to the diary)

Tante Dela with Wimke at age 7 weeks.

Wednesday, September 22

At 11:30 a.m. I have to be at the train station to meet Henk and Bert, two fellows who need a place to hide. The train arrives, but no boys. I phone Apeldoorn to find out what went wrong. My sister has sent them to the train station Lievelde instead of Aalten. I bike to Lievelde to see if they are there. Not a soul around the station. I drop into the coffee house across from the station to see if maybe they are there. Not there either. Now I have to try something else. I approach the owner. He says that two young men were there apparently waiting for someone.

Then they left on their bikes to Ruurlo. I know that this man can be trusted and I tell him what happened. "Is there a cafe or coffee house across from the station in Ruurlo?" I ask.

"Yes," he says. "The owner is a good friend of mine."

We figure that they might wait there for the train back to Apeldoorn which is not due until 3:30 p.m. He reads my mind and offers to phone. When he asks his friend if there are two gentlemen there the answer is yes, and soon I am talking to Bert. They just arrived. I tell him to bike back via the main road and that I will meet them somewhere along the way. Just before I get to Ruurlo I see them coming. By now I am hungry and we get a couple of apples and half a melon from Henk's backpack. Through the country roads and laneways we head to Aalten.

The leftover potatoes from noon taste really good.

Gerrit Houwers, from *de Bleeke*, who just happens to drop in, says that he will take one of the boys. First we go to Wikkerink's to let them know the boys have arrived and ask if it is okay that we find a place for them? We draw straws and Bert is to go to *de Bleeke*. Henk will sleep at our place tonight.

Thursday, September 23
To the barber in Lichtenvoorde. Henk helps me to work in the tobacco. In the evening our neighbour Jan Houwers from the farm *Neerhof* comes to talk. His is a big farm compared to the little one of ours. He wants to talk about the boys in hiding.

"You," he says to Oom Herman, "you have now two fellows hiding with you and I have no one. Henk should come with me. I have enough work and food for him." And so Henk goes.

Saturday, September 25
Herman Jr. is high school age and wants to make a little pocket money.

"For 10 cents I will eat four live flies," he says. Wim and I sure want to see this experiment! We each put a nickel on the table and Herman catches four flies. He puts them one by one on his tongue and together they go down his throat.

Then he says, "For a quarter I will eat a worm." Of course we want to see that too! But his mother comes in the door just then and hears him. It is not going to happen.

Sunday, September 26
Henk, Bert and I go to *Westerkerk* at 5 p.m. After church we go for a nice walk before heading home where we spend the evening.

Monday, September 27
Many planes come over during the night. NEWS: Emden and Hannover were the targets this time.

Tuesday, September 28
Herman Jr. turns 16 today. NEWS: Foggia in Italy falls into Allied hands

Wednesday, September 29
Jan ter Horst is 19 years old today. NEWS: Russians are fighting in and around Dnipropetrovsk.

Thursday, September 30
Today is set aside for plowing the field den Es. They let me try. Boy this is tricky.

Oom Herman and his son Gerrit bike home at the end of the day and I bring home the horse and wagon.

Receive a letter from home and I send an answer back. My family hopes to visit us this Sunday.

OCTOBER 1943

Friday, October 1

Gerrit and I move the cows from Hagendiek to 't Engeland. Wim was supposed to help me, but he is scared after what happened last time.

We go to the farm of Hendrik Driessen, the neighbour's son, to help with threshing the grain.

NEWS: Kremenchuk recaptured; Naples in Allied hands.

Sunday, October 3

My father and my sisters Miep and Nen come for a visit.

Back: Father, Nen, Peter, and Miep. Front: Gerrit and Dick.

We celebrate the birthdays of Herman Jr. and Jan. It is a very enjoyable day. My sister sees a loaf of bread on the counter in the back kitchen and says, "Oh what beautiful raisin bread!" When she comes closer all the raisins fly off the bread. It is only a plain loaf that the flies could not resist.

Talking about flies, there are plenty at our farm. With the cows under the same roof, the flies easily find their way into the small kitchen. Once I was sitting there with Wim, the student, when numerous flies had gathered on the round table having a feast with the spilled milk and some sugar. Wim wanted to see how many he could catch in one swoop with his big hand. Here he goes… "Wow," he says, "I must have scooped up quite a few."

"Let's count them."

I run to the pump with a pail and fill it half full of water. Wim dumps his hand in it and opens it up. The flies start swimming around and we start counting. We count more than forty, a pretty good harvest.

Tante is very frugal, not quick to throw things out. One time I am in the small kitchen and she is fussing around. On the table is a small can with milk for the coffee. In it are two flies, floating around. Tante goes to the table and sees these intruders in the milk. She picks them out, one by one, brings each one to her mouth and sucks the milk off. Then a quick pinch to kill them and out in the ashtray they go. I have never before seen anybody that could milk a fly, but she could!

Monday, October 4

This morning Miep leaves by train and in the late afternoon my Dad and sister Nen have to leave also.

Tuesday, October 5

The Germans want the university students to declare loyalty to them and their cause, to ensure no political turmoil from this corner. Wim, who is a medical student, is strongly opposed to this and writes an article against this movement. He needs extra copies for mailing to professors and illegal underground newspapers. I volunteer to type enough papers and go to the Wikkerink home where they have a typewriter. In the afternoon, while I am still busy typing, Henny comes to keep me company. She is studying for some evening courses. I appreciate her company.

Wednesday, October 6

In the morning, more typing. Afternoon sees us busy with the chewing tobacco. The tobacco has to be hung for drying.

Thursday, October 7

Before noon we work on pipe and cigarette tobacco. Another letter arrives from home.

Each night at about 8:30 or nine o'clock we eat oat porridge, hot! Tante, Oom Herman's wife, asks me to look after the porridge and make sure it does not get burned.

Recently Wim has been practicing riding the neighbour's horse. He says, "I am really good at it. I can let it trot and also go in full gallop. You should come and have a look. I am getting the horse ready."

"Okay," I say, "but I have to stir and watch the porridge. Let me know when you are ready."

Mina, the daughter, will call me when Wim is near Heideman's house. There is a large open space and we should be able to see the spectacle first hand.

After a few minutes they call me outside. Everybody is there, the neighbour, Oom Herman, Tante, Mina, Gerrit, and Herman Jr. We stand behind the farm and wait for Wim and the horse to show up. He is now on the Slatdiek and should turn left to Heideman. The trees and bushes hide our view but we can hear the horse galloping. Funny, nothing shows up in the clearing. Then we hear a voice calling. "Whoa! Whoa! Whoa!" Suddenly we see the horse coming around the corner towards the farm. Wim is not sitting on his back. A little later there comes Wim running around the corner and he is happy to see that the horse is standing quietly near us. This event turns out to be a lot of fun and we have a good laugh. Several remarks are made about his riding experience. Abruptly we stop our talking when we hear Tante calling, "Oh ..., the porridge!" This evening we eat burned porridge.

Friday, October 8
Today work in 't Goor clearing out bramble bushes.

Saturday, October 9
With an axe we clean out the young *elshout* trees around the pasture. This area is named after these trees: *Elshoek*. On our way home we take the cows from 't Engeland to 't Vree.

Monday, October 11
NEWS: In three days, the Allied downed 350 German fighter planes. Bombs on Münster in Germany. Also damage in Enschede (province of Overijssel).

Wednesday, October 13
My sister's fiancé, Berend, who is in Berlin, has a birthday today.
  NEWS: Kiev (Russia) is burning. Italy declares war on Germany! How is it possible?

Thursday, October 14
NEWS: In the streets of Melitopol is heavy fighting.

Friday, October 15
NEWS: Zaporozje liberated.

Sunday, October 17
Church at Houwers, farm *de Bleeke*. We eat there too.

Tuesday, October 19
NEWS: Conference in Moscow; Churchill, Roosevelt and Stalin.

Wednesday, October 20
NEWS: Melitopol recaptured.

We pull up several heaps of turnips for fodder.

In Apeldoorn the Resistance movement has tried to get rid of policeman Doppenberg, a member of the NSB. Also, Mr. Dobbleman has been murdered. The Dobbleman's live close to our home in Wiesel by Apeldoorn. This family owns the well-known factories of Dobbelman tobacco and soap. Mr. Dobbleman was very active in the Resistance movement and he hid a number of Jews in the *Zandhegge* area of his forest.

Thursday, October 21
Mina ter Horst's birthday today.

Monday, October 25
Clean and fix up the pigsty today. The sow is expecting and needs a place to give birth to her offspring.

Friday, October 29
The sow gives birth to seven little pigs.

Saturday, October 30
Huithorst, an NSB man from Lichtenvoorde, has been killed.

Sunday, October 31
10 a.m. church at Mateman. Dominee Klijn is preaching.

NOVEMBER 1943

Wednesday, November 3
Thanksgiving Day. Church at Mateman.

Thursday, November 4
Dick's birthday today. She is the fiancée of my brother Gerrit.

Friday, November 5
Wim Papiermole's birthday.

Tuesday, November 9
Thresh grain at Jan Driessen. The sow is to go to the boar again!

Oom Herman seems to think I will do anything for a good adventure. He wants me to take the sow to the boar. "Okay, where do I take it?" I ask.

"To te Slichte in the Giezenbosch."

"How do I get there?"

"You know we don't have a horse and wagon, you will have to walk."

"Oh well, if I tell the sow where she is going, she will probably be running all the way."

But I start having some second thoughts. It would normally be a 25 minute walk, but if Porky does not cooperate it could take me an hour. "How do you want me to get her there?" I ask.

"I'll tie her to a rope," he says, "and I think that will do it!"

"If you think so, I will try. But if I am not back at noon, don't wait with lunch because of me."

Gerrit ter Horst comes to help his Dad; he seems to enjoy this episode. When the ropes are in place I start to walk. The sow runs and almost pulls me off my feet. If this keeps up I will be there in 15 minutes. She only runs for about 10 meters and stops dead in her tracks. I must get her moving again and pull on the rope. It does not help, no matter how hard I pull. I slap her on the back; pull her ear, no movement. Then I grab her tail and pull. That does it, she sprints ahead and we walk a good distance. I hope we get past the neighbour's house in a decent way. If the girls there see me struggling, I will certainly hear about it later. Porky jumps sideways off the laneway, then turns around to go back to our farm.

"No way, you stupid thing!" and I tie a spare rope on her front leg. When I have straightened her out, I take her by the tail again and pull her in forward drive. Not bad, not bad, and I start to praise her. We are making some headway again.

Just when I think she is getting used to it, she starts making trouble again, repeating her previous manoeuvre. We are doing very well walking through *Klein Zwitserland*, then along the Selmseweg and behind the cemetery. Reaching the old Barloseweg, a paved road, she does not want to cross. It takes almost 10 minutes but finally we are on the other side and back onto a dirt road. Next crossing is the Lichtenvoortseweg and the same thing happens again. It seems she is afraid of pavement. From here on, it is all dirt road and lanes, which wind behind the Mill and on to te Slichte, the farmer with the boar.

I am not too disappointed. The trip could have taken much longer. I hope that Porky is not disappointed either.

The farmer sees me coming and is waiting for me and the pig. "This way," he says, directing me to the one barn where a boar is waiting. Porky goes into the pen next to the boar's.

"How long does it take?" I ask.

"You might be able to pick her up tomorrow or Thursday."

What welcome news. "You mean I don't have to drag her back home?"

"No, not today, Thursday will be fine," says te Slichte.

Okay with me, for I know that tomorrow or Thursday Tony's horse will be available as promised. I enjoy the walk home and arrive in time for a hot lunch.

Wednesday, November 10
Thresh grain at *Neerhof*.

Thursday, November 11
The sow comes home again after her visit to the boar.

Tuesday, November 16
Gerrit D., son of the neighbour, has his birthday party. We are invited.

Grada, the housekeeper, sees her chance to get even with Johan and me. We tease her quite often and we know she is waiting for a good opportunity to get even. The coffee is ready on the stove when we come in and she asks if everybody wants some. "Yes, of course, please."

Coffee is not filtered these days. Grounds are put in the coffee pot; water poured on, and then boiled on the stove. Sitting around the table, Johan and I are the last to be served. I notice Grada, who is standing behind Johan, shaking the pot around and around a few times. This mixes the grounds into the coffee. Now she pours his cup, then mine. Johan looks at me and I look at him. He shrugs his shoulders. What are we going to do?

"Drink it," I say, taking my cup and sipping the coffee through my teeth, leaving most of the grounds behind. I leave a little coffee in, then take the cup and empty it under the table. The others are talking and don't pay any attention. Johan does the same thing. Our empty cups are now back on the table.

After a while Grada, who has made fresh coffee, asks, "Who wants another coffee?"

Johan is the first one to reply, "Yes, please."

"And so do I."

So Grada comes with the coffee pot and we are the first ones to be served this time around. She goes to Johan, then stops, utterly amazed to see his cup empty; no grounds. Glancing over to my cup, she wants to say something but stutters something like "uuuh... ooh... aaah..., how was the coffee?"

We assure her that it was good. Next day she finds another reason to get even with us.

I must explain that the floor is not carpeted. Most floors are made of small pieces of ceramic tile and can be easily cleaned with a broom or a wet cloth.

Tuesday, November 23

For a few weeks already, I have gone every evening to the farm *de Bleeke* to sleep there in the barn with Jan, the farm hand. It is a safer hiding place. When the grain was stacked in the barn, a square space was kept open by the back wall. The barn board was loosened to get in from the outside. Once you are inside the board is tightened from the inside and there is no movement when someone leans against it from the outside or when someone shakes the board to find out if there is a hiding place somewhere. We sleep on straw, surrounded by straw. This morning as I wake up and want to dress myself I cannot find one of my socks. I feel around in the pitch-dark, but to no avail. I just have to walk back to *de Koekoek* with one bare foot.

Wednesday, November 24

Lien Wikkerink who is engaged to Johan, son of Oom Herman and Tante, was going to come in today to help Tante with the wash. She does this quite often. Tante is physically not able to handle all the chores. Today Lien cannot come, but her sister Henny takes her place.

When Jan and I crawl into our hiding place at *de Bleeke* tonight, I look for my sock again. I am feeling around, and discover a little hole and poke my hand in it. I touch something soft, grab hold of it and pull. It is my sock. A rat or mouse must have tried to take it into its nest but the sock suspender got stuck in the straw.

Thursday, November 25

It is raining and the wind is blowing.

Tim, one of the *onderduikers* from our neighbourhood, has been to the office of the P.B.H. They issue permits for having pigs, among other things. If you never had one before, you do not get a permit. On our farm we never had a sheep and there is no way we would get a permit for it. But Tim's father always had a pig, which was raised by a farmer friend.

Tim comes home from this office and is just crazy about the two young girls who work there. He really would like to go on a date with one of them.

Peter Van Essen

Both girls are called Linie. It just happens that Oom Herman's daughter Mina also works in this office. Tim asks me if I can help him get a date.

"Well, why don't you ask one of them tomorrow when you pick up your permit?"

"I don't know how to do that. I am too shy," he says.

I don't really want to have anything to do with it and I tell him so. But again, in the afternoon, he talks about it and seems to think that I can pull it off.

"Let me think about it," I say and my mind goes in full speed. When Mina comes home from the office at about 5:30 p.m., I ask her if the girls would be game for a little bit of fun. She is sure they will be and when she hears what I plan to do, she gets excited.

"I will talk to them tomorrow morning, in the office, first thing!" she says.

Friday, November 26

Last night Tim went to stay in Aalten overnight. When he arrives at *de Koekoek* later in the morning, he asks if I have come up with something. I take him aside and tell him that Oom Herman wants me to go and take a message to his daughter at the office. "When we are there," I tell him, "I will talk to the girls and ask them if we may have the pleasure of taking them home to Lichtenvoorde."

"Oh," he says, "don't let Mina hear this."

"Of course not," I say. "And then we will go outside and wait for them there. By this time it will be dark and Mina will have no idea what is going on."

He is getting excited and marvels that just today I have to get a message to Mina.

"Yes. It is amazing, isn't it?"

Tonight we will go out with the girls. When we get ready to leave, Tim is still marvelling about his luck. I wonder if he will still feel this way when he comes back home tonight. It is raining again. We arrive in time at the office and while Tim is picking up a permit for a pig, I talk to Mina. I want to know which Linie goes with Tim for he is going to get a surprise tonight. She has lots of lipstick, and also a piece of soft coal that really smudges things up. It starts to look promising. We go outside, and tell Mina that we are on our way to the barber, who is in the same town where the girls live, so we will see her at home later tonight. Outside we wait behind some trees. We don't really have to hide, for it is so dark you cannot see anything three to four feet ahead of you. Mina leaves the office shortly after, and then come the girls.

I whisper, "Who goes with Tim? He is right there."

One of the girls moves up to Tim. We chat a little, and then we are on our way. Tim and his Linie ahead, I follow with the other Linie. Close to their town is a park with a small bench and we arrange to stop there for a while. Tim and his girl sit on the bench, and Linie and I move away to give them some privacy. We now hope for the best and that things will work out as planned. We are getting pretty wet, and after a while we call to them that maybe it is time to move on. They come toward us and I ask Tim what time it is. He has a watch; I do not. This is all done on purpose, because in order to see the time we need a flashlight. I have the flashlight. The light points a little too high and shines in Tim's face on purpose. It is amazing what this girl has accomplished in such a short time. I almost burst out laughing but manage to keep it in. We now go on to town to drop them off at or close to their home. Before we say goodbye, I see Tim's girl reach for the ground and put her finger through the wet mud. She then touches his cheeks and I would love to see the results of this gentle stroke. We say goodbye and start to go home, or so I think.

Tim says, "We have enough time to go to the barber for a haircut."

This is a bad idea, for I had promised to bring Tim home so everyone could see what had happened. And everyone was going to BE home!

"Tim, the barber is closed today."

"Yes," says Linie, "that's right, he is closed. But my uncle has his barbershop open tomorrow." I know that all barbershops will be closed the next day. But Tim falls for it after asking which barbershop that is. When she mentions the name, I give up all hope, for it is the same barbershop we always go to. Amazingly, Tim does not realize this. He is so ecstatic about his night out that he cannot think straight. Off we go, home, but Tim tries once more; at the first side street he wants to turn left, to go past the barber to see if it is open. I keep going straight ahead.

"Hold it," he yells. "Where are you going?"

"Home. We are pretty wet by now and I want to go home."

"Well, if you are going home, then I go too. You have given me such a wonderful evening, and I can go back tomorrow to get my hair cut."

He carries on all the way home about Linie. "She really liked my moustache, she stroked it several times and also my cheeks. She even kissed me".

Getting closer to home, I make sure to be just ahead of him and the last 200 yards I sprint home, quickly put my bike in the barn and go inside the house. The kitchen is full, even the neighbour is there.

In walks Tim and only now do I see the full effect of the evening. Gerrit ter Horst asks, "Did you get your permit?"

"Oh yes," says Tim.

"And you also bought a pig."

"Eh… no, why?"

"Well it looks like it scratched you up a bit."

Tim turns around to face the mirror; it almost floors him! His face is full of lipstick and black coal stripes.

"Hey," he says. "I am full of scratches. Where do they come from?" Everybody starts laughing. I too have a good laugh but I feel a bit embarrassed and walk out to the threshing floor where Tim cannot see me laugh. All of a sudden he realizes what must have happened and says, "It was the girl who did it." And now he has some more explaining to do.

DECEMBER 1943

Friday, December 3
Every morning we have a problem getting dressed when we sleep in the *hol* in the barn because it is pitch dark. Again this morning. First my shirt. I put my arm in one sleeve and cannot find the other. It is backwards. My pants give me problems too. I have the buttons mixed up; zippers were not common yet. I end up with one buttonhole too many. I decide to finish dressing outside where we have some light.

Tuesday, December 7
In the town Goor, the local office where ration coupons are handled is looted by the Resistance movement. Hurrah! With many people in hiding, Jews, *onderduikers* and Resistance workers, ration coupons are needed to buy food and supplies. People in hiding do not have a valid identification to obtain these coupons and would not dare to show themselves anyway. The loot is distributed to these people.

Friday, December 10
We hear that yesterday the Resistance workers emptied the office in Eibergen. Again Hurrah!

Two English planes come flying over, very low. Beautiful to behold. It gives some assurance that they are working on our liberation. At times you ask yourself, will we ever be free again?

Saturday, December 11

Rats are a problem, especially in the barn where the pig food is stored in barrels. The pigsty in the barn is invaded by rats. Herman and I want to try to catch one. Sebe and Henk, two *onderduikers* from the farm *Neerhof*, are here for a chat and coffee. We suggest that they come and help us. Henk comes along, but Sebe flatly refuses. We make a plan of action.

The barrels are in the far corner, and the rats are in the barrels. When you open the door into the pigsty they run out, climb up on the post and into the attic or loft. Earlier today we have left the door ajar and two of us will slip silently onto the room. Number three will flip on the light when the others have reached the barrels by the post. Each one has a good size club and will start knocking against the pole and the wall. It works, Herman hits one on the tail; it loses its grip and falls onto the floor. He is able to kick it twice with his wooden shoe. The second time the rat smashes against the wall and a well-aimed hit with his club knocks the life out if it.

Excited, we go inside to share our success. Sebe reveals, "I did not want to tell you before, but I once tried to catch a rat. I had it cornered and then it disappeared. As I wondered where it could be, I felt something in my pant leg. I tell you boys, I was out of my pants before the rat!"

We have not tried to catch rats again.

Sunday, December 12
Last night the distribution office in Beverwijk had a visit from the Resistance movement and also the registration office in Varsseveld has been looted.

Monday, December 13
The neighbour has slaughtered a pig and it is the custom to visit them tonight to assess the quality of the meat and bacon. The more praise, the better.

Sunday, December 19
No church today, the alarm has sounded.

Friday, December 31
The farmer's wife makes *oliebollen* and *poffertjes*, a custom for New Year's Eve.

NEWS: The Russian Army is said to be in Poland.

JANUARY 1944

Monday, January 3
Today it is our turn to kill a pig. The neighbour's grandson, Anton, about 8 years old, has the pig's bladder. He takes a straw and starts to blow it up. When it is almost full of air, Herman, who pretends to hold it steady for him, squeezes the air out of it. Poor Anton, he gets all the air and the dirty smell in his mouth. You should see his face.

Tuesday, January 4
At noon an English plane flies low overhead; it seems to have trouble. Later we hear that it made an emergency landing near the next town. One crewman died, one has a broken leg and is arrested, and seven escape into nowhere. The pilot is also arrested. The next day the pilot is supposed to be taken to a German camp in Borken. The car taking him to the camp has to stop in the woods about halfway to their destination. The police escort, Pauli, and the pilot get out of the car and escape on bikes that had been hidden there for that purpose. They also take the car keys, so the chauffeur has to walk back to his hometown. If he had the use of his car, it would have taken very little time for the driver to warn the authorities and most likely would have resulted in the arrest of the two escapees. This was a well-organized escape.

Thursday, January 6
NEWS: The coastline of France and Belgium is bombed. We hear that nine and a half million American soldiers have arrived in England to help. Hard to imagine that many people.

Tuesday, January 11
There are many Tommies in the air. In the afternoon we see many German fighter planes going in a westerly direction. One of these is engaged in a fight with an English plane.

NEWS: There are heavy air battles over France. The radio says that 65 English and about 150 German planes are shot down.

Saturday, January 15
Today is my birthday. I am 22 years old.

Monday, January 17
Tonight dominee Zwart, a former pastor in Aalten, is preaching for the *onder-duikers* at the farm *'t Ruwhof*. There are about 80 young men. The room is too small and they have opened the doors of the built in bedchamber in the corner of the room. It is filled with men. I walk there with two *onderduikers* from the neighbour's house. We know the general direction of the farm but it is dark and we have a hard time finding the place. We walk through a lane, and come to a farm so I decide to ask inside. All these farms have the back end towards the road or lane. Because of the blackout no light whatsoever is visible. I open the back door to the threshing floor, it is even darker inside. Slowly I inch forward. Now I see a glimmer of light coming from the door to the living room. I decide to take a few large steps to reach the door and trip on some wooden shoes standing in front of the door. One shoe flies against the door with a terrific bang and causes the farmer to throw open the door, yelling, "Who is there?"

I assure him it is okay, tell him who I am and that we need help to find the farm *'t Ruwhof*.

"Oh. Come outside and I will show you where to go." He points in a certain direction, but because it is so dark, we more or less have to guess which way he points. "It's easy. You go over the hedge here and follow that direction. At the end is the farm *'t Ruwhof*."

You should know that where I came from in Apeldoorn, a hedge was a hedge. But here, in Aalten, a hedge means a strip of grassland along a ploughed field. At this time, we did not know that. The farmer goes back inside and we start looking for the hedge to climb over it. Finally we give up and start walking in the given direction. So far so good. But we end up in a ploughed field, and this being January, it is muddy! Our wooden shoes that were nicely cleaned and white before we left (after all we were going to church) are now covered with mud. And so we arrive. Since we are the last ones to come in there is not too much choice about where to sit. There are about 70 to 80 young men in the room, some eight or more sitting on the *beddestee*. But, hey, up front is one empty chair and I sit there. Should not have done it. It is right smack in front of the big stove that has to keep the room heated. No wonder the chair was left empty. Nevertheless we have a beautiful evening. I still remember the sermon about Job sitting on the manure pile scratching his sores with a piece of broken pottery. At the end we sing two verses of the National Anthem, and I never heard such singing.

Thursday, January 20
Tonight there is a young men's Bible study meeting at farm *Nooitgedacht*. All the farms here have a name. The family name does not always match the name of the farm; very interesting. We have to vote for a new Board and that causes some problems. About most of the young men, we only know their first names, and about others, we don't even know that much. One of the voters marks his ballot "name unknown, wears brown corduroy pants".

Tuesday, January 25
Another hiding place is being built in the barn under the straw. It is just above the pigsty and nobody would expect that you would sleep there, because of the smell. To get in, we go through the pen and hoist ourselves up through the opening in the ceiling. Once in, we close the board, which is on hinges, and shut the bolt across over the beam. This place has its advantages. When you have to go to the toilet during the night, it makes no sense to go all the way down to the house. You just open the gate and let the flood go down. We call it the floodgate. One time there is a sow with her seven piglets in this pen. The little pigs stand below with open mouths and fight over the stuff. Boy, they must really be thirsty.

Thursday, January 27
The Germans give an order that all farmers must turn in all barbed wire that is not being used.

I am thinking more and more about doing profession of faith in the *Gereformeerde Kerk*.

Sunday, January 30

Today we will have a professor Ridderbos from the Free University of Amsterdam preach in the *Westerkerk*. We should go early to get a seat. However, we are a little late this morning and Henk and I agree that we don't want to stand during the service. If there is no room to sit, we will go to the other church service, which starts half an hour later. When we get to the first church it is already filled to standing room only. We walk on to Ome Jan's house where we have coffee and help Mother Wikkerink peel potatoes. She forgot to do this yesterday. We leave early enough to get to the second church on time for that service. Just before the elders and deacons and the pastor file in to the service, the caretaker runs in and shouts, "*Onderduikers* get out! The S.S. is raiding the town." Many of the men jump up and go off in all directions. I take little back lanes and am quickly on my way to the farm. I arrive safely.

Later that day we learn that the first church we planned to attend had been surrounded by the German S.S. The pastor tried to stretch out the length of the service by adding extra songs. Some of the young men hid in the attic of the church, and one even hid inside the organ. 42 men were arrested leaving the church. Amazingly, a few managed to escape arrest.

Someone had thought of a very creative idea to help the young men avoid capture. Here is what happened:

> In Aalten are many residents of a small fishing village close to den Hague, the seat of government in Holland. This village is on the border of the North Sea. The Germans had built a defense line along the coast, resulting in the evacuation of many of the people. These *evacuees* are now staying with farm families in our area.

> The people of this village still wear beautiful, traditional costumes. The woman's dress consists of several layers of clothing. One of them said to a young man, "Wait a minute," before he

went out of the church. Then she started to remove her top layer of clothing and put it on the young man. She also gave him her big white head-dress with the golden clips on it. Several other women followed her example, and soon a number of young men walked out of the church in the village costume. A little later when the women left the church, the S.S. realized that they had been tricked, because these women were practically in their underwear!

One young man, wearing a woman's costume, grabs his bike and gets on it at the road. But he forgets he is dressed as a woman, and gets on the men's way, swinging his leg high over the bike. Lucky for him the S.S. is too busy and does not look his way. The other redressed men walk quietly away but, once they have rounded the corner, they start running for their lives. People sitting at home in front of the window, drinking their coffee, watch in amazement as these women run so fast and wonder what on earth is going on.

The S.S. asked someone for directions to the church that I had gone to. This person pointed them in a different direction, where they found a very small church and surrounded that. Here they arrested 6 men. When the S.S. load these men into vehicles, one escapes by jumping through the watching crowd, running through yards, and jumping over fences. All those arrested are then transported to a concentration camp in Amersfoort.

Oom Herman's son Jan is one of the 42 who was picked up at the first church. Eventually most of the men came back. They were placed with farmers in Germany just across the border from Holland. When they were given a few days off to visit home, many did not return to Germany. Not all of the men were given a chance to work in Germany and some of them died in camp. Jan came home very sick and never regained his normal strength.

A terrible day.

FEBRUARY 1944

Wednesday, February 2

That nice Wikkerink girl, Henny, is coming again today to help with the wash. We get along pretty well.

Wednesday, February 9

Thresh grain at the neighbour's. When I come home at 6 p.m. I notice that Henny is still there. A nice surprise. It is dark outside and Henny says, "I hope I can find my way to the main road."

"Oh," says Johan, "I am sure Peter will take you there."

So I walk her to the main road, and when we get there she says goodbye. I also say *daag* and we both disappear into the dark, each on our own way home.

Saturday, February 12

A bull-calf is born at the neighbour's farm. Custom requires a visit at which a glass of wine will be presented. Johan and I each receive a very small glass of wine from the housekeeper. The reason? Lately we have started to tease her good-naturedly, and she does not always appreciate it. She is getting even with us.

Monday, February 14

Henny's 17th birthday! Johan and I are going to the birthday party. Earlier today, Grada, the neighbour's housekeeper, came in to talk to Tante, the farmer's wife. When she opened the door to the little kitchen she started, as usual, with, "Uuuuuhhhhh..." but stopped abruptly when she discovered that Johan and I were sitting there peeling potatoes.

She said a few words and turned to leave again. "I will see you again soon," she said.

Johan remarked, "You may stay away for a while."

Two Allied fighter planes chase a German plane. They turn around just above the neighbour's farm, a beautiful sight. The German plane crashes just across the border in Germany.

Wednesday, February 16
I get a letter from my sister Nen saying that our brother, Gerrit, is coming home from Germany for a short furlough.

Thursday, February 17
Johan and I cut wood in the field 't Goor. Johan's axe slips and he cuts his finger. At home he says, "That axe was sharp!"

"No," says Oom Herman. "If it was sharp you would have lost your finger."

Wednesday, February 23
Henny comes to do the wash. I help her carry water from the pump in a large bucket. When the bucket is full, I lift my end just enough to spill a fair bit of water over her foot and into her wooden shoe.

Thursday, February 24
Brother Gerrit comes to visit. He gives me two cigarettes as a present. They are from my brother in Amsterdam. A real unexpected treat.

Saturday, February 26
Mother Wikkerink's birthday is on February 28. To celebrate this at their home is too dangerous, because several *onderduikers* want to pay her a short visit. The party will be at our place, *de Koekoek*. For this occasion I have put on my best suit. When Henny comes, she comments, "Are you ever dressed neatly!"

"Yes, I knew you were coming."

It is a busy evening, 38 people in all. The living room is full, and the overflow sits in the bedroom.

Beside Henny is an empty chair and I claim that one for myself. I tell her that all day long I have been hoping to sit beside her tonight. When the coffee is served, Henny brings a tray into the room, and passes it around. I am the last one served. I see that on Gerrit's cup it says *Opa*. This is enough to make everybody laugh. But wait - Gerrit looks at my cup and notices the words *Uit Liefde* (with love). We all roar and they call Henny back into the room to let her know what happened. She turns red, and protests that it did not happen on purpose. She goes to the other room to tell her mother why we are all laughing so hard, and a little later she comes back to our room to join us again.

Monday, February 28

Gerrit and I go to see Kruithof, the local barber, to see if he might have work for Gerrit, and we are told he can start the next day. When my brother was deported to work in Germany as a slave labourer, he would have loved to go into hiding. At that time the idea of hiding was not even heard of. Not until I was summoned was there talk about an organization that would help young men to hide. Being an underground activity it was hard to get information about their work, even for me at this later date.

Gerrit was placed with a Steel Foundry. Hard work and hot work. He is a barber and could not handle the hard labour. After a few days he walked into town and saw a barbershop. He went in and asked the owner if he could use some help. Could he ever! The owner went to the authorities and was able to arrange a transfer for Gerrit from the Foundry to the Barber Shop. This month, when Gerrit got a few days off to go home for a visit, he did not return to Germany but decided to go into hiding in Aalten and work at the local barbershop.

MARCH 1944

Sunday, March 4

Johan and I get a little male lamb, just born at the neighbour's farm. Johan goes to town to see if he can get a nipple to fit on a baby bottle to feed the lamb. When he returns, Tante asks, "Did Johan get his new nipples yet?"

We do not have a permit for this lamb, so we have to keep it hidden. But when we bring it into the kitchen where it is nice and warm, someone opens the door and, when he steps inside, we recognize him as one of the inspectors. Luckily Mr. Rutgers is on our side and he is not going to report us. It seems however, that we are not going to keep the lamb very long. A few days later it gets sick and, no matter how hard we try, it dies. The three of us, Johan, Henny and I bury the lamb. Henny puts a few wildflowers on its grave.

Wednesday, March 22

I have made a few *mattenkloppers*. I show them to Henny and tell her that this one costs one kiss, the other, five kisses. She takes the one for five kisses and tells me that she will pay me sometime later.

APRIL 1944

Tuesday, April 4

I talk to Oom Herman, and tell him that I would like to do profession of faith in the *Gereformeerde Kerk*.

Monday, April 10

Henny and some friends are walking near the farm. Jan Houwers, a neighbour, comes along with two Belgian horses. He asks Henny if she wants to ride the old one while he rides the younger horse. So far, so good.

But when Jan's horse starts to gallop, the old horse wants to keep up and also starts to run. Henny is not used to this, and without a saddle it is hard for her to stay on the horse. When the horse goes around a bend, I see her fall off and she hurts her knee. I run to her and pick her up. After supper, I take her home on the bike. She worries, "What will they say when they see that you are bringing me home? They already tease me about you."

Wednesday, April 12
We are asked to help at the neighbour's farm, to hoe a field of rye. It takes us all day. At lunch they bring pancakes for us. Delicious meal. Next day, same work again. We finish in the afternoon and take time for a half hour rest.

There is a lot of dry and dead grass along this field and Johan starts a little fire to burn it off. The wind is quite strong, and before we know it, the fire spreads to all sides. Johan gets worried, and tries to put the fire out with his hoe. He swings the hoe like a madman, but it does not do much good. We have a good laugh at his antics and then decide to help him put out the fire.

When we arrive home, we are sent to another parcel of land to spread manure.

Saturday, April 15
I am going to get a haircut, and then I will visit Henny who has to sit quietly with her damaged knee. During the night approximately 2,000 Allied planes came over towards Germany.

Wednesday, April 19
I have to see dominee Veenhuizen to talk about my profession of faith. He will come to the farm for catechism lessons, since it is too dangerous for me to go to his place because of German raids in town. The date for the profession of faith service has been set for July 2, 1944.

In the evening there is a warning and we disappear into the *hol*.

Thursday, April 20

We stay around the farm and start to clear out ditches. The alert is still on. In the evening we hear two cars passing along the main road. A while later they return. The S.S. has arrested Mr. Wiggers who is heavily involved in Resistance work, including hiding Jews. Ome Jan and Mother Wikkerink immediately go into hiding as they strongly suspect treason. Later we hear that 22 of Ome Jan's co-workers were arrested as a result of a traitor. Some are killed and some escape while being transported. Most of them were transported to the western part of Holland where, in the dunes along the North Sea, they were forced to dig their own graves, stand in front of them, then were shot to death. Others are also buried here. This site is now an honour cemetery called *Bloemendaal*.

Tuesday, April 25

Dominee Veenhuizen comes and we talk about my decision to make profession of faith. He wants me to do some study so this coming week I have to learn the first ten lessons!

Wednesday, April 26

For the past few weeks people have been persistently talking about an upcoming invasion. A while ago I wrote to Jan ter Horst, in concentration camp. He was very sick. Today I receive a letter from him in which he says that he is getting a little better.

MAY 1944

Monday, May 1

The S.S. is raiding the town, and also a neighbouring town, Lichtenvoorde. Several men are picked up.

Friday, May 5

Brother Gerrit visits me and he is going to stay for the night. Safer here than in town. The three of us have to sleep in the *hol*. Gerrit sleeps at the bottom end, with his head near our feet. But, this means that his feet are near our heads, and he has awful stinking feet. We cover his feet with an old jacket. It does not do much good, but finally we fall asleep.

Monday, May 9

Today we weed the barley field. Towards evening we hear shooting at the farm *Nonhof*, our neighbour who is a member of the NSB.

Dominee Veenhuizen comes to talk about the lessons I have studied and gives me some more work. This time I have to learn lessons 16 to 26. I find it quite a bit to learn in such a short time.

These days I keep myself busy with working in the fields, weeding and hoeing oats; preparing the vegetable garden for planting; planting beans; cleaning hay bins, the stable and the threshing floor; moving cows from one pasture to another. I also work in the potato field, which is growing fast.

Sunday, May 21

During the night we hear many planes on their way to Germany. A cloudy sky is an advantage for them. It makes it harder for the searchlights to detect them. Duisburg is being bombed tonight. Also the alarm is sounded again, and we dress to be ready to go into hiding.

Monday, May 22

People expect that the invasion will start this week. We better listen to the BBC tonight. Again we hear hundreds of planes during the night.

This week I do some more work around the house, mowing the lawn with a scythe, cutting wood, milking cows, and cutting wood for the neighbour.

We receive word that the *Landwacht*, also known as *Groenen*, is active tonight. These are Dutch people who sympathize with the Germans. They can be recognized by their green uniforms.

Saturday, May 27

Today I clean the lower outside walls of the house. These are whitewashed and need a good cleaning. We are expecting visitors and it has to look nice.

Monday, May 29

It is nice weather, and I lie on my back in the grass. Here comes Gerrit Wikkerink with his sister Henny on the back of his bike.

"Here is company for you," he says, "as long as you bring her back home tonight."

I promise to take care of that if Henny agrees with it. After supper, at about 7:30 p.m., I take her home. We had a nice time together and with the rest of the family.

JUNE 1944

Tuesday, June 6

Dominee Veenhuizen comes again to the farm to give me catechism instruction. On July 2nd I hope to do profession of faith in the *Oosterkerk*. Dominee Veenhuizen mentions that the invasion has started. The Allies have landed in France.

Wednesday, June 7

The doctor's wife comes to the farm with a message that Jan ter Horst can be picked up in the town of Winterswijk. He was arrested in January with the other 41 young men at the church, and was put into a concentration camp. They have now let him go. He arrives home at 3 p.m., more dead than alive.

Wednesday, June 14

I have to go into town to pick up my watch. It is 2 p.m. and I remember that Henny has to go to catechism at 2:30 p.m. I decide to bike in the direction of her uncle's farm, where she is staying. I really want to see her again; there is something special about her. I take the country lane by Landsbulten and wait there. It takes quite a long time, but finally I see her coming around the bend. She is surprised to see me and thinks that maybe there is something wrong, and that I have bad news. I assure her that everything is okay and that I had counted on her coming this way. "I wanted to see you again," I tell her.

Sunday, June 18

A visit from Henny, her sister Jo, and Bep Jamoel. Jo and Bep are active couriers for the L.O. I have a little time alone with Henny, and I tell her about my feelings for her.

Monday, June 19

Johan and I have to transfer the cows again. One of the calves takes off, and this makes Johan mad. He gives it a good kick. He kicks so hard that the leather strap of his wooden shoe breaks. Now he has to walk the rest of the way home with one bare foot.

Once in a while, when we help out at a neighbouring farm, we have lunch there. Occasionally there will be some paper money under the plate as a small thank you. This usually ends up in the collection plate on Sundays, as we really do not need to buy anything.

JULY 1944

Sunday, July 2
Today I do profession of faith, together with 18 other young people. The organist plays: "*Boven de sterren daar zal het eens lichten.*" "Above the stars there is the eternal light."

Thursday, July 6
Ome Jan's birthday party. Johan and I go there at 7:30 p.m. Jo, Henny's sister, has a game called Love, Friendship and Hate. I don't let on that I know this game, and when I am asked if I hate anyone, I say, "Yes, I hate Henny." She gives me a funny look. But at the end of the game, those who hate have to make up for it by giving that other person a kiss. Henny now realizes that I must have known the game, and we are good friends again. I have the feeling that her mother looks at me in a strange way, and I notice that it is getting very warm in the room.

Back at the farm Johan says, "I have a feeling that something is going on between the two of you." He is right!

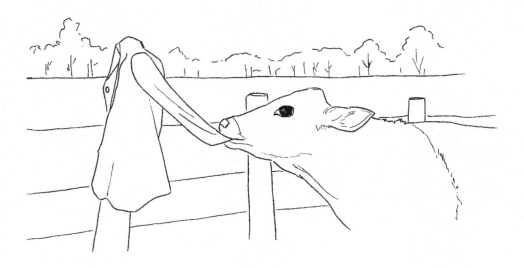

Saturday, July 8

Cows and calves are supposed to eat grass, but here is one who likes jacket sleeves. We are working in one of the pastures and my jacket is hanging on a post. At lunch hour we try to catch wild ducks, and when we come back one of the calves has eaten the sleeve out of my jacket.

It starts to rain and we take a break. The ensuing conversation is very interesting and we forget the time. Johan says, "Why are we still sitting here? It is dry again."

Oom Herman says, "Oh, we are waiting for the next shower."

Thursday, July 13

We did not sleep well last night. The sow made lots of noise. Later we find out why. She is about to give birth, and by the end of the day there are nine little pigs. One of them is nearly dead, and Oom Herman puts it into a pail of water. That does the trick. With a big scream, it comes to life again. The mother sow is unwilling to feed her little ones. We have to pull her up off of her feet with a rope, so the little ones can get some nourishment. This procedure has to be repeated every two hours, day and night!

Thursday, July 20

Today I have to go to Henny's home to talk about our relationship and to ask if her father and mother have any objections about us building a future together. Her father is not home yet, but when he arrives, he asks me to help him dig some potatoes for his sister in Driebergen. No objections, but a warning that Henny is still very young. We are now unofficially engaged.

We hear that the Führer, Hitler, has been attacked. He is said to be slightly wounded and has a concussion. The war takes its toll on Germany. Everywhere many soldiers are taken prisoner. Each night many Allied planes bomb German cities.

Sunday, July 30

Henny comes to the farm after supper and stays until 8:30 p.m. I take her home, not knowing that they are raiding the town for young men. When we come close to the police station, we notice a commotion and see several Germans and *Groenen*. It is too late to turn back, and we just keep going. On both sides of the road are German police and we see that they have arrested some young men. They don't even look at us, which is fine with me. Our hearts beat a little faster, and we are very, very thankful that we pass through unhindered.

Monday, July 31
We are playing a little game with Herman Junior, youngest son of Oom Herman. He likes to earn money, and will do almost anything to get it. He can earn 10 cents if he is able to drop this coin into a funnel that is tucked into the belt of his pants. The 10 cent coin is placed on his forehead, with his head bent backwards. While he is standing in this position, face up, waiting for us to tell him to start, we take a glass of water and pour it into the funnel. Would you believe it? The coin fell on the floor.

Rumour has it that Warsaw in Poland has been liberated by the Russian army. Also that General Rommel (Germany) is dead in Normandy.

AUGUST 1944

Friday, August 4
NEWS: The Russian army has reached the German border. Rennes in Normandy has been taken by Allied troops.

During the night Henk vander Meulen, an *onderduiker*, has been arrested by 15 men from the *Landwacht* and Dutch S.S.

Sunday, August 6
The son of a neighbouring farmer comes flying into our kitchen. He is being chased by the *Groenen*. Together we go into the hiding place. The *Groenen* search at another neighbour's farm, but do not show up here. Last night an *onderduiker* was picked up at Vervelde's farm.

Monday, August 7

We are harvesting oats. When we come to this field we see five German soldiers resting under the oak trees. We decide to go to a different field, where we catch a rabbit. There is a warning that the *Groenen* will most likely be in our neighbourhood tonight. Be sure to spend the night in the hiding place.

Tuesday, August 8

When we get up for breakfast we hear shooting at the farm next door. I take off and leave the house for a five minute walk through small woods and fields. When I come to a wooded area, I feel safe enough to rest for a while. It is 8:30 a.m.

I must have fallen asleep for I wake up at 10 a.m. I see four other young men heading for a field of oats and follow them. Together we hide in this field, not knowing that the farmer has seen us. At about 10:30 his wife comes with a large coffee pot and some cups. "You stay here and we will tell you when it is safe to come out again," she says.

When we are finally able to go home, it is almost dark. The shot we heard this morning was at our neighbour Houwers, farm *Neerhof*, where the *Groenen* arrested a French soldier who escaped from a POW camp in Germany, and an *onderduiker*, Henk Walchien. Henk ran away and was shot at. The other *onderduiker*, Sebe, succeeded in getting away by fleeing into a field of rye. The rye was high and the *Groenen* lost sight of him.

Later we hear more details of what happened at the farm *Neerhof*.

The Houwers had two *onderduikers* and a French soldier hiding at their place. The French soldier had escaped from a POW camp in Germany. The German *Groenen* seemed to know that he was somewhere in our area. When they came to the Houwers, farm *Neerhof*, and stepped through the back door, they heard a noise on the threshing floor. They became suspicious that someone was in the hayloft, hiding. They were right. The three men had just crawled into their hiding place.

They were ordered to come out with the threat that bullets would be shot into the hayloft. One by one the men came out. Outside the *Groenen* were deciding what to do. Sebe said to Henk (in Dutch, which the Germans could not understand), "When I count, One Two, I will push one policeman into the other and we will both run." Sebe is big and strong, and at the right moment he pushed, hard. Henk sprinted along the laneway towards our farm and Sebe across the laneway into the rye field. Sebe got away, he cannot be seen anymore. Henk was not so lucky. He was in full view and they shot at him. He let himself fall, then started running again. Another shot, and by the time he fell and got up again the *Groenen* grab hold of him. This was the shot we heard at breakfast. We thought it was a bicycle tire that blew. Another neighbour who saw what was happening took his bike and raced to our farm to warn us. "Get away," he yelled. I left through the back door, but took along my egg, a spoon and… a little bit of salt. I planned to eat my egg later.

In another district, Heurne, five boys are picked up. Two of these were shot and wounded and are now in hospital.

Tonight we are going to sleep in the cornfield. When it is dark we pick a good spot and put some straw down, then on top of that, a horse blanket. Jan and I settle down for the night. All of a sudden Jan whispers, "I see somebody standing there." When we look closer, we realize it is the scarecrow.

The moon and the stars are very bright. We wake up in the morning with the dew drops falling off the leaves onto our faces. Had a very good sleep.

Thursday, August 10

The Resistance workers have raided the distribution office in Doetinchem and got away with most of the ration coupons. Hooray!

NEWS: The newspaper reports that 33 people in Holland received the death sentence and were shot to death. Allied troops are approximately 75 kilometres from Paris.

Friday, August 11

Watch out, a strange car is seen near the clubhouse of the people who sympathize with the Germans. This time the *Zwarten*, who are just as bad as the *Groenen*, are in our area. The oldest son of farmer Houwers is picked up by the *Zwarten*.

While riding my bike to do some errands, my pant leg gets stuck in the chain. This happens four times. An awful job to get it out. I might as well walk - it would be faster.

Saturday, August 12

We hear that the *Zwarten* and the *Groenen* are searching for one of their men, Beckers. Beckers is a member of the militia that sympathizes with the Germans. Apparently he is very dangerous and the Resistance movement is convinced that he should disappear. The Germans won't find him. What we hear later is that Beckers was taken to a farm, shot and killed by the Resistance. He was buried in a field which was immediately ploughed under by the farmer.

About 40 German police are roaming around in the area and are terribly mad. They pick up eight boys but they all find a way to escape. One jumps off the motorbike, another jumps out of a car. A third escapes on a bike. One of the policemen stands with two boys at the City Hall when one boy takes off. The policeman runs after him and number two runs away in the other direction. One of the *Groenen* falls with his bike and his rifle goes off. He runs away thinking somebody is shooting at him.

The Resistance has freed one of the men who were jailed.

Sunday, August 20
Extra warning. Tonight they expect a big raid in town and surrounding area.

Monday, August 21
Ome Jan and Tante Dela come in the afternoon and stay for supper. It is safer here at the farm than in town. During the night two Jews are picked up in town.

Wednesday, August 23
Allied troops are 100 kilometres east of Paris. We still have to be on the alert. *Groenen* and *Zwarten* are raiding surrounding areas. They have caught another man.

Saturday, August 26
The sound of sirens can be heard from across the border. A few minutes later the airplanes are flying over and then all hell breaks loose over Germany. A terrible noise from exploding bombs just across the border.

SEPTEMBER 1944

Friday, September 1
NEWS: Allied troops have advanced through France and are 15 kilometres from the Belgian border.

The *Zwarten* are raiding town again.

The neighbour's cow has to give birth to a calf. She is in the pasture behind the farmhouse. The farmer thinks that things are not going as they should. He is going to run home to get the ropes to pull the calf out. In order to run faster he leaves his wooden shoes behind and goes barefoot.

This is our chance. We pick a fresh thistle leaf and put this in his wooden shoe. Now we just wait for him to return and see his reaction when he jumps back into his wooden shoes.

Here he comes. He steps into his *klompen* and walks away without noticing anything. Amazed, we look at each other. He must have hardened skin under his feet!

Sunday, September 3
NEWS: Allied troops marching on very rapidly. They are approximately 60 kilometres from the border bewtween Belgium and the Netherlands.

We don't see any more V-1's coming over on their way to England. In the afternoon and evening we hear sounds of heavy rumbling in the distance. There must be heavy fighting across the border.

Monday, September 4
NEWS: Allied troops are in Maastricht (province of Limburg) and are marching north very quickly. In the next few days city after city is being liberated and the German soldiers are running for their lives. The Germans change our curfew from 9:30 p.m. to 8 p.m.

The Canadian troops are in the western part of Holland, the English in middle and Americans in east. The Dutch sympathizers with the Nazi's are fleeing the southern part of Holland and are coming by droves into our area. It is getting crowded and a bit uncomfortable. Another heavy bombardment in Germany, many airplanes coming over.

The mayor of a nearby town is a traitor and was getting scared; he has fled to Germany. Also one of our neighbours, farmer Bulsink from the farm *Nonhof*, who is a Nazi sympathizer, left for Germany.

Saturday, September 9
Nine *onderduikers* meet with the bank manager. When the war is over we want to present the people of this town with a memorial for all their help to us. We

have set up a committee and will start to gather names and money to build a monument. Eventually this results in a very moving ceremony after the war. Across from the railroad station a nice fountain will be erected to show our thankfulness to the local people for their kindness, courage and unselfishness. This is now known as The Hiders' Monument in Aalten.

Sunday, September 10

Henny arrives at the farm in afternoon. We go to church together. This is the first time. It was always too dangerous to get into town, but there is so much confusion and fear among the *Groenen* and *Zwarten* that it seems safe to try. Henny leaves the farm at 7:30 p.m. so she can be home at 8 p.m. curfew.

Wednesday, September 13

8 a.m. A warning not to go into town today. City Hall personnel are on strike because they do not want to follow up on a German order to recruit men for defence purposes. They now expect the German police to raid town. All men are in hiding; women are delivering things and doing all the kind of work that men normally do.

Johan and I go into our hiding place early.

Friday, September 15

Since our mayor is in hiding the Germans have appointed a local man who is a Nazi sympathizer as temporary mayor. A couple that wants to get married has to go home again because this mayor does not know the procedures. At noon there is a warning for our area. Danger is all around. Two men from town come to hide at our farm. The whole town is devoid of men.

Peter on the ladder, Frans van Tienhoven near the roof of the haystack. When the onderduikers had to hide here, the farmer
took the ladder away after the men had climbed up.

At night we try to sleep in the big rye-stack. We climb in using a long ladder
which is then taken away. We now are on our own. It is not all that warm
either, because it is outside. We are awake quite early but cannot get down
until the farmer gets up and puts the ladder back up.

There are many NSB men in town who are fleeing the approaching Allied
forces. The farms around us are flooded with these people. One gets 21,
another 16 of them.

All of the men are supposed to register for work of defence. The Town Hall employees, who are now in hiding, have taken all registers with them so that names and addresses are not available to the Germans.

Sunday, September 17

No church this morning. People are coming back warning not to go to church. German's are picking up young girls and women to work for them and do kitchen work, washing, ironing and other chores.

Hundreds of planes come over. Germans order all bikes to be handed over to them. In town five *onderduikers* are being chased. None are captured. In an outlying area one *onderduiker* is wounded but not captured.

Electricity is cut off and we improvise with candles.

A new curfew is imposed. We now have to be in at 7 p.m., starting today. We hear this at five minutes to seven and we have a visitor. She has to stay here for the night.

Monday, September 18

We wake up because of a noise on the roof of the rye stack. Somebody is throwing apples on the roof to wake us up. The farmer is already standing on top of the ladder looking in at our bedroom. He wants us to hear the latest news. NEWS: More towns are liberated and 80,000 paratroopers have landed north of the river Rhine in Holland. So that's why we saw all these planes yesterday, hundreds and hundreds of them.

6 p.m. Time to do the milking. Johan comes out of the hiding place to go to the house but sees a German soldier and a civilian. The German had walked behind the farm, looked through a little window just as my brother was going into the hiding place.

He must have seen him. The three of us go and check it out. We take some shovels and an axe along. When we come to the house the men have left again. All they wanted was eggs.

They say that Arnhem is in Allied hands. This is close by. Unfortunately they have to retreat, and there is worse still to come.

Even farmers from this area hide in ditches and wooded areas to escape from being rounded up. Those that are caught are being put to work digging defence ditches close to Arnhem.

The situation is so bad there, that some of the bravest are running for it, back home. Thousands of people fleeing these areas come our way. Also many German soldiers.

Many planes fly over. German fighter planes come to meet them. We see some exciting action. Four Allied planes are after a German plane. They shoot and shoot until the German plane starts burning. With a trail of smoke behind it the German plane dives head first to the ground. The pilot floats behind it and we see his parachute open. It seems that the Allied planes shoot at everything that moves.

Thursday, September 21

I take the day to go around and collect money for the onderduiker monument. At one point I hear several airplanes coming. They are low. Must be looking for targets. I jump off the bike and fall flat on the ground. They fly past shooting like madmen. Don't know if they aimed at me or not but I am glad I stopped moving.

NEWS: Heavy fighting by Arnhem and Nijmegen. Bridge over the Maas in Allied hands.

The noise of the fighting is heard very clearly.

Every day we listen anxiously to the news from BBC. The fight in and around Arnhem is terrible and the bridge there is still in German hands.

Tuesday, September 26

We see and hear a strange item flying through the air. Very high and very fast. Never saw anything like it. Later we learn that this is Germany's secret weapon developed by Werner von Braun, the V-2. Another one in the evening on its way to England where it creates havoc.

In town, an announcement that every man from 17 to 50 years of age has to report for duties of digging fox holes and trenches. You have to bring a shovel, blanket, fork and spoon. The whole town runs empty. Nobody reports for duty and the result is that we get another chance. If we do not report our homes will be burned down. A number of men show up at our door to hide and so it is in all other districts surrounding the town. Still, 17 men have shown up for duty. For some reason seven of them are exempted and sent home.

Thursday, September 28

Bombs fall at a neighbouring town. A terrible noise. Four more times another attack. A totally different scene behind our farm in the lane where the 80 year old farmer Eppink, who has dementia, is holding the reins of his old horse. He is sitting on the two-wheeled wagon heading home; his horse knows the way. A beautiful sight – a symbol of peace that I have to preserve with a photograph.

Farmer Eppink heading home.

We are warned that the *Groenen* and the S.S. are going for a big hunt tomorrow morning.

Friday, September 29

The lady from next door comes to tell us that the *Groenen* are at their house looking for *onderduikers*. The four of us quietly and quickly disappear in our hiding places.

Airplanes are constantly overhead and we conclude that they are dropping something. We hear a terrible noise in the distance. The German soldiers are leaving town and it is believed that no more raids are planned for today. We come out of hiding.

OCTOBER 1944

Sunday, October 1

There is no more going to church; it is too dangerous. We have now, for some time, organized church services at the farms in our area.

When we come home from the service we hear that the *Zwarten* are at a nearby farm. We hear shooting and decide to disappear. There are five of us and we all manage to get in our *hol*. We see young men all over, walking through fields and wooded areas.

Henny comes to visit. She was going to church, but since there are no elders and deacons church is cancelled. Town is full of *Zwarten* and *Groenen* and all men from 16 to 60 years of age are arrested. In the evening we get another warning. The farmer was in town and saw six transports full of men leaving for digging duties. No news on the radio tonight, it is too dangerous to listen.

Monday, October 2

The postman has started early today to warn everybody that there will be another hunt for men today. Sure enough, somebody has spotted them in our area.

Four American airplanes are bombing the railroad south of us. The first two come diving out of the sky and drop their load, then the other two. It is a wonderful sight and we hope they have destroyed the rails so no German trains can pass by. Tante comes running outside and tells us to come inside, but we think it is too interesting so we stay outside to watch.

We get a warning in the afternoon that the *Zwarten* are now very close. They are at the neighbor's farm. We decide to hide. Since we have not finished our warm meal we take our plates along. The first one in takes our plates and then we hoist ourselves up into the *hol*. Now we have to eat the rest. It is pitch-dark inside and to find the food we have to feel with our fingers where it is and if there is anything left on the plate.

The neighbour is getting worried about his son. He should have been home a long time ago. The *Zwarten* have been chasing him and almost caught him. He got away and has been hiding somewhere until it was safe to go home.

We transfer to the hiding place in the barn. We have some light here and can read a little bit. This place is above the pigs in the pigsty. Frans who has to go to the bathroom opens the floodgate and lets it go down in a steady stream. The little pigs are standing there, looking up with open mouths.

Word comes that they are still raiding the area. By now they have been almost at every farm, except ours. After 6 p.m. things seem to calm down and we come out of hiding. I am sitting in the small kitchen by the wood stove trying to update my diary. Mina, the daughter, remarks, "It must be very interesting that diary, especially for your children and grandchildren."

We have not had such a restless day as this one.

At one farm, Wiggers-Salomon, three young women are arrested because the men are not home. If they do not show up before 7 p.m. the farm will be burned down.

The men do not show up, the farm is not burned down and the three women are let go.

Tuesday, October 3

Henny's sister comes to get some milk at our farm. This is a regular routine. One of the family members comes to fetch some milk each day. It is strictly forbidden by the German police. If caught, you can be punished quite severely. It is still not safe in town and they talk about the police going back to the farms to catch more men.

Someone mentions that in Apeldoorn, where I come from, several people were shot to death and left on street corners. All because of sabotage and men not reporting for digging and other duties.

In another town, Gorssel, the S.S. wanted to arrest six people who were then going to be killed for a similar reason.

One of Henny's uncles is on the list of six. He was in church and managed to escape. Another man is not at home when they come for him, so they take his son who is sick in bed. After these men are shot, they are rolled in sheets and taken to a cemetery on a flat bottomed cart and put in a mass grave. This all happened within one hour.

Throughout these years it is very difficult to keep your clothes in decent shape. You cannot buy anything new that is reasonably good. Even a pair of socks is luxury. You hang on to what you have. Especially socks, they slide down your feet all the time. If you can get a pair of sock suspenders you are in luck. My brother has a pair, but they are getting to the point they cannot do the job anymore. He tried to fix them with safety pins which worked for a while, but no longer. Tante will try to do something about it with thread and needle. She is doing a remarkable job, considering the lack of suitable yarn. I tell my brother to hang on to the safety pins. They might come in handy for use on the diapers of his future children. "Two is not enough," I say. "You need three pins."

"You need four pins now," remarks my brother. "Nowadays they fold the diapers in a square."

Frans, the other *onderduiker*, comes in and I ask him how many safety pins are used on a diaper. "I don't know," he says.

"Well, put your pants down so we can see," says the farmer.

"Four," says Frans. "Nowadays they fold the diapers not in a point but in a square." After some more discussion we decide that a diaper folded into a point needs three pins, and the one folded into a square needs four pins. And my brother has to find a few more safety pins.

Allied armies must be making some progress. We see German soldiers in the area. Two soldiers in front of our house. We sprint inside and into the hiding place. The two soldiers move on.

Wednesday, October 4

American planes, quite low, are shooting over town. It must be small bombs, the explosions are not very loud. Railroad station is their target. Part is destroyed.

Lumberyard's boiler room is flattened; chimney stands on a dangerous angle.

At three p.m. more planes, this time 16 in total. Railroad to the west being bombed. The first two planes come down and each drops two bombs, then the next two, and again. The railroad has suffered enormous destruction. Very interesting sight.

I have to go to a nearby country store to get some groceries. The name of the store is Dahlia. On my way there I meet a German soldier. I wonder what his reaction will be to see me. He says *Guten tag*. I don't say anything but keep going on my way to the store. When I get to the store they are amazed that I, an *onderduiker*, am coming to get some groceries. Nobody, and that is nobody, shows himself outside in this whole area for fear of being picked up.

I didn't know it was that bad.

After supper we have to milk the cows. Frans comes along and he will milk the Red cow. It is only his second time milking a cow, but he is doing pretty well.

Shortly after seven we bring the cows inside. Now it is time for me to bring my diary up-to-date.

NEWS: The Allied forces are making good progress. They drop 6,000 kilograms of bombs on the island of Walcheren in Zeeland (a Dutch province). Canadian troops are forcing their way up north, from Antwerpen (Belgium) towards Breda (province of Brabant). They are within 35 kilometres of this city and the Polish army is 25 kilometres from Breda. In Aken (Germany) the Allied forces have broken through the Siegfried line. This is a very strong defence line of the German army.

Also the news mentions that Warsaw (Poland) is back in German hands.

Thursday, October 5

After we eat breakfast and peel the potatoes, we go to the potato field to gather the leaves for compost. Mr. Wiggers comes in to buy 100 pounds of potatoes. While we are busy with this the Allied planes fly over. You never know what they are going to bomb next, so we keep a close eye on them. They pass over and this time it is the next town Winterswijk where the bombs fall.

A little later we hear the sirens in Germany full blast. We call this the German National Anthem. And yes, there they come. The sky is loaded with hundreds of Allied bombers, a sight to behold. The sun reflects brightly on these silver birds. Like beautiful birds they glide through the sky holding their eggs until they are over German territory just a few miles away. "*Alles, Alles, Uber Deutsland.*" "All good things will come over Germany."

Around one o'clock they return. Some fighter planes fly quite low and suddenly begin to shoot. It is so close by that we stay in the kitchen for safety.

Friday, October 6

We are up before seven o'clock. While we are washing ourselves by the pump outside, four American fighter bombers fly overhead. They are going further on over to Germany. After we have taken the cows to the pasture and had our breakfast, Gerrit, Frans and I peel potatoes, and we sing all kinds of songs, especially folk songs. We feel good because the air attacks seem to be too much for Germany and we might be closer to liberation than we think.

In the afternoon the sky is filled again with many, many planes. The German fighters also come. One Allied plane is burning and makes an emergency landing close by in *het Klooster*. I don't know if there are any survivors.

Saturday, October 7

After we have done our morning duties we drink coffee at 10:30 a.m.

We get a little scare when we see a gentleman in a brown suit on a bike coming to the house. Johan takes off in a hurry to hide but before I can get out of the kitchen the man is already inside. Just before he came in the door I had seen somebody else right behind him, Ome Jan. It could not be dangerous. The man in the brown suit is one of Henny's uncles from the town of Gorssel, he is a brother-in-law of Ome Jan. Since I have finished my coffee I go back to the pasture to continue work. A little later Ome Jan comes to where I am and introduces me to his brother-in-law, also an uncle Jan.

I really appreciate this. Henny's father treats me as if I am already one of the family too.

At noon when we are eating we hear many bombers fly over. Later, working in the field behind the house, we hear a terrible noise in the direction Emmerick (Germany). The bombers are doing their work. An awful noise, you cannot describe it. Our legs shake from the strong vibrations in the air. It takes about an hour before it calms down. I now have a terrible headache. We see a heavy column of what looks like smoke or dust rising in the distance and it does not take long before the air above us and around us is filled with smog. It has a strong burned smell. In Aalten pieces of burned paper and cloth float down out of the sky.

Since it is Saturday, I clean around the house, raking, and sweeping. Then I have a nice bath and put on clean clothes. The bath consists of a pail with warm water which I take to a cleaned out stable in the barn. You have to wash with a bar of soap that is not soap at all. It does not create any lather, smells strange; you might say it stinks a bit. But then, nobody has any real soap.

Shortly after 9 p.m. I go to bed. Because of all the stress, being away from home, hiding in uncertainty, the battle front coming closer, bombing all around us, planes shot down, boys and men being picked up at random by the Germans and the Dutch organization *Landwacht*, I have a good crying spell and amazingly I fall asleep.

Sunday, October 8

Today church at our farm. Gerrit is reading the sermon. There are 19 boys. The collection nets 5 guilders and 4 cents. Nobody earns any money here. At 3 p.m. we dare to go to the real church in town. Today they celebrate the Lord's Supper. Very few men are in church, it is too dangerous. Johan and I sleep at Wikkerink tonight in a real bed with fresh sheets. What a treat!

We hear that the Allied troops are making good progress in the south of Holland. Many members from the NSB movement flee to the more Northern provinces. One of them, appointed mayor of a town, has fled too. He gets into an argument with a German soldier who in turn smashes his head in. The mayor is in a hospital! He has a major concussion.

Monday, October 9

On our way home to the farm this morning we suddenly come upon two *Landwachters*, Dutch men who joined a German controlled militia. They are armed. We come out of a small path to reach the main road. They don't seem to notice us, but for security we do not take the main road but scoot across it into *Klein Zwitserland*. A winding path through trees and bushes gives us good cover. When we come to the farm there are four German soldiers right in front of us busy setting up a field telephone.

In the immediate neighbourhood 't Villekesderp we hear a lot of shooting. The *Landwacht* is in action with about 30 men. Hunting for men. The *onderduikers* fly in all directions. One is shot in the shoulder, another in his leg. Nobody is captured. Around five o'clock Ome Jan comes to the farm. I wonder if he has somehow been involved in this conflict. Hiding escapees?

In the afternoon we do some work in the field with sugar beets. Wow, here come 20 *Landwachters* but they stay on the road. And pass towards the neighbour. But then there are two *Moffen* by our farm. It is a relief to see them pass by too.

In the evening my brother Gerrit and I go and listen to the news of the BBC. NEWS: Our Queen Wilhelmina is preparing to leave England in order to be ready to go to Holland where a large part of the southern country is liberated.

Some Allied planes return from their mission over Germany. Two planes are shot down.

Tuesday, October 10
Watch out. One hundred *Zwarten*, sympathizers with Germany, are in Aalten. They are hunting for men.

Wednesday, October 11
This is going to be a strange day; it seems to get more dangerous by the minute. First a *Landwachter* walks over the path about 100 metres behind the house. We keep an eye on him but keep working as if nothing happened. And nothing is happening. Then four of them approach through the neighbor's pasture and head straight for us. I say to Frans, "If they don't change direction we have to run." But they do change direction and suddenly they start to shoot. However, they are hunting for other wild things. Rabbits and hares this time.

The *Moffen* are also busy. They need bikes for the soldiers. Germany is running short on transportation. My brother, Gerrit the barber, is at a nearby farmer to give him a shave. When he sees the German soldiers coming he is as quick as lightning to get away. He is just home at the farm when two other

Peter Van Essen

soldiers show up. We run to our hiding place until they have disappeared. NEWS: The BBC says that in Utrecht (the Netherlands) 4,000 men are picked up and put to work to make new defence lines for German soldiers. Dangerous work. Allied planes are always aiming at this activity. In Aalten the Germans demand that by tomorrow morning at nine o'clock 80 men have to report for work.

Thursday, October 12

We see more and more *Landwachters* and decide not to hide anymore. They are all on their way north to escape the war zone, and probably more scared than we are. We cannot play hide and seek all day! In the afternoon we work in the bean patch. German soldiers are again hunting for bikes. In front of our farm, three Germans are using their telephone. One of them, about 19 years old, says, "You better hide your bikes, and then the war will be over sooner." Then suddenly there are the bike thieves, rifle on the shoulder. They don't find any bikes. A little later another three Germans; they cannot find any bikes either. One of them says, "You people are smart; I would have hidden my bike too." And with that he marches on.

I get a letter from home and also two pair of socks. One pair is for day and night, the other for night use only. We sleep with our socks on for it is very cold in the loft of the barn.

My family tells me that on October 2nd in Apeldoorn 12,000 men have been picked up in a *razzia*. They needed 14,000 men to work in the war zone near the towns of Dieren, Doesburg and Rhenen. To intimidate people and scare them into registering, the Germans have killed some men and put their bodies on several sidewalks, and left them there for more than three days.

My uncle Frits from Apeldoorn, who was to pick up *evacuees* moved out of war zone, was shot in the leg.

NEWS: The Allied troops are now west of Arnhem and it is expected that very heavy fighting will follow.

Friday, October 13

The calves are in the pasture and I have to make sure there is enough water in the trough. When I look up, I see some NSB's coming. They start shooting at something behind me. When I turn to see what is going on they walk through the next field with sugar beets to locate a rabbit they have shot.

Instead of a rabbit they come up with a bike. It is the bike from the neighbour's son Gerrit. He had hidden it there.

We find out that they are temporarily stationed in a neighbouring farm and that is where this bike ends up. When Gerrit comes home at five o'clock he does not waste a moment. He goes straight to this neighbour and comes home with his bike.

When work in the barn is done and the dishes are cleaned, I start again with my diary. The old lamp, running on carbide, starts to stink and it gives hardly any light so I have to stop. I still have one candle, but Mina, the daughter, needs it to do some sewing. So I have to quit again.

Saturday, October 14

We are working in the barn when we hear the sound of airplanes. Better have a look. Here they come, right overhead. And are we getting a show! A swift turn in the air and the first two planes dive towards earth. Two bombs fall from the last plane and a few seconds later they explode with a terrible noise. Then come the next two and we see the same thing again. Seven more planes repeat this activity. Their aim is the railroad, but the damage should have been much greater; they did not hit their target as well as they should have.

The window in our little kitchen fell out from the noise of the bombing and we replace it to keep the heat in.

At night I write a letter to Henny by the light of a small candle in the little room upstairs.

Sunday, October 15

1 p.m. Trijntje Rots comes to our farm. She lives in town and by the look on her face you can see that something is wrong. At noon the *Landwacht* and a German soldier surrounded the house of the Wikkerink family. Ome Jan is

the head of the Resistance movement in this part of the country. They captured three men, Ome Jan, Anton Nusselder, a Resistance worker, and Joop Winkelman, an *onderduiker*. This is indeed terrible news; everybody is shocked. The three are locked up in the station of the *Rijks Politie* which is a regional police service.

Later we hear more details.

At the breakfast table at the home of Ome Jan this morning, the Bible reading is Psalm 91. Read this to understand the significance of what happens later in the day. The family attends the morning church service and comes home for a cup of coffee. While they enjoy this with their visitor Anton Nusselder, a Resistance worker, the house is suddenly surrounded by German soldiers and *Landwacht*. Three men are arrested: Ome Jan, Anton and Joop. They are marched off to be jailed. City Hall and jail are close by while the *Rijks Politie* jail is further away. If they were to end up at the City Hall, it would mean certain death for the three men. At the *Rijks Politie* station, Ome Jan has friends and helpers. It takes about five minutes to walk to City Hall; halfway there is the turn off towards the barracks and jail for the *Rijks Politie*. Ome Jan prays constantly that they may turn right, and it is a long three minute walk. Coming to the crucial point, they do turn right, into Slicher van Bathstraat. The rest of the walk is a prayer of thanksgiving.

The three are put into separate cells and the *Rijks Politie* takes over for now. After the Germans have left, a policeman approaches Ome Jan and asks, "How are we going to arrange your escape?" A plan is made and executed in minute detail. The guard is knocked out with ether after a physical struggle, some black marks and blood on the wall, and some other necessary little details. In the meantime three bikes have arrived and the prisoners are on their way out.

Someone from Aalten is talking to a farmer telling him the shocking news that Ome Jan was picked up about an hour and a half ago. "That cannot be," says the farmer. "I just met them on their bikes, riding out of town."

Lien goes with Johan to Aalten to see what they can do. At 4 p.m. they return to the farm and Henny is with them. Henny looks very pale. In Aalten there is a rumour that the three men have escaped already. Oom Herman goes to Aalten to see how things are. When he comes to the house of Ome Jan the

Germans are there and take him and Mother Wikkerink to the City Hall for interrogation. Oom Herman is let go shortly after but Mother Wikkerink is kept until eight o'clock and she can just make it home in time. Curfew is at 8 p.m.

The younger children Janny, Ineke en Dikkie come to our farm in the evening. The rumours seem to be reality. The Germans are seething mad and pick up several VIPs in town who will be punished with death if Ome Jan does not turn himself in. We learn later that nobody ever told Ome Jan about this for had he known he would most certainly have given in to them. We don't sleep very well this night. NEWS: BBC mentioned that special prayer services are held for the people in still occupied Holland.

Monday, October 16

After breakfast, I do the dishes together with Henny. Frans helps me to peel potatoes; there will be twelve people for dinner.

Henny and I go to the little room in the attic to pray together for the situation with her father and the VIP's and then she leaves to go to her uncle's farm *de Haart*.

Mina is going to Aalten again to see if there is anything she can do for Mother Wikkerink. The town crier is going around with a message from the Germans. All men ages 12 to 60 years have to report for work. Dominee Gerritsma, one of the VIP's who was arrested, is released again.

In town the Germans pick up every bike they see. Mother Wikkerink was ordered to report again to the City Hall. They want to know where her husband is. She does not know and eventually she is allowed to go home again.

In this area there are many activities against the Germans.

We suspect that the farm of Wiggers-Salomon is used for meetings of the Resistance movement. The Germans must have some suspicion or knowledge of this and this must be the reason they have the house and property expropriated.

I write this poem:

Helaas zijn er ogenblikken
Duisterer nog dan des afgronds nacht,

Die een Christen's moed verschrikken
Terwijl hij op God's redding wacht..
In our life there are some moments
Darker than the darkest night,
When a Christian's faith is tested
And he waits to see God's light.

Tuesday, October 17

Dora Hei comes to let us know that the house of Ome Jan has been burned out by the Germans. The VIP hostages are free again. The plan was to kill all hostages if Ome Jan did not turn himself in. Everybody is very relieved and thankful for answered prayers.

Wednesday, October 18

People are being picked up again, this time as new hostages. Farmer Rietman, Scholte Eppink, Farmer Vervelde, Deunk from Bara.

This is a new way of getting men to register for digging trenches. Tomorrow morning men and boys have to report for duty before noon. If they don't, 12 hostages will be killed. When they come to our neighbour's farm, farmer Jan is not home. His sister Hanna has to hand over her personal identity papers and she can pick them up again within a few hours. When she gets there they don't know anything and send her home without her papers.

Frans, Herman, Johan and I have been in our hiding place all during the raids. Many, many times we spend time there when we receive warnings about raids or sudden attacks.

At 3 p.m. Mother Wikkerink comes with Wimke. A little later Henny comes. What a nice surprise. She stays until the next morning.

Oom Herman, Tante and Henny are darning a pile of socks. Since you cannot buy any new socks you always wear the same ones and it shows! Mine are really bad and Henny scolds me for it. I try to tell her it is not my fault. There is not much sock left to begin with, it is all patched-up holes. She does not go for it, but lovingly fixes them.

Our farm *de Koekoek* seems to be an emotional refuge.

Thursday, October 19

Many from the neighbourhood drop in and ask what to do, to report or not report for digging duty. The pastors of town have printed a pamphlet about this and it is written in such a way that it will, in my opinion, encourage people to report. It does not take long and we hear that many men are reporting for duty.

Dominee Veenhuizen drops in at our farm and we talk about it. I don't agree with him at all and say, "You tell me to report for work with the Germans. I refused to work for them in Germany itself and decided to hide instead. The Resistance movement, risking their lives, made it possible for me and others to do so. Should we now turn around and go along with digging their trenches against our liberators? It would make a mockery of the heroic work and activities of the men and women in the Resistance movement".

The children of dominee Veenhuizen, who had come with their Dad, have to go to the farm of Wiggers. Johan will take them there. It happens that the *Zwarten* are in that area and they have spotted Johan when he snuck away. Eight-year old Jan Veenhuizen is asked, "Where did that man go?" He points in a totally different direction, keeping Johan out of their hands. Johan comes home safely.

NEWS: Diggers: 600 were requested and 1,200 reported. Allied troops in Holland making good progress.

In Venray (Province Noord Brabant) five kilometres gained. In Yugoslavia, Russians gain 50 kilometres over a 250 kilometre wide front line. In Holland, Allied are planning a big offensive.

We have changed the *hol* where we sleep so that it can hold three people. This *hol* is in the loft, way back in the barn.

Friday, October 20

Oh, oh, we already have a third person to sleep with us tonight. When we laid the straw as bedding yesterday we did not realize that the sides were a fair bit higher than the middle. I chose to sleep in the middle - nice and warm. But at midnight I wake up to find myself buried under two other sleepers. I cannot move to the left or right. I finally get myself out of this awful position. *Luctor et Emergo.* I struggle and emerge. I will try to sleep again but now on my side, and not on my back.

A funny noise comes from the stable underneath. One of the cows opens the floodgate and does a pee! Have you ever heard a cow pee? There is lots of it and there is no end to it. But the worst is still to come. The smell! It is overwhelming, it almost knocks you out. And you try to sleep. It takes a long time for it to waft away, but eventually it gets bearable.

I think the mice awoke from it. They are busy gnawing on the boards we used for a bedside. I try to scare them away by hitting the boards. This wakes up Gerrit, my brother, and he is going to help me. He only hits once for he forgot that there were boards on the side, and they are hard.

Glad to be called out of bed at 6 a.m.

I forgot to mention that last night Henny's little seven year-old brother Dikkie was here. Mina puts him on Johan's neck, a leg on either side of his head. Johan says, "Hey go away you, with your stinky behind." Right then Dikkie lets one go and tries to slide down in a hurry. There is a chair behind him, the kind with a high backrest that has a long narrow spindle on either side. Dikkie's pants get caught around one of these and it rips his pant leg apart from bottom to top.

Johan is assigned to get the news tonight. NEWS: The Betuwe is filled with Allied troops. Allies started a new offensive by Bergen and Rozendaal in Noord Brabant. Belgrado in hands of Russian army.

Saturday, October 21

Mina's birthday.

Some grain has been threshed and the straw is to be stored or stacked in the barn. We first do our straw and then we help *den Eume* next door. In afternoon I fix up the garden; it needs weeding. Suddenly I hear a loud noise as if something big is being fired. Then twice again a similar sound. I know that something is coming down on us. Cannot see anything but there is a strange sounding movement in the air. It is coming closer. I go to the front of the house, but nothing to detect in the air either. It seems to lose altitude. Suddenly... quiet... a few seconds... then a terrific blast.

Gerrit, who was out shaving some clients, comes back with the explanation. Just over the border in Germany they launched a new weapon: the V-2, a guided missile. They are far from perfect and many do not reach their target in England, but crash either in the Netherlands or even return and head back for Germany. Some are intercepted by the Allied planes.

At 5 p.m., after all work is done, I wash up in the cow stable with my small bathtub, the pail. However there seems to be some more work and it is 8:30 p.m. before we are finally finished.

At 9:30 p.m. we go to bed and I sleep in the *hol* above the pigsty with brother Gerrit. Frans is in the *hol* over the cow stable in the back of the farmhouse. He has strep throat. We are just bedded down when a Tommy flies overhead. It rattles its onboard machine gun like crazy. Three times it returns, and then it disappears. Johan calls us out of bed. Two big flares are hanging in the sky. That is something we must see. We let ourselves out of the hole, walk through the pig manure since we are in a hurry, and come outside to see... nothing! They just burned out. One came down by our neighbour *Neerhof*, the other landed close to our house.

Sunday, October 22

Mina comes into the stable and loudly wakes us. She is excited and tells us that Herman Junior found the parachute from the flare. It landed on the other side of *Neerhof* on a piece of land that belongs to our farm, Boesveldsland. This seems to be important news, for shortly after Tante comes to tell us the same. And then a few minutes later the farmer does the same thing.

At 9:30 a.m. church at our farm. At about nine they start coming. As always the *onderduikers* arrive from different directions. Nineteen in total. Johan reads the sermon that Mina just picked up from ds. Veenhuizen. It is based on the Heidelberg Catechism, Sunday 39, "Sovereignty". The collection brings in 5 guilders and 8 cents.

The afternoon is quiet. 6:30 supper and at seven o'clock there comes Henny and her sister Lien.

We enjoy a nice evening. Totally different than last Sunday, when Ome Jan was picked up. He is safely hiding after an amazing escape. When Henny and

I are doing the dishes there is a noise by the kitchen door outside. It is Jan who wanted to listen by the door and find out what we were doing, dishes or kissing? He ran into a pot, making a lot of noise.

Tante Gerda has a new baby named Johanna, Hannie for short. At 11 p.m. we all go to bed.

Gerrit and I have received new underwear from the L.O. organization. Wow. They think about everything.

Monday, October 23
Up at 6 a.m. The rest of the men who reported for digging duty are expected to come today for transport to Bochholt (Germany).

At our farm everybody is up and busy. At seven o'clock Henny is going back to *de Haart* via her grandparents. She has left her bike there for safety yesterday and pedals the rest of the way. Lien is going home at ten o'clock and she is taking the collected church money, 27 guilders, for the Resistance movement to use as they see fit.

Rijk vander Meulen comes to do some work on the *kelder*. He cannot start yet because Opa Wikkerink (father of Ome Jan) has not arrived yet. And Opa is the Boss. Rijk passes the time by smoking one cigarette after another and we see our tobacco diminishing by the minute. However, he is a nice guy and jokes around and laughs a lot.

We keep ourselves busy until early afternoon, but then we can take it easy. Not much left to be done.

At 9:30 p.m. we go to bed. Rijk, who is going to continue work on the *kelder* tomorrow, stays here for the night. Johan, Rijk and I sleep together in the *hol*. My brother Gerrit goes to the neighbouring farm *Neerhof* to sleep. It does not take long for Johan to fall asleep. Rijk and I talk for about an hour. He is a very nice fellow and very open with me.

NEWS: Heavy fighting by Den Bosch (Noord Brabant); Breskens (Zeeland) liberated.

Today Lien is coming to do the wash for Tante. I am appointed to help her and do the turning, by hand, of the handle on the washing machine. I help Gerrit who is putting up new tobacco leaves for drying. When that is done we move the geese to a new piece of pasture where we close in a small section with chicken wire for them.

Rijk needs a haircut and would like Gerrit the barber to cut and shave him this afternoon. After the haircut Gerrit starts to make him ready for a shave. Lots of soap on the brush and in no time he looks like Santa Claus.

Johan, Lien, and I are hanging around and we have a good time with the five of us. But Rijk, making fun of things, starts to joke about Henny and me; how we like each other. We all laugh about it. But Rijk laughs with his mouth wide open. I see my chance and grab the brush, indicating to my brother to hold off with the sharp razor and stick the brush straight into Rijk's mouth. I have never seen anything like it and we never laughed so hard. Rijk jumps up from the chair blowing and spitting soap all over the place. I am standing at a safe distance.

Supper time. Frans wants to tell us something. We call him Happy Frans since we have never seen him angry or mad. He tends to talk slowly... he also walks slowly. A good-natured fellow! "Yeah," he says: "Once I was sitting on the bank of the Gouwe." This is a river in Western part of Holland where he comes from.

He hesitates before he continues and I interject with, "Oh yah, and you fell in the water?"

"No," he says. "I did not fall in."

"Oh that is too bad," a number of us reply. He has a good laugh and we all share in it. I don't remember what the story was all about.

While we do the dishes someone bangs on the kitchen door. I open the door and in steps *de Guste*. Not a nice name, but she is a very large woman. Her husband is an active member of the *Landwacht* and they live a couple of houses behind us on another small farm. So far they have not caused any danger to us or anybody in our neighbourhood. She was inside so fast nobody had any chance to get away out of sight. And there were four *onderduikers* in the kitchen.

She asks for a litre of milk. I step outside to see if there are more persons there and sure enough, by the barn is another person. They both walk to the front of the farm. The second person is not her husband Fanny, but another woman.

NEWS: Allied troops have reached the limits of Den Bosch but not liberated it yet. Troops in Brabant have cut off German supply lines towards Zeeland.

Wednesday, October 25

I had a very good sleep. Up at 7 a.m. Set the table and then after breakfast take the cows out to pasture. Dishes done, peel potatoes with help from Frans and help Gerrit to hang up tobacco for drying.

In the afternoon we get fodder for the pigs off of the field. Johan and I are going to turn over the compost pile in one of the pastures. Lien comes and brings another pair of underwear for Gerrit and for me. Allied planes are very busy when dominee Veenhuizen arrives. He is in need of some milk and a few other things. It is strictly forbidden to get milk or grain from a farm. Everything is rationed and the Germans are milking our country dry. Things are so bad that people in the west of Holland starve for lack of food.

Frans is going to make his bed. He takes the pitchfork along and we get a good laugh. Why do you take that along Frans? "Well I have to loosen up the hay of course." Hey, that is pretty smart.

I start a letter to my family in Apeldoorn.

NEWS: Allied troops are street fighting in Den Bosch.

At 9:30 p.m. we crawl under the blankets.

Thursday, October 26

I take the cows to pasture. Johan and I clean out the chicken coops. Frans and I peel apples. Since yesterday there has been no hydro in a wide area.

Pigsties are washed out, scrubbed and whitewashed.

When we are out in the sugar beet field the Tommies are again very busy overhead.

At 5:30 p.m. we bring the cows into the barn. They are always taken care of first. When they have their food in front of them, it is our turn. So at 6 p.m. we can start eating. We are just enjoying our meal when somebody knocks at the door. Tante calls loudly, "Get away!"

She should not have done that. Gerrit and Frans sneak out through the back door. I remain in my seat. It is obvious by the number of chairs and plates that there have been more people at the table. Luckily the visitor is not a bad person.

While I brush my teeth another person comes to the farm. He is looking for an *evacuee* from Scheveningen who lives at Scholte Eppink. This *evacuee* has to go to work for the Germans in Bochholt tomorrow. Then comes Keus, another *evacuee*, and his son Ben. They also have to go to Bochholt tomorrow and need two bikes. Do we have bikes for them? How do they dare to ask? Of course we don't have any to give to them. If the Germans want people to work for them they should provide transportation. He is mad at us and lets us know in no uncertain terms. Then they leave.

NEWS: Russian army is marching into Norway; this is official. City Den Bosch (Noord Brabant) half liberated.

Because Allied troops march further north (they are now in southern part of the Netherlands) the Germans put many troops along the West Coast of the Netherlands. This is coastline and already strongly fortified. Now all people living along the coast have to move inland. We call these displaced persons *evacuees*. Many from Rotterdam, Scheveningen and other coastal towns are sent to farmers in the eastern part of the country. Our area around Aalten gets more than its fair share. But they are taken in like family. It takes a little time and planning to bed them all down. It must be awful to be driven out of your home and be totally dependent on strangers. Many are very thankful for the warm reception they receive and they are willing to help out where they can.

Friday, October 27

My brother Gerrit is working for a local barber, Kruithof. Kruithof is also involved in Resistance work. One day he is arrested at home. He asks permission to change clothes before they take him away. Permission is granted, and he goes upstairs to his bedroom climbs out of the window on to the roof of an attached building and lowers himself into the neighbour's yard and gets away. The Germans are mad. They lock up the shop and brother Gerrit comes to our farm. He will operate from here and any money is given to Mrs. Kruithof so she can take care of herself and the children.

By now my brother Gerrit has learned a number of expressions in the *Achterhoek* dialect. At the supper table he says, "My, this food is *miege* fatty." Our food is very fatty, but not *miege* fatty. Everybody starts to laugh, leaving Gerrit looking puzzled. He has heard the expression *miege nat* which he thinks means very wet. The word *miege* is used for horse urine. He now realizes that *miege* fatty does not make sense.

After dishes are done I peel potatoes. My brother Gerrit is at the neighbour's helping to cut firewood. He has to come home to the farm where some customers are waiting for a haircut. The farmers in the whole area like to come here for a haircut, it saves them time and there is less danger to be picked up than there is in town. Also *onderduikers* come for haircuts. They don't dare to go to town these days when there are so many *razzias*.

In order to keep busy I start polishing any shoes available. The pigs need some extra food and I go to the field to cut some grass and some green leaves from sugar beets.

The geese seem to be crazy about beet leaves and I decide to give them some as well. Overhead several V-1's are heard but not seen. Too much cloud. The V-1's are launched just across the border in Germany and we can hear the launching.

This morning only six men report for digging duty.

In afternoon when Johan and I dig up some carrots, Lien and Ineke, two daughters of Ome Jan, come to the farm to tell us that again there are *Zwarten* in Aalten. Two by two they go in all directions on their bikes and most likely are going to pick up hostages. Of course the reason is that only six men have reported and the hostage-taking is to scare people. Going for digging trenches is now very life threatening and people know it. Later that afternoon we hear that several hostages are already picked up. Gerrit, Tony's grandson, has been shot through the leg.

Something of totally different nature, in town City Hall has put up a notice that again there is opportunity to get married. This Mayor has a license where the previous one did not.

Nowadays most good mayors and police have been replaced by members of the NSB and most of them are totally incapable to carry out this work. We hear stories about couples who had already registered to get married who now cancel. They don't want to be married by a member of the NSB. Also there are apparently a few children born that are not registered either. We are sure they will sort it out later. No man is going to risk being taken hostage while registering for a marriage license or birth certificate.

5 p.m. Johan and I are getting several wheelbarrow loads of *knollen* from the field behind the farm. Then we bring the cows in again.

At 6 p.m. set the table. After supper I do the dishes with Frans.

NEWS: Greece fifty percent liberated. Den Bosch in Noord Brabant liberated. Allied make good headway in Zuid Beveland (Province of Zeeland) and in Noord Brabant (Province) troops are marching in the direction of Roozendaal, Breda and Tilburg. Japanese fleet two-thirds destroyed.

By Zevenaar (close to Arnhem) many men are escaping from their digging duties and head for home. One of them, Oom Derk Wikkerink, is back in Aalten.

In Amsterdam a Gestapo agent is killed by one of his colleagues. The Gestapo is one of the worst German military units. Mean, deadly, no pardon. According to the news, 29 persons from Amsterdam are taken hostage and killed and another 30 hostages are taken and held prisoner.

Saturday, October 28

In the morning I help the neighbour *den Eume* cut straw for his cows. When I have a free moment after that, I begin a letter for Henny, but Johan asks me to help him clean the big *mantelpot* in which we cook food for the pigs. The stupid geese are once again outside the small pasture. They always find a way to get out from behind the chicken wire. When that is fixed I finally can finish my letter.

For lunch today we have *snert*. Really good food.

I have to get a few more wheelbarrow loads of *knollen* and while busy with that I have a real good opportunity to look at the Tommies. Hundreds of them come from the direction of Enschede (north) and turn east when above us. They are now heading for Germany. It is only a short distance to the German border, about 4 kilometres. At about 3:30 p.m. I see an airplane accompanied by several fighter planes. It has been hit by enemy fire. About two kilometres north of here I see smoke coming out of the plane and it dives straight down. Then I spot a parachute slowly coming down to earth.

At 5 p.m. Frans and I go to wash up. I go into the little sheep stable and Frans is over by the rabbit hutch.

The town crier makes another announcement. "All men to register so the hostages can be released."

After supper Frans and I go for a little walk. He has to vent himself of some frustration and I can identify with that. He complains bitterly, "It is no life on the farm, you're never finished. And, my goodness, how many potatoes I have peeled; there is no end to it. It is enough to make you crazy. Oh, I will be so happy when I will be home again. And look at when you want to take a bath, you should laugh about it. Before, I would walk in a big circle around all the cow poop, now you are washing yourself right next to it?"

He is right, but we do not have a choice!

And we must be thankful that someone is willing to take us in and give us food. The farmer does not want any money for it, we just help him out wherever we can and for a change he now can take it a lot easier and do things he could not before. Here we are at a farm with seven cows in the stable, four or five pigs and they have five children. Four of them are old enough to work for others; the youngest is in high school. These people are poor compared to many others. But they have a very strong faith; the sound of laughter is heard many times. A strong conviction that you help out wherever you can, in times of need. And the need is getting even greater.

Many people from western Holland come east across the country to our area looking for food. Some on bikes, many walk with a little cart or wheelbarrow. Amazing to see how the farmers are trying to help. And the price is right… there is no overcharge.

When a farmer threshes his grain, the noise is carried over a large distance and in no time people arrive with their bags, wheelbarrows and other contraptions. And they all get something. At one farm at the end of the day when threshing was finished the farmer ended up with only a few bags for himself. And to know that from every crop a certain percentage has to be set aside for delivery to a German depot. Not to do so is considered sabotage and can be very dangerous.

I want to mention here that the "hungry from the West" have to cross some large rivers on their return home. As these bridges are guarded by German soldiers, the travellers have to show what they are carrying. All too often the soldiers take away their food, leaving them devastated.

NEWS: Den Bosch liberated and also Vught. In Vught there is a concentration camp; a bad place and more like a death camp. The guardians of the camp are now the prisoners.

Sunday, October 29
After breakfast I have a shave and then start to work on my diary. When I put the potatoes on the stove at 11 a.m., look who is coming, Lien and Henny. What a nice surprise. Henny and I go for a long walk in the afternoon and we are back in time for her and Lien to go to the three o'clock church service in town.

We *onderduikers* have a service at the farm of Houwers *Neerhof*. It too starts at 3 p.m. 18 young men show up. Collection 6 guilders.

Brother Gerrit gets a letter from his fiancée Dick in Apeldoorn. She writes that two factories there have been bombed, the Talens and the Nettenfabriek.

After supper we bring the geese into the barn. Normally they stay outside, but nowadays nothing is safe there. The Germans steal anything that can be eaten. Chicken, geese, sheep, goats, calves. There are reports that calves and young cows have been slaughtered right where they graze, in the pasture.

A plane came down in Zinderen yesterday and the pilot parachuted out safely. German soldiers, as always eager to catch him, go after it. They meet a young man who tells them that the pilot has already been captured. The German soldiers take it easy but finally decide to have a look anyway. When they get to the spot the pilot has disappeared. He is safely hidden at one of the farms.

This is usually what happens when someone bails out of an airplane. The Resistance workers who hunt for the crew member are assisted by some of the farming community to locate the exact spot or are told where the person is hidden. They take over from there. The crew member is changed into a farmer; coveralls, wooden shoes and a bike and taken to a safer place until he can be transported to Belgium, through France, over the Pyrenees into Portugal. This is a neutral country and from there they ship people back to England.

NEWS: City of Tilburg in Noord Brabant is liberated.

Monday, October 30
Someone stole three geese overnight.

NEWS: City of Breda (Noord Brabant) in Allied hands.

We have a quick breakfast and then off to *de Bleeke*, a nearby farm. We help with threshing oats and buckwheat. Frans and I do not take the road but go through field, over ditches and barbed wire. When we get to *de Bleeke* we are told to watch out. The *Zwarten* are raiding a neighbouring district to get *onderduikers*. Last night German soldiers visited the Woldboom, close to our farm. At farmer Rensink's they took a *schinke*, at another farm a large chunk of bacon and some bikes. Even underwear was not safe as they took some of that as well. They must have been in need of warm clothes and farmers do wear some pretty heavy long-johns.

In the district of Barlo three fat pigs have been taken from a farmer.

NEWS: Goes in Zeeland is liberated.

Just before noon we are finished at *de Bleeke* and this time we don't have to walk home. Frans and I have a ride on top of the wagon with straw.

By *de Bleeke* four letters arrived for *onderduikers*. One is for me.

"Wouldn't it be nice if there was a letter for me too?" says Frans. As luck will have it, in the afternoon they bring another letter and it is for Frans. "This is a really good one," he says. "It says that I became an uncle for the third time."

Before we have our lunch we unload a wagon load of straw into the barn. After lunch another load of straw over the threshing floor in back of the barn, and then one for the neighbour in his barn.

The big cooking pot in the barn needs to be fired up to cook food for the pigs. In between I make the beds in the small boys' bedroom in the house. Then with three of us, we set the table and bake potatoes. 6:20 p.m. supper and dishes.

At 8 p.m. Johan is going to listen to BBC news.

In meantime we hear that the pilot from last Saturday landed by Rutgers in Varsseveld. The airplane was one of those that are seen over our area when bombing small targets. They could see him come down and open his parachute. It looked as if he would land on the house, but then he started to walk through the air with both hands and feet and missed the house by a few feet, landing in the garden. The *Moffen* who arrived shortly after to take him prisoner of war came too late. He was gone and nobody knew where he was!

NEWS: In Noord Brabant, Roozendaal and Oosterhout are liberated. Allies making good progress there.

It is different by Rotterdam. Moerdijk bridge has been bombed a few times, but it was very difficult. Too many anti-aircraft guns. German troops have withdrawn behind the bridge. But they feel the pinch. In Den Haag people have to provide blankets, winter coats, undershirts and underpants for the German army.

Those who bring any of these will receive a paper as proof and this is to be placed behind the window in front of the house.

At 9:30 p.m. I go to bed. The day has been long enough.

We were able to get a sheep. It is doing very well. Sheep are usually kept outside, but since the Germans steal animals right out of the pasture, it is safer to bring the animal inside overnight. Oom Herman suggests that we clean the pigsty which is empty, so we can put the sheep there when it is not safe to be out in the field. The sheep goes back outside as soon as the day breaks. It is not good to keep it inside for too long.

The *hol* where we sleep is above this pig pen. We have to go past the sheep to crawl into our hiding place. During the night often one or both of us has to get up and do a pee. Instead of going all the way down and outside it is much easier to go on our knees, open the trap door and let it go.

After about a week, the farmer notices that the sheep is losing its wool, especially on her behind. It does not get any better, and a few days later he asks the vet to come and have a look. The vet has no idea what has caused this, except maybe the sheep has been inside too much. He prescribes a bottle of liquid to rub on the bare patch, and advises the farmer to leave the sheep outdoors more. We leave the sheep outside every night, rub the liquid on faithfully, and sure enough, after about ten days the *kale kont* starts to grow wool again. When she is almost back to normal, Oom Herman thinks it is safer to keep her inside overnight again. So we do! A week goes by and the whole process starts over again. Sheep loses wool, vet comes, more liquid, leave sheep outside at night. Vet scratches his head and writes out a bill. It does not take long and the sheep starts to grow wool again. Since we are getting more pigs that need to go into the old pig pen, the sheep will be bedded down in a new place. This finally solves the problem of her losing her wool.

Frans and I have carried this secret for a long time for we never told the farmer or the vet what the real cause of the bald spot was: using the trapdoor as a chamber pot.

Tuesday, October 31

Up at 7 a.m. Set the table, eat, and do dishes. The neighbour Driessen, who is 70 years old, needs help to stack a wagon of oats in the loft above the threshing floor. He lives with his son Gerrit and housekeeper Grada in the same building as us. This is a double farm; not many like it exist. Each has a front door to the living quarters. From the living quarters you enter the threshing floor. One threshing floor is used by both farmers. In back of this floor are the stables for the cows and pigs, one on each side. Over the threshing floor each has his own loft for hay, straw or any other storage.

After potatoes are peeled, Johan and I fence off another section of grass for the geese.

Lunch at 1 p.m. Dishes done. I clean the pigsties. I am always overwhelmed by the smell.

Since we have tobacco and the cigarettes you make from it do not taste too good, how about making some cigars? Might as well try it. It does not look too bad, but when we try them a few days later they taste very bitter and it is hard to suck on them. It makes you tired!

I clean up the barn again, get more pig food *knollen* from the field and notice that one of the cows has broken loose. No sense putting her back in the pasture so I take her to the cow stable in the house.

At 6 p.m. milk the cows with Frans. Then supper and whatever comes with it. This takes until eight o'clock. My brother is gone to *de Bleeke* to shave the farmer and a few others. Johan, who goes for news, comes back with nothing. The farmer could not listen because he has visitors.

We are not allowed to listen to BBC, may not even have a short wave radio. More than a year ago this type of radio had to be handed in to the German occupation. Some people did, many more did not. It means that you cannot leave it in your kitchen or living room. The radio is hidden, and listening to it is done secretly. If you are caught it could mean concentration camp.

NOVEMBER 1944

Wednesday, November 1 Thanksgiving Day

Up at 7 a.m. Set table, eat, wash dishes, shave and change clothes because at eleven o'clock we have church service here at our farm. Dominee Gerritsma will come and preach right after he finishes the service in the *Westerkerk*. He comes at exactly 11 a.m. A good sermon, nice service and good conversation afterwards.

Present 20 *onderduikers*. Collection 16 guilders and 30 cents.

While we have our coffee, dominee Gerritsma relates to us how he was picked up as a hostage on October 15. Three Germans and Fanny came to his house. Fanny had to do the talking because he is Dutch. When dominee Gerritsma came to the door Fanny said, "I.., I.., have to a…rrest you". He was so nervous, he almost started crying.

"What have I done," asked the pastor.

"Tha… tha… that, I don't know."

On the way to the City Hall Fanny said time and again, "I cannot help it pastor, I cannot help it." Bah, what a miserable guy. Fanny lives on a small farm in our immediate neighbourhood with his wife who we call *de Guste*.

NEWS: Noord Brabant and part of Zeeland liberated. Troops are now at the river Maas in province Noord Brabant. At Moerdijk 3,400 German soldiers were taken prisoner of war. Total since the invasion on June 6, 1944:

600,500 POW's. Fighting starting on island of Walcheren in Zeeland. Russian army 70 kilometres from Budapest.

This morning the S.S. picked up Mr. Delleman. We don't know for what reason. The S.S. is also picking up young men in Lintelo, a neighbouring district of Aalten. Linus Johan and his whole family have gone into hiding. Their house is confiscated.

In late afternoon many Tommies fly over. We count approximately 200.

5 p.m. supper, dishes and clean up. Then we bring in the geese. Gerrit and Johan are going to listen to the news at Mele Jan.

NEWS: Allied making good progress in Zeeland by the city Vlissingen. Canadian troops have crossed the dam Sloe and proceed towards Middelburg. Near Helmond in Noord Brabant, a German counter offensive has been thwarted. Street fights in Knokke (Belgium). Gelsenkirchen, Hamburg and Keulen bombed. City of Vienna bombed.

At 8 p.m. we see a beautiful display of fireworks outside. Red, green and orange flares hang brightly in the sky and we see very bright lights from exploding grenades.

9 p.m. It's early to bed again this night.

Thursday, November 2

After breakfast we march the geese out to their little grazing field. I pull up some more carrots.

In the afternoon, at 2 p.m. when we go and get the calves from 't Goor, we again see many planes in the sky. We come home at 4:30 p.m. My feet hurt badly. I am glad to sit down but not until the geese are herded inside.

The calves ate half of one sleeve of my jacket. Mien and Mina have tried to fix the sleeve and it will do for the time being.

While I take a rest, I sort out tobacco leaves for drying. Gerrit is going for news tonight. Meanwhile we have a discussion about honouring the Sabbath day by resting and hallowing.

NEWS: New offensive started by Aken in Germany. Fighting in the streets of Geertruidenberg (Noord Brabant). Domburg and Zoutelande in Allied hands. Allied troops established bridgehead over the Mark. Russian army 50 kilometres from Budapest. Knokke liberated; Heist last stronghold in Belgium. The Ruhr area in Germany is blasted by 1,000 bombers accompanied by 900 fighter planes. Target – oil refineries and railroads. From Italy 750 planes bomb Vienna.

At 7 p.m. we have another fireworks similar to last night's.

Friday, November 3

It will soon be time to preserve endive for the winter. This is kept in wooden kegs. One of these barrels has steel bands around the outside but they have come loose. My job to fix it. I give it a try, taking my time and I manage to do a fairly good job.

I try to make a few cigars from the tobacco we grew. They look pretty good but when we try to smoke them a few days later it is impossible to get air through it. You can suck all you want but to no avail. Frans and I pick some more *knollen* in the field behind the house. We notice some commotion in the pasture and see that the Red cow and her calf have broken through the fence.

We might as well pick them up and bring them into the stable.

For supper we fry some potatoes and afterwards Johan and I do the dishes. At eight o'clock it is time to get the news and Johan goes to listen. I start a letter to the family in Apeldoorn.

NEWS: Vlissingen (Zeeland) liberated except the northern part. Still heavy fighting by Aken in Germany. By Heist in Belgium fighting has ceased and Belgium is now completely liberated.

They can start celebrating their freedom but we still have to wait. For how long?

Saturday, November 4

Today is Dick ten Have's birthday. Frans and I peel potatoes.

The mailman brings a letter from my brother Teun and his wife Stien who live in Twello. Nice to get some news from relatives. You need it to keep your sanity. Teun writes that their house lost all its windows when the railroad station was bombed recently.

Johan and I do some work and we hang the last of the tobacco to dry. I bring two wheelbarrow loads with *mangels* into the *schoppe*. We do it today because tomorrow is Sunday. Also, around the house and barn some cleaning with broom and rake needs to be done. The geese have to come inside and now it is time to clean myself. A good scrubbing in the barn in front of the rabbit hutch. That feels good.

This afternoon we see many V-1's being launched just across the border in Germany. At six o'clock another two are launched. We first see a big red ball of fire that rises with a great speed. Every time it gets a new burst of power it moves; it veers sideways. After a few seconds the big fire is out and you cannot see it anymore. We eat at 6:30 p.m. but dishes cannot be washed until 7:30; the water is not hot yet. We have to heat water on the wood-fired stove in the kitchen and it was neglected. When the dishes are done and put away it is eight o'clock and I can clean and wash the milk cans. Put them on the wooden stand outside to dry so they will be ready for tomorrow. This was another long day! Back at my home we always tried to have our work finished early in the afternoon on Saturdays. Wash and clean up and have a relaxing time. But not here and that is kind of hard to get used to.

Once when I washed and cleaned myself up right after supper they asked, "Where are you going?"

"Nowhere," I said.

"Oh, you look so nice." I felt awkward, almost guilty. It was certainly not an encouragement to do it again.

But Mina who has been in Aalten has a nice surprise for me. She tells me that tomorrow afternoon, after church, Henny and Lien are coming and they will stay until Monday morning. That makes everything good!

Wim has bought a goose for 25 guilders. Frans is asked to cut its throat and he is trying very hard. He says that the knife is not very sharp. I believe it. You should see him struggle, poor goose. Finally he has managed to do the job and hands the goose back to Wim who, together with Johan, is going to pluck the feathers off.

In the early evening more planes overhead. Sirens go off in Aalten to prepare for possible air raids.

NEWS: BBC gives good news from different fronts. Budapest under fire, Germany bombed constantly from Italy. Canadian and American troops unite at the established bridgehead over the Mark. Canadian troops have gained two kilometres at 't Sloe.

Sunday, November 5
After breakfast I brush my teeth. Can only do this once a week since tooth-paste is no longer available.

Today church is at *de Bleeke*. Dolf reads the sermon. We are the only ones that still have a church service. All other outlying areas have stopped because of the danger involved. 20 young men show up. Shortly after we have started someone comes to warn that the *Groenen* are in the area. We put four watchmen outside to keep an eye out for danger. Suddenly a loud bang, the windows rattle, and we wonder what is happening. English planes are bombing small targets again. We can finish our service and are back at our home farm at 11 a.m.

In Aalten they have started a campaign to relieve the diggers in Zevenaar for a few days. Volunteers are requested to replace them. This has been approved by the Germans. Not much has been learned apparently. Those who have not reported on behalf of the hostages will certainly not report to replace trench diggers.

Lunch time. I have eaten too much. The meal was delicious. We had *haantjes soep*, potatoes with apple sauce, a nice piece of chicken and pudding as dessert. In the afternoon some of the group plays checkers and I try my best at the old organ.

After supper Lien and Henny come for a visit. We do dishes together and clean up. Henny brings a letter from Tante Gerda for me.

We go for a nice walk, Mina and Dirk, Lien and Johan, Henny and I. When we come home it is nice to sit around the stove with a cup of coffee. Outside the wind is howling; inside it is warm and cozy. We sing some songs, standing around the organ, and Gerrit goes for the news.

NEWS: Schelde is cleared of German soldiers, now they have to remove landmines from the water. At Geertruidenberg Allied forces have reached the

Maas. Zevenbergen liberated. Troops now five kilometres from Moerdijk. Near Dinteloord two kilometres from the Volkerak. Northeast from Domburg heavy fighting. A new offensive at 's Hertogenbosch. Allied troops now use flame-throwers. This weapon seems to be very effective especially to burn out positions across a river or canal. In Germany by Aken troops advance 221 kilometres. Utrecht (Holland) a factory is bombed with 12 direct hits.

Peter Van Essen

Before we retire for the night, Henny and I go to a small room to pray. The situation is very critical. Many soldiers on both sides are dying, homes and other buildings destroyed, the western part of Holland running out of food and other necessities. In the cities trees are cut down and used for heating homes. Also the wooden ties from under the tram rails are being removed for firewood.

I have to write down here what happened a few days ago in the neighbouring district Lintelo.

The German raiders paid a surprise visit to Lines Johan. In the stable was Johan Heideman who was previously captured and sent to a concentration camp, from there shipped to Germany, and escaped back to Lintelo. He was milking the cows. The Germans took him to a room and ordered him to wait there until they came back to get him. He managed to get away but could not get out of the house as there were too many Germans outside. He decided to hide somewhere in the farmhouse. On the threshing floor was a big mixer for grain. He crawled inside this *mengmolen*. The Germans, who didn't find him in the room, were pretty mad and started to search for him. They knew he did not get outside because the farm was surrounded. Some tracks led to the mixer and they were sure he was in there somewhere. Lifting a board here and a lid there they still could not find him.

"He must be in here."

"I will throw a hand grenade in it," one of them said. "Then he will come out." For some reason they didn't do it and this was Johan's good fortune. He stayed where he was until eleven o'clock in the evening. He had been in the mixer since 8 a.m. Most of the Germans had left but one guard was still outside. Johan managed to sneak out unseen.

Mina's fiancé Dirk brings a half pound of yeast. We can now bake our own bread again. *Eigen gebakken wigge* is so good.

Monday, November 6
Had a good night's rest but wake up very early. At 6:30 a.m. I get up and set the table. Oom Herman, Dirk, Mien and Henny eat before the others for they are to leave soon. At 8:30 Henny leaves. Oom Herman goes to the

Schaarsheide to bring home our sheep and those belonging to Houwers from *Neerhof*. It is too dangerous to leave them there. Last Thursday two sheep were stolen.

Johan and I get busy with the compost heap. It needs turning over. At 10:30 a.m. it is our pleasant duty to drink coffee. Although this time I get the unpleasant surprise to find a big *hooiwagen* on the bottom of my cup. Brrrr … I remove the daddy-long-leg spider from my cup. Then a little later I get a pleasant surprise when Hendrik Jansen drops in with a letter from home. Amazing what a letter once in a while will do. You get a big lift from it.

At home in Apeldoorn all is well. Train station in Aalten was bombed again but no direct hits. A number of people dead or fatally wounded.

Gerrit D., son of *den Eume*, came home from digging in Zevenaar yesterday evening. He is not going back.

At noon we bring the cows outside so they can graze for a while. We also finish work on the compost heap.

Tommies flying off and on. Bombers, fighters; the sky is filled. We hear explosions and loud bangs on every side; north, south, west and east. We even get a glimpse of a good fight in the air but then lose sight of them; the sky is too cloudy.

Frans and I take in the geese and gather some *knollengroen*. After this we prepare ourselves for a good supper.

This coming Sunday it is Opa Eppink's birthday. Opa is Mother Wikkerink's Dad. He will be 81. On Monday Johan, Lien, Henny and I have to go there for a little party.

Gerrit and Johan go for news. NEWS: The Moerdijk bridge blown up. This is a big one and may set back the advancing of Allied troops. Klundert, Dinteloord and Geertruidenberg liberated. Budapest partly surrounded by Russian troops that are now about 20 kilometres north of this city. In Germany, Hamburg and Harburg are targeted with bombs. 1,100 bombers take part in this attack. Stalin speaks on the occasion of the 27th anniversary October Revolution.

Dirk mentions that in Lintelo, where he lives, the *onderduikers* are leaving to go home. I think this is a bit premature. Too early, we are in for a bad winter yet.

Tuesday, November 7

Marching the geese and then the last of the *mangels* picked up to bring in the *schoppe*. The corn has been taken in some time ago but now we pull up the stalks. The rest of the morning is spent in idle time and coffee drinking. It starts to rain. When we look outside we see the geese walking on the road behind the farm. It is hard to keep those energetic fowl behind a wire fence.

Gerrit, Frans and I go to do some work for our neighbour Papenborg. Papenborg is very ill, suffering from severe arthritis. There are some tree trunks in his meadow that have to be removed.

After supper Frans washes the dishes, Gerrit dries and I put away. Like most evenings I bring my diary up-to-date while I try to smoke another of our home-made cigars. Dirk has brought us some more cigarette tobacco.

NEWS: Willemstad, Veere and Middelburg in Allied hands. Heavy fighting by Moerdijk bridge. Air raids on Arnhem and Utrecht. A few kilometres gained by Aken in Germany. Gelchenkirchen and Coblenz bombed. At Westkappelle (Province Zeeland) 25 ships tried to land. Five of them are successful. I have no note of what happened to the rest. Plan was to bomb the area for 45 hours prior to landing, but bad weather prevents this. They fight heroically and many are killed. It was so far the most difficult landing performed during this war. Up until the end of September 1944 the number of troops that landed in Western Europe totalled 10,000,000. Of these, 200,000 have given their lives **for our freedom**.

Wednesday, November 8

Up at 7 a.m., wash myself with water only. For some time already there is no more soap and you cannot buy any either.

Johan and I go to work on the tree trunks. Some of these are big and tough. After a morning of hard labour it is good to go home for a meal. I manage to eat two plates with some potatoes and applesauce and one plate with potatoes and beets. Then for dessert a plate with buttermilk porridge. By now I feel like never eating again.

Some of the NSB are moving on again. The ones that stay at the Hoopman's farm and *Nooitgedacht* leave for the city of Hengelo, which is further north and away from the frontal zone.

In the afternoon Johan and I go back to the neighbour's tree trunks. At 3 p.m. Tante calls me home. There is someone to see me. It is Henny's uncle, Jan from Gorssel, and we talk until 5 p.m. It is now time for him to go and for me to feed the cows and pigs.

After supper Johan and Oom Herman do the milking so I have to wait to do the dishes until the lamp is back in the kitchen. We have no hydro and oil for the lamps is very scarce. We burn only one lamp at a time.

To pass time I play a bit on the organ in the dusk.

When the milking is done Gerrit, Frans and I do dishes and at 8 p.m. my brother Gerrit goes for news. He is so good at this job that it is mostly he who is asked to go for it. Gerrit is a barber and barbers can listen and talk well. When one of us would go for news we would come back with a one to two minute report. When Gerrit comes back with the news he talks for half an hour. It helps us pass the time in the evening.

NEWS: At Oostkapelle the last German stronghold destroyed. At Moerdijk and its bridge, very heavy fighting. Roosevelt elected as President of USA for a fourth term.

At 9:30 p.m. I want to go to bed. Bed is above the cows in what we call the *hol*. Since we burn only one lamp, I tell everyone, "Don't worry, I will manage. I have crawled into the *hol* so many times, I know the way, even in the dark." I should not have said that. It is different when it is dark and I mean DARK. I slowly move along the wall toward the back of threshing floor where the stable is. Hitting a sack I move around it, letting go of the wall. Now I am somewhat unsure where the wall is, but after a few very small steps I stand in front of the cows. I want to move ahead to reach the wall leading to the very back of stable where you have to hoist yourself up to get in the *hol*. The Red cow is blocking my way, she is lying down. Moving a bit to the right I find that the White cow is lying down as well. Did not know it at first. I step on her leg when I try to get by her. Of course she jumps up. This helps me to get by her. I must now be standing at the edge of the *gruppe* where the cows drop their poop. I don't want to step in it with my wooden shoes so I carefully move my wooden shoe ahead to feel for the edge. When I feel it I take a big step to get across. Wouldn't you know, I now stand with both feet in the middle of this *gruppe*. I try to figure out what went wrong and conclude that I stood sideways by the *gruppe*. I realize that I am not in bed yet. But WHERE am I? I must be on the right side of the stable and the *hol* is on the left. Better start moving. My hand against the wall I move ahead. One step and I have reached the end of this wall. This is funny; I must have been on the left side and not the right.

The *hol* must be just overhead and I will have to cross the *gruppe* again. I decide to take it very easy, slowly reaching for the other side. My wooden shoe hits something. It is the hind leg of the Red cow and she kicks back, hitting my pants but not my leg. Now that I know where I am I hoist myself up into the *hol* ready to crawl in my bed of hay. I should have cleaned the manure off my wooden shoes first. Who cares!

Thursday, November 9

Opa Wikkerink and Dikkie's birthday. This morning I make a few cigars to take along to Opa Eppink on Monday.

The mailman brings a pamphlet written by the pastors and priests. It is another request for volunteers to replace diggers in Zevenaar. All of us here think it is terrible to pass around such a paper. I am sad, angry and everything else at the same time. Johan seems to be worse than I. It is in total conflict with the actions and attitude of the Resistance movement whose members risk their lives and have paid with their lives for us.

We go to pick up a sheep at the farm *Neerhof*. We have a good laugh as Gerrit, who tries to catch it, falls face first in the pasture, missing the sheep by inches.

Johan asks me to help him fix the grindstone. When that is done we sharpen two axes and try these out on the big tree trunk at the neighbour Papenborg.

5:45 p.m. supper. Dishes by Gerrit, Frans and me. Diary updated.

NEWS: Johan reports - No news! German defence by Moerdijk silenced. Tilburg is celebrating their liberation. All the fighting is still below the big rivers. The news about Allied movements is going to be curtailed. We may now have to wait a few days before we hear what happened and when. Same day reports will give away situations to the enemy and may counteract any surprise attacks by Allied troops. Good move.

Friday, November 10

This morning, as usual, I wash myself by the pump outside. No soap, just water. It is raining. Johan and I again attack the tree trunk in Papenborg's field. It is big. After lunch we go back there and work on it whenever the rain stops. When it pours we take shelter in Papenborg's farm and have a nice talk with him. He tells us about the old days. We drink coffee together and go home at five o'clock.

Frans and I get some *knollen* for the cows. Johan and I do the milking and make sure that the milk cans and pails are washed and put away to dry.

Brother Gerrit gets a letter from Dick ten Have in Apeldoorn saying that an airplane fell on the palace stables in Apeldoorn. Bombs fell on the outdoor ice rink.

Saturday, November 11

Opa Eppink is 81 years old today.

Saturday is cleanup day. I clean the sty of the old sow, then the rabbit cages. Afternoon, the other two sties get cleaned out. Sweep the floor of the whole barn so it is neat for Sunday.

Many planes pass over from and to Germany.

Mantelpot fired up for pig food. We have to pull up more *knollen* and then cut off their leaves. It is now time to clean myself and I take the usual bath: pail of water, no soap, in the calf stable in the barn.

At 6 p.m. when we are still at the supper table enjoying a restful evening, *den Eume* comes to warn us that the *Groenen* are in our district Dale. Right where we are! They are looking for deserters from Zevenaar. Since this is really dangerous, we go to bed in the *hol*. About eight o'clock we get out for a bit of fresh air and a cup of coffee. No one has showed up yet at the neighbour's but we stay inside and go to bed again at 9:30 p.m.

NEWS: A dredging machine is cleaning out the waterway Schelde (province of Zeeland)

Sunday, November 12

Birthday of our neighbour Tony Driessen.

Many deserters have been picked up in town. They still have not been next door. Gerrit D, Tony's son, left Zevenaar unauthorized a few days ago. We are sure they will come and look for him and might search the whole farm and all its buildings. Oom Herman wants us in the *hol* all day; awful. Gerrit and Frans leave for a while, and come back at 10:30 for coffee time. We keep a good watch the rest of the day and are happy that the *Groenen* do not show up. The morning church service was cancelled and we plan to have it this afternoon if possible.

At 3 p.m. all is still quiet and we meet at Hoopman's farm. I have to lead the service. Title "Ask and it will be given unto thee".

Attendance 15 young men, one young woman. Collection 4 guilders and 47 cents.

Henny's uncle Jan dropped off a letter from Frans de Vries this morning, asking me to bring in the money collected for the monument.

While we were at church service, we had a few tense moments when some German soldiers came by the house.

Hannie Hoornenborg was baptized today.

NEWS: Ex-Prime minister Colijn died in Berlin of a heart attack.

Monday, November 13

I have collected 373 guilders and 25 cents for the monument so far.

The leek in the garden needs to be peppered up and we put some liquid manure at their disposal. Carrots stored for winter, this is done outside. A hole in the ground, straw at the bottom, a layer of carrots and then more straw on top covered with soil.

I remember that today it is six years ago that we celebrated my mother's last birthday.

Polishing shoes for tonight. Have a nice shave.

Look after cows. Harvest some more *knollen*. Make a few cigars. Get the sheep inside. Afternoon, Lien and Henny arrive. A quick bite to eat and then off to Opa Eppink. We stay until 7:30 p.m. and we accompany Lien and Henny to the Pol, and then turn around. We all have to be inside at 8 p.m. for curfew. At eight we are at the farm again. Weather is really bad and the sandy roads are awful. When I arrived at Opa's I had one wet foot, I now have two wet feet. All the ter Horst's are next door at *den Eume* to celebrate Tony's birthday. We may as well join the party.

Tuesday, November 14

Today is going to be a wet day. We will have to do a little work in between the downpours. Dahlia's have to be taken out and stored for winter and when that is done I have a chance to pull up some *Brussels lof* which is to be stored the same way as the carrots yesterday.

I manage to finish my letter for Apeldoorn. We need better black paper in the stable to cover the window so that no light shows through to the outside.

I have time to make our bed before I start making porridge. After supper the diary gets an update. Although we do not get much news lately, we are sure the war's front-line is coming closer.

Yesterday and this afternoon the Germans set up a piece of heavy armament in the field by the neighbouring farm *Nonhof*. This farmer is sympathetic to the German cause. Several times we hear shooting, perhaps practice?

No NEWS tonight.

Wednesday, November 15

The farmer slept in today, and using this opportunity, so did we. We had a night frost and it is cold outside.

We have to move the geese to more edible stuff. I till a piece of land with a spade. Fairly heavy work. After supper Lien comes to tell us that she and Henny are planning to go to Apeldoorn tomorrow. They can get a ride with someone, take their bikes along and will continue to Driebergen to pick up Jo who is staying with their Tante Riek and Oom Ap. Plan to return here on Saturday. Gerrit and I get busy to write a letter for home as the girls are going to drop in at our home in Apeldoorn. Tante and Mina gather some good food, pack it, and they will take some of this along for Dick ten Have and for my father and sister Nen. Food is very scarce in the cities.

Gerrit and I are quite nervous and we have many mistakes in our letters. When we finally hand all these things to Lien it is dark outside and Oom Herman takes Lien back to her home. Oom Herman quickly kills a goose and it too is on its way to Apeldoorn.

No NEWS tonight.

Thursday, November 16

Today is my father's birthday; he is 60 years. A pity we cannot be home. But it is very nice that Henny and Lien will drop in to see him. Gerrit peels potatoes. I till some more land in the garden. Some customers come for a haircut and I take over the peeling from Gerrit. I may choose what we shall eat today to celebrate father's birthday. Very thoughtful of Tante, I really appreciate this.

I may choose between *karnemelk sause,* a concoction made with buttermilk (which is not my favourite) used as a gravy, or gravy made from meat which is my very favourite. I pick the last, of course. Tonight we will also get something special to drink, a glass of wine.

In the afternoon Ome Jan comes in to bring back the goose. The girls could not take all the stuff along. Understandable.

At 4:30 p.m. I am outside and Mina comes to warn us of two men who are next door. She thinks they are Germans and she says: "*Ie mot mar effen an de ziet.*" "Better keep out of sight." I make myself invisible in the pig barn where I try to make some more cigars. Ome Jan comes in to help me and has some real good suggestions about cigar making.

Frans, who has been gathering branches from under some trees, comes home. The wood is for a widow in town who is running out of stuff to burn for cooking.

While we spend a *gezellige* evening with a bowl of strawberries *op sap* and a rusk, I have time to update the diary.

Friday, November 17

Tilling land. The neighbour had a wagon load of straw to be stacked in the barn. When this is done I clean out the pig pens.

The strawberry plants in the garden need thinning and cleaning. It starts to rain and it is time for me to go inside. The barn is just the place and I can make a few more cigars. Looking through the window I see *Moffen* in the pasture next door. Gerrit is looking for work and he is going to cut my hair. We hear that English fighter bombers dropped their loads near the next small town of Lichtenvoorde. We could hear the bombs explode.

German troops are moving back to regroup in Germany.

Because of the bad weather and awful darkness nobody goes out tonight to hear news. This day has a sad ending. With a lot of stress on everybody and uncertainty on many sides, occasionally there is an outburst of bad words. And it always seems to be between father and son. I try to keep out of it but it is not nice to hear all this. Not fair to either of them. I don't want to hear any more of it and decide to go to bed. It is only eight o'clock when I reach the *hol*; my reaction is a good cry. Shortly after I fall into a deep sleep.

Saturday, November 18

We put up new wire and chicken wire for the geese and sheep. Clean the barn. Cows need water. Clean pig pens and pen for geese. Gather more *knollen*. Take a bath.

The airplanes are busy again. NEWS: Allied have started a new offensive stretching from the border of Switzerland to Limburg (the Netherlands). The Ninth army takes 1,800 prisoners of war by Aken (Germany).

Many Germans came into Aalten again yesterday and overnight. Came from Willemstad and Numansdorp (southwest in the Province of Noord Brabant).

Later in the evening we see a big flare in the sky. It could indicate a dropping of material for the Resistance. Yes, we now hear a plane and it flies over, very low.

Peter Van Essen

NEWS: Hilden in district Peel liberated. Gelsenkirchen in Allied hands. City of Ivietz attacked from three sides. Frontier by Aken was bombed with 2,200 bombers and 800 fighter planes taking part.

Sunday, November 19

Church at our farm *de Koekoek*. Dirk is in charge. Sermon title "The power of Jesus in heaven and on earth". 19 boys. Collection 5 guilders and 35 cents.

Gerrit, Frans and I take a nice walk. We talk about how our friends and others would react to threats by the German authorities. At 8 p.m. Gerrit goes for news. An airplane flies low overhead, just like yesterday. Two flares hang in the sky above 't Villekesderp about 250 metres from here. Everything is lit up. There is a drop-off spot not far from here and in other areas. Later this evening more flares are seen above Lintelo, de Heurne and Woldboom. The plane makes several passes and a few times fires its onboard canon. The *Moffen* in Aalten shoot at it with their rifles. We hope the plane had a safe landing. This makes you feel thankful, that others are fighting for your freedom.

NEWS: Street fights in Metz, Germany.

My thoughts have been a lot with Henny and Lien today. I hope all is well, wonder where they are.

Monday, November 20

Today it is 4 months ago that I went to Henny's parents to ask if they had any objections about the friendship that had developed between Henny and me.

I am very thankful for these past months and for what I have received in friendship and understanding.

The night was very unrestful. At one o'clock an awful noise in the direction of Aalten. We hear that a vehicle with explosives or ammunition exploded beside Oom Johan the butcher's house. All the windows were blown out of the house and also parts of a wall blown out.

I have to clean up our Sunday clothes that are still in the *hol*.

Prepare more land for winter *knollen* and bring manure to the field with the wheelbarrow.

In the afternoon Gerrit Wikkerink comes for a haircut. He tells us that Henny, Lien and Jo not will return before Wednesday. I had hoped that maybe I would see them today.

Ten minutes later, who comes along the path by Papenborg? The three Wikkerink sisters, Henny, Lien and Jo. They have had a lot of bike trouble, mainly flat tires and walked all the way from Vorden to here, about 30 kilometres. In Apeldoorn everything is okay. They brought apples and honey for us. It is only a ten minute stay and they head on to their own home in Aalten. Next time we will talk about everything. It is good to have them back, safe and sound.

We discuss what the situation after the war will be like and how to deal with it.

Gerrit ter Horst, who has been sick for some time, is allowed to get up from his bed for one hour a day. Maybe at the end of the week for a whole afternoon.

NEWS: In the Northeast of France the German army retreats steadily towards the Saar district. Helenaveen liberated.

More airplanes and flares.

Tuesday, November 21
During the night an airplane flew over very low. Maybe another dropping.

We bring more manure to the land by wheelbarrow. When that is done we give the big tree trunk another attack. Finally we win and we can lift the last piece out. Within ten minutes we see four V-1's being launched from across the border. These are dangerous. Malfunction is normal and some of these go in big circles. You never know when and where they come down.

Frans is appointed to crank the washing machine by hand. He does not like it at all and every chance he has he disappears for a while.

After supper the planes come again. Many searchlights by the border, anti-aircraft guns fire steadily and with deadly accuracy. Several planes are downed. When a plane is caught in a searchlight it does not have much chance to escape and is almost certain to be downed. We count at least 30 searchlights probing the sky.

German soldiers yesterday tried to steal a sheep from farmer Hoopman. The farmer and his son noticed it in time and when the soldiers ran away son Gerrit gave chase. However he had to stop following because they started to shoot at him twice. In Lintelo soldiers stole a bike and two chickens. The *Ortzcommandant* made them return everything. The chicken was already killed and ready for the pot, but they were ordered to buy another chicken on top of what they had taken.

NEWS: In Germany, Duren liberated, Mulhausen reached but not liberated yet. In Eindhoven (Noord Brabant) a 12-hour strike or protest because there is a lack of food. Of all things. This is a shame. They seem to forget that all of the Netherlands just north of them is still occupied by Germans. And how in the big cities people are dying of hunger. They seem to forget very quickly. Do they not remember what the Allied troops suffered and the paratroops that are dropped just north of Arnhem? Many, many of them paid with their lives, some have been without food or sleep for days on end, for our freedom.

Wednesday, November 22

I want to till some more land, but the weather is too bad, it is very wet. Stay inside and try to keep myself busy. The church collection money has to be made ready for pick up. It totals about 31 guilders.

My socks need to be darned, and I give it a try. It does not take very long to know that this is no work for me. I will finish this pair, but hope it is my first and last attempt at darning.

The calf shows an indication that it wants to go to the bull, although she has not developed as she should and is still quite small.

Oom Herman asks me if I will take it to Houwers at farm *Neerhof*, where they have a good sized bull. Johan will accompany me. Frans comes walking over and says, "I would like to come along; I have never seen this before." Johan and I talk to Oom Herman and we tell him that we plan to play a trick on Frans. Johan and I discuss how we will do this, and then go ahead to the neighbour to ask his co-operation. When Jan Houwers comes with the steer, he will ask Frans to help by standing behind it and push against the steer's big behind, when it jumps on the calf.

When we arrive at *Neerhof*, we see that some German soldiers are ready to take some of his chicken, geese, sheep and pigs. When the farmer asks them to see their papers for authorization they don't have any. He threatens to go and see their *Ortzcommandant* in town. They don't seem to like this idea and leave without taking anything.

It is time to put our plan into action. Johan holds the calf by its rope, and I am in front of her grabbing her nose, thumb and finger inside, pinching. This will keep her standing still. Out comes the steer and Jan tells Frans to be ready. The steer jumps up and Frans starts to push. Johan and I are having a good laugh. I am standing bent down in front of the calf. All of a sudden, Jan shouts, "Peter, watch out!"

I look up and there is the steer almost on top of me. I jump aside, just in time. The steer slides head over heels over the calf which is almost lying flat on the ground by now. To top things off, Jan yells at Frans, "Frans, you are pushing way too hard."

It is not just Frans, but we all have seen things today we never had before.

NEWS: Allied 50 kilometres from Strazburg. First French army has established a 30 kilometre long front along the river Rhine. Mulhausen liberated. Also Baarlo in Limburg (Holland). The V-1 launching pad by the border bombed.

Thursday, November 23

When I get up after a good night's rest it is only 6 a.m. It is wet outside and I will have to keep busy inside. My sock suspender needs fixing. It takes a while before you have found the necessary yarn or thin rope. It is the same with socks. Nowadays we even use binder twine to darn heavy work socks. But it hurts your feet. The rest of the morning I keep myself somewhat busy with a crossword puzzle book.

We have to get some more *knollen* from the field behind the farm. Johan is going to help me because it is raining cats and dogs. The field is so wet and muddy; we have to jump from one spot to the other. Johan misses a few times and the mud runs over his wooden shoes. "I don't care anymore," he says and walks through mud and water seemingly having a good time.

Later we drink tea by the burning stove and the neighbour comes to invite us over for Sunday evening. It is Jan's birthday. This is at farm *Neerhof*.

NEWS: Street fighting in Strazburg. First French army eight kilometres north of Mulhausen. Second English army fighting in Blerick near Venlo (province of Limburg). Troaj in Hungary liberated.

Another letter from home.

Friday, November 24

Work on the land, and take geese to their piece of pasture. Last night Frans was going to get the sheep from the pasture. He came back without a sheep but with soaking wet feet. "I could not get it," he says. He kept running after it through the wet watery field. I offer to go with him to try again. When I come to the field the sheep comes walking up to me without any trouble.

"*Dat kreng,*" Frans says. "Nasty beast. He does not know me of course."

I write a letter to Janny and Adriaan, my oldest sister and her husband.

NEWS: Mr. A. den Doolaard warns Amsterdam that BIG raids are coming. Russian army has taken island Osel by the coast of Estonia. Estonia liberated. In Koerland, 30 German divisions pinned against the Oostzee. The Lapps liberated.

Saturday, November 25

Cleaning day. Chicken and goose coop cleaned out. Also pig pens. After cleaning up a few other things in and around the barn, I help in the kitchen and mop the floor.

I help peel potatoes for potato flour and prepare red beets for supper.

NEWS: Strazburg in Allied hands. Eight kilometres away from Duren. Two kilometres from Venlo. By Geilenkirchen they bombarded a town with 20,000 grenades and 10,000 mortar bombs. Aken attacked with 1,000 cannons, each firing every three seconds. The Ruhr has overflowed its banks and is now 300 meters wide, double its normal size.

This morning I got a letter from my sister Bep and her husband Wim.

In Aalten some bombs have been dropped close to the community entertainment centre.

Jan ter Horst is sick with pleurisy.

Sunday, November 26

Church at farm *Neerhof*. Johan in charge. Sermon title "Don't get discouraged". Attendance 17 men, collection 7 guilders and 32 cents.

Mina comes to warn everybody that the *Groenen* are in Aalten. I go home and want to finish a letter for Apeldoorn to my Dad and sister. Mr. Toop, one of the *evacuees* from Scheveningen, is going to Utrecht and will deliver my letter. After this I go for a nice walk. We are invited again to come to farm *Neerhof* this evening, Gerrit, Frans and I. Johan comes a little later.

I count 16 people around the table.

I forgot to mention that I wrote a letter to Henny this afternoon. Mina will give it to her right after church in town. We cannot go to the real church anymore, it is too dangerous.

NEWS: By Venlo two villages liberated. A Dutch submarine has torpedoed a 45,000 ton Japanese ship. 60,000 Japanese prisoners of war and 30,000 died in the jungle. Four enemy strongholds still active by Metz.

The weather was nice today.

Monday, November 27
Nice weather. Dr. Schouten brings a letter from my sister Miep.

First I pick some more *knollen*, and then help with the wash. I crank the handle of the washing machine. Jan Eppink comes to kill and butcher a pig. I like this kind of work and am allowed to help him. Then back to kitchen duties. Fried potatoes and setting table.

Supper and then a fair bit of argument about whether they should make sausages or not. Gerrit is glad he can leave for a while. Comes back with a lot of news. Everybody is quiet and willing to listen.

NEWS: Some bombs have been dropped on certain targets in Amsterdam and Hilversum. In Germany, Keulen and Munchen covered with bombs. Cordell Hull resigns as US Secretary of State. General Petrov pushes ahead in East Slovakia over a frontal line 50 kilometres wide.

Tuesday, November 27
It seems that a decision has been made. Johan, Gerrit and Mina are going to make sausages. Oom Herman and I are going to work in the pasture called 't Vree. We have to clean and straighten out the kitchen. While we are busy we see 13 *Moffen* coming our way. And there are lots more in the whole area. They seem to exercise; all around we hear shooting from rifles and other equipment. But then we get some other visitors, the Tommies. One group comes

and goes; another follows in its wake. When the *Moffen* are in the pasture beside ours we see four fighter planes coming and they are low. Better watch out, if they have spotted the Germans, there will be an attack. The Germans are about 20 meters away from us and fall flat on the ground. The planes pass without shooting and the Germans want to stand up. Another set of planes come and again the soldiers lie flat until they have passed. Now the Germans are quick to move and take off in the direction of Lintelo. A little later we hear that the planes drop light bombs and also use their onboard guns.

We are home again at 11 a.m. Now planes fly over the road from Varsseveld to Lichtenvoorde. Five in total. They use their onboard guns and not just a few rounds. Terrible; what a noise. After about 15 minutes they move on.

At noon we eat mashed food with *gris*. Afternoon, cut tobacco. Harvest *knollen*. Get water for cows.

Turn washing machine crank. Peel potatoes for tonight. Trim and clean oil lamps. Set table and after supper do dishes with Gerrit and Frans.

Johan may go for the news this time. NEWS: Her Majesty Queen Wilhelmina speaks to the people in Holland. She praises the railroad workers for their courage to go on strike.

Wednesday, November 28

Today I spend all my time working in the garden in front of the house. Many planes overhead, bombers and fighter planes. Some planes carry extra fuel tanks which are discarded when empty. We see four of them come down in the surrounding area.

Some bombs fall in district Haart where Henny is staying at the farm of her aunt and uncle. We have an exciting moment when an English fighter plane chases a German plane. They disappear in the distance. Jo comes to drop Ineke off at our farm until tomorrow. My sister Nen does not get any more news from her fiancé Berend who is working in forced labour in Berlin.

NEWS: Venlo has turned into a real battle field.

Jan is getting a lot better and Gerrit may get up from bed all day and go for a 15 minute walk.

Thursday, November 30

Work in the garden and finish the work. At farmer Jansen an *onderduiker* from Arnhem was working in the field and got picked up by the *Landwacht*. Willem Scholten and Bernard Stronks received a letter to register for digging trenches.

Jo, who comes to pick up Ineke, has trouble with her bike. When it is fixed she can go home and I hand her 38 guilders from church collections. Ineke is staying here until Saturday.

The cherry tree is to come down. After sharpening the axe, we try it out. It works very well. When this is done we get a load of *knollen* from the field in den Es. Gerrit from next door will use his horse and wagon for this job. It is too far to go with the wheelbarrow since that would take days or weeks.

For food today we have some special items. This morning we had *balkenbrij*; at noon potatoes with endive and a delicious piece of meat and nice dark gravy. Evening, fried potatoes, homemade bread, and a plate with oat porridge. Tante who went to town to do some shopping came home with a full pack of matches, 12 boxes. She gives me one of them. A precious gift!

DECEMBER 1944

Friday, December 1

The branches of the cherry tree have to be bundled up and stacked. They will be used to heat the *mantelpot*. We borrow a long saw from the neighbour at *de Bleeke* to cut the tree trunk into small pieces. This saw is called a *kortiezer* as it is used to make the wood shorter so it will fit into the wood stove.

We hear that Amsterdam is in an emergency situation. A pail of water costs 2 guilders and 50 cents. Potatoes are sold one at a time for 1 guilder and 50 cents each. Antwerp's harbour is operating again. 20,000 trucks go up and down each day to transport all kind of things.

It is a custom here to eat some *pap* at about 8:30 p.m. You get used to this quickly, and look forward to it each day, especially after a day of hard work. Frans likes his porridge but cannot eat it too hot. Often he is very tired in the

Above the Pigsty   145

evening and almost falls asleep waiting for his *pap* to cool off. This time we are in for a treat. It is like a skit, with Frans performing very well.

Tante is scooping up the porridge. There are seven of us around the table. Frans sits between brother Gerrit and Herman Junior. The *pap* is hot; Frans is sleepy. While we are talking, we see Frans' eyes getting heavy, his head nods. We look at each other and have the same unspoken expectation. His head goes lower and lower and we giggle. He looks up and wonders what is going on. Everybody is looking in another direction and there is just the normal conversation. Satisfied, he closes his eyes again. The other six pairs of eyes turn in his direction again. His head goes down a little to the left. Herman moves Frans' bowl of porridge toward Gerrit. When Frans' head moves to the right, Gerrit moves the bowl toward Herman. By now Frans is almost asleep and suddenly his head takes a deep plunge straight down. Herman is waiting for it and the bowl is in the perfect place. When his nose lands in the hot porridge, Frans wakes up with a shock. Loud laughter is the result from our side. Frans suffers from a red nose for the next few days. Someone asks, "What are you going to tell Riekie, Frans?" Riekie is Frans' girlfriend.

Saturday, December 2

We have to cut down the other cherry tree as well. Jo comes with Dikkie who needs a haircut. I clean out the goose pen and the barn itself. After that I can give myself a bath.

Gerrit goes for NEWS: Russian army advanced 30 kilometres and is approximately 145 kilometres from Austria's border. Karlsruhe and Koblenz bombed. This news was aired by Radio Herrijzend Nederland.

I write a letter to Mr. Henk Wolf. We are warned about raids; they need more men.

Sunday, December 3

Church at our farm. Gerrit is in charge. Attendance 19; collection 6 guilders and 85 cents. It is good we have the service in the living room because two German soldiers step into the kitchen without knocking. To our relief they are not looking for men; they want to buy something. The farmer tells them we do not sell on Sunday, and they leave.

After church Johan and I get ready to go to Patrimoniumstraat to see Lien and Henny. We are just about ready to leave when Lien and Henny arrive to pay a visit to the sick: Gerrit and Jan. After the visit the four of us walk to Patrimoniumstraat. The weather could not be any worse, raining cats and dogs. Since we are walking we arrive with four pairs of wet feet, but in good humour. What else do you expect when you can spend an afternoon and evening with your best friend, Henny? Supper is almost ready when we arrive and it tastes delicious.

Nice meat, liver sausage, cheese etc. When I count around the table, there are thirteen people. But three are missing and that is too bad. However they are safe and sound. Mother Wikkerink makes the comment, "We can be so thankful that after seven weeks we are all together again, except three of us."

The three are Ome Jan, Anton Nusselder and Joop Winkelman. They were picked up in October but managed to escape. They are still in hiding! I appreciate Mother's comment. She is such a lovely person and it makes me think about my own mother. When we walk to Oom Derk's, Henny says, "I am sorry I did not know about your mother's birth date, November 13th. We could have talked about it." My mother died July 1939. I am sorry I did not share this with her, and tell her that her caring attitude means a great deal to me.

We have a nice evening at Oom Derk's place. We listen to Jo play the organ and Lien, Jo and Henny sing. We are not allowed to join in the singing because the house is too close to the street and it is nobody's business that there are men in the house.

10:30 p.m. bed time. I sleep in the *hol* with Johan ter Horst, David Kodde and Gerrit Wikkerink. I am awake most of the night. So much noise from German soldiers with cars, trucks, horses and walking. On the farm it is much quieter.

Monday, December 4

Glad to get up at 7 a.m. NEWS from last-night: British making good advance along the Maas in Limburg (Holland). Russian troops 100 kilometres from border of Austria. Allies near the river Saar. Fighting in Saarlautern. In Hungary, Kaposvár and Dombóvár liberated. Budapest liberated. Bombing of Hagen, Dortmund, Frankfort and Heidelberg. A warning is issued to Germany that no atrocities will be tolerated against members of the Resistance movement, because these are now fighting along with the Allied troops and are to be treated as soldiers. On island of Crete, good advance. Tokyo bombed for third time. Germany has a new division of soldiers made up of 16 year olds.

When we come to Opoe Wikkerink, who lives next door, Henny and Lien are busy making some breakfast and tea. We leave for the farm at 7:30 a.m. and Dikkie comes along. He needs a haircut *(mot zich de heure loaten snie'n)*. Miserable weather, wet, hail, rain and snow. Also some thunder.

Dikkie has to go back home and begs me time and again to accompany him up to the main road. Of course I am willing to do this. When I get home, back at the farm, I set the table and we eat.

Afternoon, fire up the *mantelpot* to make slop for pigs. Get more *knollen* from the field. Frans helps me faithfully.

After supper my diary updated.

8 p.m. I am the one going for news tonight. It is pitch dark, very wet and you cannot see where you are going. Once I step into a large puddle of water and a little later twice into a big mud hole. Over town I hear a plane, very low. It starts shooting with its' guns and the sound comes closer. Then it stops shooting.

NEWS: The Allied have reached Roesi in Italy. At Saarlautern the bridge over the Saar in Allied hands. Blerick liberated (or taken). The Germans blew up the Rijndijk by Arnhem. Likely to inundate the Betuwe.

Prime Minister Gerbrandy was in Nijmegen. One quarter of the homes are totally or partly destroyed. Offices of army staff in Amsterdam, Rotterdam, Hilversum and Utrecht bombed. People are urged to move from these areas. Tonight I sleep with Frans because Johan is sick. Will be a second night without much sleep. He does not lie still but moves around in bed.

Peter Van Essen

Tuesday, December 5

I did get more sleep than expected. Cleaned the kitchen and lit the stove to improve the temperature.

A number of planes in the air search for enemy targets. Suddenly they come down. Aim for the railroad by 't Halt. We count three bombs which explode with a terrific bang. Interesting sight.

Washing machine crank turned. Feed cows in afternoon, then gather some more *knollen* and back to turning washing machine. The Tommies are very active again. Very low, six of them fly over. We see them turn around, come back in our direction and dive down. We hear a lot of shooting and the sound of exploding bombs is in the air. Oom Herman and Frans crawl into the bomb shelter when one of the planes comes a bit too close for comfort. Target: German troops moving on the Heelweg.

We need more carbide to burn the lamp and our neighbour at *Neerhof* has promised some. When I return from *Neerhof* it is time to eat. Frans and I do the dishes and at seven o'clock I find a little time to update my diary.

NEWS: An all-day bombardment of Venlo. Also Berlin and Munster. In the Betuwe a foot of water due to the blown up Rijndijk. The road and rail-road between Arnhem and Nijmegen still okay for traffic. The *Moffen* regroup behind the Siegfried Line, the strong defence position at the river Rhine. The 3rd and 7th American armies have passed the Saar and progress very well. In Italy the city of Ravenna taken. Two-thirds of Hungary in Russian hands. In 't Wurde a train is attacked in which men from Apeldoorn were transported to work in Germany. This must have been the train in which Wim Riphagen, the son of our neighbour in Apeldoorn, was killed.

Wednesday, December 6

The first thing I did this morning was look in my *klomp* to see if *Sinterklaas* had left some presents for me. Nothing in my wooden shoe.

I have noticed that the washing machine is pretty dirty and should be cleaned. After this Frans and I are going to pull up some more *knollen*.

Afternoon, Frans and I first do the dishes. While in the kitchen the atmosphere gets bad. Harsh words fly back and forth. I feel sad about this and ask myself if we, the *onderduikers*, are the cause of it. Of course there is a lot of tension with the war carrying on all around us and who knows for how long yet. Since the invasion in June only half of the Netherlands is liberated. We will probably face a very hard and trying winter.

I go to the cow stable where it is quiet. I remember that the *hol* where Gerrit and Frans sleep is very drafty. I try to fix it with old burlap bags and boards.

Dominee Veenhuizen comes to visit the sick. We talk for more than an hour about the letter the clergy have written asking men to consider reporting for digging duties.

In Aalten, a car arrives with wounded people from the bombed and bullet-riddled train in 't Wurde. All men from Apeldoorn. Also in Lichtenvoorde many have arrived and are in hospital there.

After the dishes are clean we try to get the lamps going. It takes a long time before we get one of them burning and I can now do some work on my diary.

This afternoon we kept ourselves busy trying to turn a bicycle into a light for the living room. We might be able to rig up something.

NEWS: Allied troops crossed the river Saar in six different places. Bergstein captured. The last six months, six million Germans have died, been wounded or captured. This probably includes the dead in bombed cities?

At Winkelhorst in Aalten everything has been confiscated. I do not know why.

All day I am working on the new light fixture. It is ready in the evening. And now we all have to pedal. Maybe I should not have tried to make it work. They might hate me for it! It would be much nicer to go and bike with your girlfriend.

I write a letter to home in Apeldoorn.

No news - Gerrit does not want to go. "It is too dark," he says. He is right, it is pitch-dark!

Friday, December 8

We have to get potatoes from the *koele*. Potatoes are stored for winter in a hole in the ground and covered with a thick layer of straw and soil. *Mantelpot* fired up to cook slop for pigs.

Changes have to be made on the bike light. We rig up Gerrit's bike with two generators on the rear wheel. The rear wheel rests on a wooden stand and wires run from the generators to the ceiling and down the middle of the room. A small piece of plywood holding two bicycles bulbs will give us a fair amount of light depending on how fast you pedal.

At first we all enjoy this contraption, later it becomes more or less a pain in the neck. But then, you have to do something to be able to read, darn or sew at night.

I remember one night when Tante was sewing, and I was biking. By this kind of light threading the needle was not the easiest thing to do, but normally she managed. When Tante started to put a new thread into the needle, I pedalled just a little slower. She got up from the chair to get a bit closer to the light. I reacted by going yet a little slower, and she reached her arms higher again to get more light. Then one more time, and by now she realized what was happening; the light was almost out. She scolded me and we both had a good laugh about it.

Ineke, who came to *de Koekoek* yesterday, keeps me company all day long. We eat pancakes with bacon tonight. Delicious.

I received a letter from home and one from Jo Nijdeken who used to hide here but went back home some time ago.

In Aalten, the town police have gone into hiding.

Starting a letter for Henny.

NEWS: German troops have had some successful activity near Haguenau. We don't know exactly what they accomplished.

Saturday, December 9
Improvements to the bike light. After gathering *knollen* for the cows we bring the remaining bicycles into the loft under some straw.

I give my wooden shoes a thorough cleaning and they are now hanging outside to dry.

By farm *Neerhof* are two *Landwachters*. They have to transport NSB members to Winterswijk and need a horse and wagon.

No news tonight.

Sunday, December 10
Church at *de Koekoek*. Lies van der Male in charge. Sermon based on John 1:11 & 12. Collection 8 guilders and 29 cents. Present 19 young men. After church I continue my letter to Henny and start another to Henk in Driebergen. Also one for home in Apeldoorn. I get a surprise when Lien comes to visit Johan and hands me a letter from Henny.

In the afternoon we go for a walk, Gerrit, Frans and I. By the farm *'t Nonhof* we find a nice long galvanized wire which the Germans have left there for some reason. Since they stole our clothesline this morning we feel free to take this with us. Tante is very pleased and has now a much better clothesline than before.

In the evening we enjoy sitting around the stove and I take my harmonica and play for more than half an hour. Later, when I am in bed, ten German soldiers arrive and ask for directions to the next town Lichtenvoorde.

Johan sleeps in the *hol* with me again tonight.

Monday, December 11

Drika Houwers from farm *Neerhof* is going to Apeldoorn tomorrow and will take along some food for home. I see they have already made quite a parcel.

In afternoon the *Zwarten* paid a visit to neighbour Papenborg. Bernard is ordered to dig trenches every two weeks near Zevenaar.

We crawl into the *hol* for about one hour. For safety's sake.

Tuesday, December 12

Feed animals. Clean up attic in barn. Bring fire wood inside the shed. Crank washing machine.

To *Neerhof* to get a postage stamp for Henny's letter. Gerrit and Johan keep busy hanging the bacon and sausages in the *wieme*. I start frying potatoes for supper.

In Aalten announcements are made again that men are demanded to report for digging. We can expect some serious trouble in the coming days.

NEWS: 7th American Army breaks through Maginot Line.

Wednesday, December 13

First feed the cows. Light the stove so we have some heat in the kitchen. Next I make a kind of ceiling in my hiding *hol*. We have trouble sleeping as the hay contains small hay spiders that continue to fall down. All too often they fall in your face when you are asleep. I make a kind of ceiling from lightweight boards, just over our faces, hoping it will do the trick.

A letter written to Ome Jan. Lien will take it with her coming Sunday when she is going to visit him at his new address, his hiding place.

Drika from Neerhof is back from her trip to Apeldoorn and brings clothes for Gerrit and me and also best wishes. Mr. Walchien from Apeldoorn, one of the men in the train bombed at 't Wurde, is hospitalized in Bochholt, Germany. He was shot in the shoulder and lost one finger. When they rounded up these men in Apeldoorn they also paid a visit to our home. They even lifted the lid off the toilet to see if there was a man hiding in it.

I finish the ceiling in the *hol*. Johan and I trim some small trees along the pasture and bind up the branches which are used to fire up the *mantelpot*. It was a nice sunny day today.

NEWS: Fighting starts in Budapest. Essen and Hannover bombed.

Thursday, December 14

After the cows are taken care of I wash my hair. When I go to work on the land I come around the barn and I stand face to face with Henny accompanied by Jan Hoornenborg. What a surprise. She does not have much time, only to tell me that the letters for my brother in Amsterdam should be delivered to their house by tonight. Also I may come to spend Christmas at the farm of Hoornenborg where Henny is staying and helping out. Best of all, Henny will come to *de Koekoek* Sunday night.

Help *den Eume* with the *knollen*. After this feed and water the cows.

In the neighbour's pasture in front of our farmhouse stand some very big poplar trees. The neighbour wants them cut down to be sold for making wooden shoes. The woodcutters come to set up shop.

We see and hear the launching of another five V-1's.

When it is dark outside we go in to enjoy some reading and other activities. *Den Eume* comes in to have another look at our bike light. He cannot get over this marvelous contraption and starts to explain himself… "*Daor kuj een heel ende op weg fietsen so 'savonds. Daor kom iej wel mit tut in Arem (Arnhem)… hu, hu, hu! Wisse we! Jao, Jao!! Ik sitte dan ok nog wel is op de fietse, maor dit ze'k oe Herman, as ik daor biej de Beddingsgere binne, biej dat zwette paedjen, dan hef ut werk da'k recht an kan fietsen. En dan geet 't 'tran, dat wit ik wel, daor praot ik niks um hen; Joa, Joa, das miej eerlijkwaor bedag."*

"You can bike a great distance on that in an evening. You would almost get to Arnhem, ho, ho, ho. What do you know! Well, well. I sometimes sit on a bike too, but I tell you this, Herman, when I get to the Beddingsgere, by that black path, then I have trouble keeping the bike in a straight line. And then it gets difficult..., I know that for sure, I'm not just talking through my hat here. Yes, yes, that is really a great invention."

No NEWS today.

This afternoon they have spotted four *Zwarten* going direction Woldboom, a section of our district Dale.

Friday, December 15

We have to watch out today and stay inside the house more. Among the tree cutters is one man we don't trust. Oom Herman calls him a *slamierus*.

I take care of the animals, and then sweep the kitchen clean. My brother Gerrit cuts my hair and I think I look a lot better.

We have a new name for our indoor-outhouse: *Tante Betje*. It needs to be whitewashed. When this is done *den Eume* calls me to assist with the birth of a calf. The vet, Jan Eppink, is already on his knees in the stable behind the young cow. Johan comes to see what is going on and helps me pull. No matter how we try it does not come out. Wow, it sure is stuck. Jan says, "We cannot get it out alive." When the calf is half-way out the vet cuts the first part off with a chain saw, after which we pull out the remainder. The cow has suffered a lot. It is almost 12:30 in the afternoon and we go to the kitchen for a nice cup of coffee and a good meal, *boerekool met worst*.

While we were busy in the stable, the airplanes were very active in the air shooting with their guns. We wonder about their targets.

Polish shoes, peel potatoes and apples, fix the light, make beds. I have to lead the church service on Sunday and I read over the sermon to prepare myself.

Saturday, December 16

Gerrit Driessen has his birthday today.

Cleaning day. First the pen for the geese, then chicken coop and pig pens. Cows and pigs fed and fresh straw. Jo Bosman from Amsterdam visits us.

Cleaned wooden shoes; toilet cleaned. And finally a wash job for myself. In evening once more I reread the sermon. 9 p.m. bed time.

Sunday, December 17

Church service at farm *Neerhof*.

When I announce the opening song a few more young men walk in and mention that there are two *Landwachters* by the farm of Gerrit Jan.

We discuss what to do and decide to continue. Two men are posted outside, one in front and one in back of house. A little later we find out what the *Landwachters* wanted. All farmers get an invitation to come with their horses to the market tomorrow.

The German army is in bad shape; it is going to move the NSB members further north away from the war zone. It is an encouraging sign. We now continue with our church service, or not?

When I am half way the second page of the sermon our lookout man sees a *Landwachter* running towards our farm. He is from farm *'t Nonhof*, who is also a member of the NSB but has never yet done anything harmful or dangerous to the people of the neighbourhood. The result of this visit is a quick reaction and movement of the church. In no time every one of us is gone; to the manure barn connected to the stable. The pulpit made up of five heavy books comes along too. Five minutes later we are back in church and it is as if nothing has happened. Why did farmer Bulsink come and scare us? To tell Jan, the farmer, to be at the market tomorrow with his horse.

We close our church service with a prayer of thanksgiving and sing the second verse of Psalm 98. Attended by 20 men. Collection 4 guilders and 50 ½ cents. Yes, we still had a half a penny in those days. Today even pennies have disappeared.

Our neighbour *den Eume* also had a visit from the *Landwacht*. He lives in one half of the farm building; *de Koekoek* is in the other half. Oom Herman does not have a horse... *den Eume* does.

At about five in the afternoon Henny comes and we go for a nice long walk later after supper. Back at eight o'clock with some wet and muddy feet. *Onderduiker* Rijk vander Meulen comes to stay for the night. In Lintelo district where he is hiding are many S.S. These are the worst; very fanatic and trained hunters. Rijk does not dare to stay at his place. We go up together in the *hol* and talk for almost an hour before bed.

We get a strong warning about planned raids tomorrow.

NEWS: German troops break through a bridge head in Luxemburg and Belgium.

Monday, December 18

We are ordered to stay in the *hol* today, at least till noon. Although I have to spend approximately four hours in the dark, the time seems to go quite fast. Dinner is ready and we can come out to eat.

Menu: Kale with sausage and porridge for dessert; a very good meal again. The S.S. is busy in 't Grevink, half a kilomtetre away; very close. Two boys are picked up at Scholten. A little later, watch out, two S.S. are at the neighbouring farm *Neerhof*. We now expect them any moment at our place. However the Lord has His ways to deal with this problem. From *Neerhof* the S.S. heads back to town. Jan Houwers, the farmer, gave the two men a good meal; they were hungry. Apparently satisfied, they stopped hunting for more men.

At 5:30 p.m. Oom Derk Wikkerink comes to pick up Rijk. S.S. has moved out of town and the area and we are allowed to come out of hiding. We are so thankful and relieved that we jump up and over each other in our cramped space messing up our beds, straw and blankets, before lowering ourselves through the trap door.

Tuesday, December 19

My socks have to be darned and I am trying my darndest to do something decent with the burlap thread and binder twine.

Besides looking after the cows, pigs, and geese, Frans and I thresh brown beans. Dried bean plants are put in a burlap bag which is then tied up. We put the bags on the threshing floor and use the flay to beat out the beans.

After my turn to bike for light, I feed the cows, then milk them and bring them water to drink. The stable needs fresh straw and after this is taken care of we can have our supper.

Letter written for home to Apeldoorn, and my diary needs updating since Sunday afternoon.

Wednesday, December 20

Johan and I make a new clothesline.

Lies Beumer will take letters to Apeldoorn so I start writing again to my sister Janny and brother Teun in Twello. We depend on people to play mailmen for us. Trains, buses, in fact anything that moves is not safe on the roads.

We hear rumours that police in Apeldoorn have gone into hiding and that the *Landwacht* has to go for training to go into battle alongside the German soldiers. *Opgeruimd staat netjes*, a saying which means it feels good to get rid of the junk.

Jan Hoornenborg comes for a haircut but the barber is not in. "Sorry," says Jan, "I was to bring a letter for you from Henny but I forgot. Tomorrow I will be back - with the letter." I hope so!

Tante Dina from Domme Anleg in Barlo comes for a visit. She tells us an almost unbelievable story. Two girls who work in the office of Hoens, which looks after agricultural affairs, went out with two *onderduikers* one night. The *onderduikers* picked them up at the office. It was quite dark and one of the girls had a piece of soft coal. She was able to smear the *onderduiker's* face with black dirt without him noticing anything. But when he came home the secret was revealed!

The whole district of Barlo seems to be talking about it. Well, we had a good laugh about it, without revealing the truth. Tante Dina has another story.

Dominee Veenhuizen and dominee Klijn both go into hiding at a farm. They have to sleep in the loft at the front end of the threshing floor. They struggle up a flimsy wooden ladder, step onto the loft covered with some straw. One of them puts his hand into some cat poop as he crawls through the straw. Finally they are lying in the makeshift bed, a pair of old blankets spread out on the straw. Later the farmer comes home and yells, "If you have to do a pee, there is a wicker basket standing in the corner." I think both the dominees were a bit shocked.

Tonight we hide the bicycles again. I mop the little kitchen floor. Also peel potatoes. Frans is cleaning a goose for Papiermole, an awful job to get all the feathers and down removed.

I receive a pair of *klomp* socks from family Wikkerink. This is easier on my socks. *Klomp* socks are thin leather slippers that fit over your socks before you put on your wooden shoes. This reduces the wear on your regular socks.

While biking for light I do some reading in my diary. NEWS: German troops 29 kilometres from Luik.

Thursday, December 21

Jan and Gerrit come for a haircut. I get my letter from Henny and write a short one back for her. Afternoon, we need more beets for the cows and I keep busy with this job. After feeding and watering cows I help with milking. Update my diary in evening. German soldiers have taken the meat out of the *wieme* at some farms.

Friday, December 22

Fire up the *mantelpot*, the food kettle for pigs. Polish shoes. Afternoon, still polishing shoes. We have a big family.

When Johan and I go outside to cut some wood there is a young German soldier, neat and polite, asking if we have something to sell. He is about 18 years old. We suggest that he ask the farmer. Oom Herman gives him five eggs. We really do not have much to give away. Ours is a very small farm and many mouths are to be fed these days. But the boy walks away happy.

The neighbour from *Neerhof* comes with a hare and wild duck and asks us to clean it so they can eat it. They are very good neighbours who are always ready to help. They seem to keep close watch how we are doing with our enlarged family. At their farm they have two *onderduikers* and once were hiding a French soldier who had escaped from a POW camp in Germany.

Sebe, one of *onderduikers* at *Neerhof*, goes with horse and wagon to Doetinchem to bring Christmas presents to trench diggers. A dangerous job.

Saturday, December 23

First frost. It's cleanup day again. Starting with the goose pen, then pig pens and the barn floor. Bring fresh straw for cows' stable. Rake and sweep outside around the farmhouse and barn. Clean wooden shoes and take a bath.

After feeding animals I can start making porridge. Ready at 5 p.m. That's early. I don't think this has ever happened before. In the evening Frans and Dick peel potatoes for tomorrow, while brother Gerrit shaves some of the other members of the family. Sebe has returned safely from Doetinchem. We crawl into bed at 9 p.m.

Sunday, December 24

Brrr... It is cold. The tears are running out of my nose.

Church at Hoopman's farm *de Krieger*. Gerrit is in charge. Attendance 20 young men, collection 7 guilders and 80 cents.

When we leave a church service or other meeting, we never all leave at the same time. Just two or three, the rest waits a few minutes. We hurry home because it is still very cold and we long for a nice cup of coffee. I play a game of chess with Gerrit before lunch. I do dishes with faithful Frans and do some more work on my diary. In the afternoon we all have to go to *Neerhof* to celebrate Sebe's birthday. He turns 25 today. We eat there too and I count 14 people around the table. Later in evening another 12 people show up. We had a very pleasant evening.

Monday, December 25 Christmas Day

Today we have a real minister to preach to us, dominee Gerritsma. Church is at our farm and 21 young men show up.

This is Christmas far away from home. Not alone but still somewhat lonely. But it is an occasion worth remembering, Christ coming into this world for me too. It fills you with thankfulness and it gives joy and peace to your soul, even when you feel lonely at times.

I am reading and enjoying a book titled "When the Leaves Fall".

Geert Lammers comes for a short visit. I am amazed how much weight he has gained. 17 years old and he weighs 175 pounds. It is because of his bout with sickness since April and he is always in bed.

Later in the afternoon Lien and Henny show up. I don't understand it. Henny was supposed to go away for a while. She explains that Opoe Wikkerink is not doing very well and that her father, Ome Jan, came home to see how things are with his mother. She and Lien are staying here until tomorrow morning.

After supper I have to take my turn to bike for light and after this Henny and I go for a long walk.

When we come home we all sing around the organ and then it is bedtime.

Tomorrow we have to get up at 6:30. We will celebrate Second Christmas Day in Aalten with the Wikkerinks. Going to town while it is still dark is much better than in full daylight.

Tuesday, December 26

I sleep like a log and get up too late. After breakfast we leave, Johan and Lien, Gerrit and Mien, Henny and I. It is cold again and we start running to get our feet a little warmer. The ladies are going to church this morning, Henny takes along a *stoof* to keep her feet warm in church. No heat is available anymore for churches and schools so you have to improvise.

After dinner Henny and I walk to Patrimoniumstraat to look at their house that was burned out by the German police after Ome Jan escaped. I had not seen it yet. It looks awful. The family is living in a temporary shelter which they have named *Nooitgedacht*, which means never imagined.

We have church in the afternoon at home. For this occasion dominee Kuiper brings his Christmas sermon from this morning's service. Johan does the reading. 14 people attend which includes David Kodde, Maarten, Hans Wikkerink, and Joop.

When the girls are busy making supper the little kitchen is full of people. Jo is cutting sausage and meat. As I watch her, she shoves the odd piece to the side where I stand. It tastes good!

The evening is *gezellig,* sitting around the table. My thoughts go home and I wonder how their Christmas is. All kinds of memories come and go. Henny calls me back to reality when she asks, "What is wrong, you are so quiet."

10:30 p.m. Bedtime. Her father takes Henny and me by the arm and pushes us into the laundry room for a few minutes of privacy. We thank the Lord for a nice day and His protection. Gerrit, Johan and I sleep in David's hiding place. This *hol* is a lot nicer than ours at the farm and not so cold either.

Wednesday, December 27

Up at 7:30 a.m. A cup of tea and a slice of bread and away we go back to the farm. When we arrive back from town we first have a good breakfast. After cleaning the kitchen we cut some tobacco, and then care for the animals. The sheep needs *haksel,* so we make that. After supper I pedal on the bike in between reading and a bit of playing the organ.

Before we left the Wikkerink's this morning, Henny said that I could come on Sunday to their place to celebrate the New Year. Mother Wikkerink will be away and we can keep Jo company. Lien will come to *de Koekoek* to be with Johan.

Thursday December 28

Den Eume, the neighbour, asks us if we would like to cut some *haksel* for his cattle. We gladly accept; anything to break the monotony of the day. Johan, Gerrit and I are busy for a number of hours and earn one guilder each and enough real tobacco for one pipe. We have time yet to thresh some beans in a burlap bag. I get the collected church money ready for Lien who will be in later to pick it up, 25 guilders.

When Lien arrives she is accompanied by Mrs. Dikkers from Driebergen. Tante Riek, also from Driebergen, has come to Aalten as well.

They are here to collect food. Western Holland is getting desperate and will face a severe winter of hunger and cold.

Tomorrow they travel back to Driebergen and Henny is planning to go with them to carry some of the goodies on her bike. There will be too much for just the two of them. Johan will bring all parcels of food from our farm to the Bredevoortsestraat tonight.

You may have wondered why women and girls do all the errands and trips. Men cannot travel safely. There is always a raid somewhere and crossing one of the big rivers is definitely a no-no. German soldiers are permanently posted at the bridge and in many other places.

Johan and I thresh barley. This is done secretly. Normally you have to get a permit for it and an inspector comes to count the sacks of grain of which a good portion has to be set aside and delivered to a special depot for Germany. Not this time!

At four o'clock we go to the Stronks' farm and help them thresh some of their grain. Finished at 5:30 and home again at 6 p.m.

JANUARY 1945

Missing part of diary
December 29, 1944 through January 7, 1945
Reason? No paper available.

The last three notebooks which I used to record my daily experiences were given to me. I have used every page and there is no more paper to write on. You cannot buy paper either; no store has this luxury item in stock.

But after a few days this problem is solved in a very unexpected way, and I get a New Book #4.

There is no paper available anymore, not even toilet paper! For this last purpose we use newspaper. Not always available either except for a little paper issued by the NSB and one issued by a communist party. We do not read this garbage, but the paper is quite soft and we like it for what we use it for, in more than one way.

On January 8, I pay a visit to *Tante Betje* and, of all things, for lack of any other paper, there is an old book explaining the doctrine of the Reformed church. The back of every page is blank for study notes. The paper is thick and shiny, not really suitable for use in a bathroom, although three pages have been used already. I claim it for a diary. Happy with this find, I ask for permission from the others in the family. Permission is granted, but please find something else to replace it and do it soon!

Monday, January 8

It started to snow early this morning. The ladies have left for Driebergen, we hope they have a safe trip. Frans and I peel potatoes. When we see the others start a snowball fight we hurry up so we can join them. Johan takes a few photos.

After the snowball excitement I fix my blue suit - a button on the jacket and another on the fly. I read Henny's account of her last trip to Driebergen.

Afternoon, another snowball fight. Oom Herman is the first one outside joined by Johan, Herman, Dirk, Gerrit, Frans and I. Gerrit takes a few pictures.

After the fun we go back to work. Turning the washing machine is my job again. Oom Herman mentions that the *sterker* will give birth to her first calf during the night. Ooh... ooh... we don't like it if this happens during the night.

Herman comes home and tells us that by Houwers at farm *Neerhof* the *Moffen* wanted to take bacon out of the *wieme*. They threatened with a machine gun and a pistol. However, they did not count on the women at home. The ladies were furious and said that one of them had already gone to town to see the *Ortzcommandant* to complain. That did the trick, the soldiers left in a hurry.

Tuesday, January 9

It is 3 a.m. Johan called me out of bed about 15 minutes ago. Oom Herman went to the vet at one o'clock this morning to let him know he would be needed very shortly. He then called Johan to light the stove for some heat and hot water. I appreciate that I could get an extra hour of sleep.

I wonder how this young cow will make out with her delivery. When I get dressed, Johan is on his way to call the neighbours, *den Eume* and his son

Gerrit, to help. The front legs have already come out. The birth of this calf goes a little different from the last one at the farm.

While waiting for the vet, I make some coffee. Since we do not have real coffee, for a long time already, we have to improvise. I take barley and grind it in the coffee grinder. The kitchen *fornuis* burns nicely and it does not take too long for the coffee to be ready. We butter some black bread and I notice *schinke* hanging above the stove. A slice of that tastes good on a slice of bread. Johan cuts tobacco while talking to Gerrit, and I use my time to update my diary.

The snow is piling up, about 20 centimetres by now.

At 3:30 a.m. Oom Herman is back with the vet, and *den Eume* has managed to get out of bed and is ready to help. The vet announces that the calf is facing the wrong way; it might get a little complicated. However everything goes fairly smoothly and I am back in bed at 4:45 a. m.

At 9:45 a.m. I hear Oom Herman calling us to get up. After breakfast Gerrit ter Horst, Frans and I peel potatoes and work with the tobacco and before we realize it, it is noon, and time to eat again. We cannot do any work outside for there is too much snow.

My grey Sunday socks need fixing. What a chore without the proper yarn! I manage to get one done and just then it stops snowing. I walk to our neighbour Papenborg and his wife Bessy. She is a saint; he is bedridden with terrible arthritis. This is an old, old farm, very cute to see, but cold and wet. With weather like today's you have to clean the snow away from the loft above the living room and bedroom. It blows through the openings between the roof tiles. This picturesque farm home belongs to a *Scholteboer* and is one of many that are leased out. The Papenborgs have lived on this very small farm for many years and it is no wonder that he is no longer able to move about. Neighbours do most of the farm work from beginning to end. Also a cousin, Bernard, comes regularly to do chores.

When I get to the house, Hendrik Jansen, another neighbour, is already busy and hands me another broom. Bessy invites us for coffee and conversation after the snow is cleared away.

Back at our farm I manage to darn my second sock. It's time to prepare for supper and start to boil potatoes and set the table. After supper I help do dishes while enjoying the warmth of the stove.

Wednesday, January 10

Frans and I peel potatoes. Poor Frans, he does not complain with words, but when I look at his face it shows his feelings. Herman Junior and his friend Johan Stronks are out tracking hares and rabbits in the snow. Frans' face lights up and it is amazing how fast we are able to finish our chore. When we look at the finished product in the pan, some of the potatoes look back at us with their remaining eyes.

The boys found a track leading into the woodshed. Now we get really busy. A lot of wood has to be removed. Under the wood is a wooden box in which the farmer has hidden copper, brass and other items. From time to time Germany demands these items to be handed in for use of war equipment. They are melted down.

Then Gerrit spots a furry animal way down in the box, but neither he nor Johan dares to reach in. Somebody has to get it out, so I reach down and grab hold of it by its skin. It is a rabbit, not very big but I am sure it will end up in one of our meals.

Johan takes a stick and gives it a good blow in the neck. Not quite dead. Oom Herman, who loves these kinds of activities, takes the rabbit's head and gives it a quick 180 degree turn. This does the trick.

It seems this event makes us all hunting crazy. We decide to go for more. Look at the bunch of hunters; Herman Junior, Johan Stronks, Bernard, Oom Herman and me. Walking through the snow along the ditches we disturb a huge hare. It jumps out of hiding and runs towards *Neerhof*. Lies van der Male, another *onderduiker*, joins us and we give chase.

Through a number of pastures and over ditches we, Bernard and I, end up by the small river Slinge and the farm *de Bleeke*. The rest of the gang could not keep up. When we reach the dam in the river we spot the hare partly buried in the snow about 10 meters away. Lies and Herman catch up with us and we hear that they got hold of a rabbit but it escaped and is hiding in one of the barns by the farm *Nooitgedacht*.

Gerrit Hoopman who also saw the hare running, and us too, joins us with a big stick. We keep going after hare when it runs to farm *Nonhof* and from there to Papenborg. Over half an hour of running and walking and we have come almost full circle. We go home to eat. The others have started already. After lunch we give it another try, now it is Johan, Frans and I. At farm *Nooitgedacht* we check the whole barn, but no rabbit in sight. But with the help of farmer Neerhof we do catch a rabbit. This coming Sunday it will become part of our meal.

The electricity in our district Dale is working again except at our farm. No choice but to keep biking.

Thursday, January 11

We spot a hare in the field next door. Gerrit ter Horst, Frans and I will give it a try. It has buried itself in the snow in the middle of the field. Gerrit has a plan of action that should work. He walks into the field in a wide circle around the hare and comes now from behind towards the hare's hiding place.

A pitchfork in hand, he throws it into the burrow when he is about 15 feet away from it. I never saw anything like it; the hare jumps about 10 feet in the air and runs for his life straight toward us.

We are standing at the barbed wire fence with a big stick in our hands. The hare veers off to miss us and hits the barbed wire with a terrible force, leaving behind wads of hare hair.

By *den Eume* it runs into the *viemhoop* and that is the last we see of it, or so we think.

When I am cleaning up around the farm two days later, on Saturday, I see some hair by the edge of the grain stack, and some blood. Curious, I kneel down and see that it seems to continue under the stack. I poke with my rake, and when I pull back, out comes a good sized hare, dead as a doornail. I would not be surprised if this is the same one we chased a few days ago. I put it back under the haystack and clean up the blood and hair as much as possible. Gerrit, who threw the pitchfork at the hare, is inside and I call him outside. When I tell him what I found, he is surprised. We both think this is a golden opportunity to play another trick on Frans. While I call Frans, Gerrit remains at the haystack, very excited.

He yells at Frans, "Get a pitchfork. I just saw a hare crawl under here." While Frans runs for the pitchfork, I grab a hay fork and Gerrit finds a good sized stick. Gerrit directs Frans to stand in the middle, where the hare is. Gerrit stands on the left and I am on the right.

"Frans, get your pitchfork ready and throw it, really hard, at the hare. Don't miss it now! If it jumps out we may be able to get a shot at it."

Frans does not miss, he really threw it in there and he yells, "I got it!" pulling the hare out with his pitchfork. Both Gerrit and I tell him that he probably used too much force for the hare seems to be bleeding so much. Frans cannot get over it at first, then he starts to have some doubts, and eventually expresses his unbelief about whether he has actually killed the hare. It cools off his excitement, but not Tante's; she is happy with the find and the next day we have stew with meat, lots of meat.

Sebe comes in. He is just back from Apeldoorn and has visited our home. Dad has trouble again with rheumatism and is home from work. It must be bad. Gerrit and I will write him a letter urging him to take his pension. Sebe also has visited his brother in Apeldoorn and the family Walchien. Henk Walchien is the other *onderduiker* who stays with Sebe at farm *Neerhof*.

The family Walchien has given him some cigarette paper for us and two packages of coffee substitute for all the coffee their son Henk drinks at our place. This is a welcome gift especially with my birthday coming up. We can now offer the visitors real coffee substitute.

Gerrit gets a letter from his fiancée Dick ten Have. She writes some very welcome news about Berend Gerrits. Someone from Berlin has visited his parents in Apeldoorn and this man had spoken with Berend as recently as December 27. He was doing very well.

My sister-in-law Janna from Amsterdam has taken their son Alex to Apeldoorn. The situation in Amsterdam is getting worse, food is especially scarce. They cannot even feed their children with decent food. My brother

Henk in Amsterdam made a hiding place under the floor and found a big surprise, a fair bit of wood. Now they can make the occasional fire for heat and cooking.

In Amsterdam and also in Apeldoorn another big raid is expected soon.

Frans and I take care of the livestock, feeding, watering, and clean straw. After supper we do dishes together and since we are low in butter I churn some cream. In between things there is always one of us on the bike providing light.

Lately people from the cities come out in droves to buy food. Some come with their bikes, some with baby carriages, and others with little carts, often homemade. We have had people from The Hague, walking all the way from the West to us in the East, a distance of at least 175 kilometres. Many people die in the cities. Around Christmas in The Hague, 89 bodies were stored above ground awaiting proper burial.

This afternoon the S.S. was in Aalten searching for men who had disappeared from trench digging. They picked up te Lindert from den Es.

It is not as cold but we got some more snow this afternoon.

Friday, January 12

After breakfast the small kitchen gets a good cleaning. Don't ask what Frans and I are doing after this; of course peeling potatoes.

We are warned that by Hoopman three *Zwarten* have been spotted. We keep a watchful eye on things until noon when Jan Heideman comes to tell us that they were the men of family Keus. No wonder they were mistaken for *Zwarten*. These men are from Scheveningen and always wear black suits.

We rig up another small light fixture on the bike so we can do some reading while biking for light. Oom Herman first had some objection thinking he would not be able to see enough. He agrees that it is not too bad after all.

German soldiers gather in the pasture next door and set up some guns. They even start shooting.

Frans and I are cutting some dry wood when his suspenders break. "I have to fix it," he says and starts to take off his pants. You have to be Frans to do such a crazy thing.

Peter Van Essen

We try to fix it with paper rope since nothing else is available. It seems that it might work, at least for a little while.

Frans remarks, "Oh, if my mother would see this, she would get tears in her eyes."

"And if my father could see this, he would have a good laugh."

"We better hide in the barn," says Frans, when he sees somebody walking toward us through the field from *Nonhof.* So we hide behind the barn door. Oom Herman wants us in the *hol,* but we just wait and he meets the man outside. It is someone who wants to buy pigs.

Saturday, January 13

Who is peeling the potatoes for tomorrow? Cleaning out pig pens etc. today. Clean a whole bunch of wooden shoes. Johan blames me for something about work. I feel hurt, for it is absolutely not true and I tell him so. Later in the day I talk to Oom Herman about it for Johan had mentioned it to him. We have a very good and uplifting conversation and part as the best of friends. I confessed that I could be sharp when expressing myself, especially when upset. Oom Herman said he was the same and no bad feelings. We both feel good about this talk.

From neighbour Houwers at farm *Neerhof* we get some wool for socks.

Sunday January 14

Church at *Neerhof*; Sermon from dominee de Vries, Tilburg. Attendance 21 young men. Collection 6 guilders and 70 cents.

Johan and I would like to go to the *Oosterkerk* where there is Lord's Supper. On our way to Opa and Opoe Wikkerink, to meet Lien and Henny, our walk is interrupted. Allied fighter planes are in the air, six of them. Are they ever low, about 20 meters above ground and about 500 meters apart. When they pull up they start shooting with their guns. We wonder; they must be shooting backwards.

We are on a side road and look, on the main road we see, a short distance away, a bike lying on the side of the road. Then a German soldier crawls out of a hole onto the road. But the planes return and start shooting again. Amazing how fast this guy disappears again. Once again the planes return with more fire which this time seems to be directed at a spot a little further away from us. Later it is confirmed that a German vehicle was totally destroyed, one soldier dead and one wounded.

Shortly after, some Allied and German fighter planes attack each other above Barlo district. Three German and one Allied plane are downed. We did not see this fight but heard about it later in the day.

Without further interruptions we arrive in the Bredevoortsestraat. Henny, who has to come from her Aunt's place at *de Haart*, tells us that she too had to lie on the ground for fear of being shot by airplane fire. She also mentions that German soldiers stole a pig out of their pig pen.

At 2:45 p.m. we go to church. Jo, Lien, Johan, Henny, Dikkie, Ineke and I. We carry some *stoofs* to warm our feet in church and we all got half a peppermint to suck on while listening to the sermon. Dominee Gerritsma preached and read the forms for celebrating the Lord's Supper. It was good to participate, I felt blessed.

After church Henny asks if I would like to come along with her to *de Haart* and stay until tomorrow morning. I would love to, but have to decline because tomorrow morning we have to start early by helping at *Neerhof* threshing grain. I accompany Henny about halfway to the farm then go back to Opoe for supper. From Ome Jan I get a letter for my birthday. From Henny a beautiful present, namely a pair of socks knit by her mother, Tante Dela, from sheep's wool. She is still working on it and when I see the one that is finished I remark, "How nice, socks with a *kabelsteek*."

"How do you know it is a *kabelsteek*?" says Mother Wikkerink, surprised.

"Well, my first pullover vest was made by my mother and it had the same stitch. She called it a *kabelsteek*."

Before Johan and I go back to the farm, Ineke and Dikkie want to have a story. I read the very exiting record of what happened to the wolf and the seven little goats and also the story of Hansel and Gretel. Ineke sits on my lap and Dikkie is all ears on a chair beside me. This is fun and relaxing.

It takes us half an hour to get home. Very dark and muddy. Frans has also just arrived from his girlfriend's home. Gerrit, my brother, is still at *Neerhof* and will most likely come home after the news. Yes he arrives with news and, as usual, has lots to report.

NEWS: Russian army starts a new offensive by Warsaw. It is 60 kilometres wide and 40 kilometres deep. Another little news item is that Jan Driesten has been wounded. He is an *onderduiker* and I have a suspicion that he is somewhat involved with the Resistance groups.

Monday, January 15

Today is my birthday, the second one in hiding. I am now 23 years old. Gerrit gives me 20 guilders; from Gerrit Driessen, 2 guilders and 50 cents. Oom Herman and Tante also give me 2 guilders and 50 cents. The others got together and I am amazed when they hand me 100 sheets of writing paper plus 100 envelopes. From Henny I will get the socks that are still in production. From neighbour Houwers at *Neerhof* I get wool which Henny is going to spin so it can be made into another pair of socks. What a beautiful birthday, it makes me quiet.

We are now heading for the neighbour to help with threshing. It has been cancelled, there is no hydro. I stay for a while to talk while the daughters are busy cleaning and spinning wool. They say spinning is easy and I believe them.

"May I try?" Eagerly they put me behind the old spinning wheel. I try it. Now I don't believe them anymore.

When I arrive back at the farm the cream is waiting to be turned into butter. I know how to handle this piece of equipment; it is easier than spinning wool.

We have been told that there is a simple way to get the hydro back on. Take a copper wire and connect it to the two cables that extend from the hydro pole. Gerrit and Frans are eager to try it, but how?

The three of us form a think tank and come up with an idea that just might work. Since we don't have a long, very long, extension ladder to climb the pole we look for the tallest bean stalks and put these together with paper binder twine. We cut a slit in the top pole for the copper wire and it now looks like a Y with the tops slightly curved, sides A and B. The trick is to get A and B to rest on the hydro wires, then to release this copper wire from the beanpole by pulling the pole down. This puts tension on the hydro lines and causes the copper wire to shoot straight into the air when released. We have to start all over again.

Eventually they succeed and we will have light tonight. At four o'clock Henny, Lien and Gerrit Wikkerink arrive and we get things ready for the party. The floor in the *waskamer* gets a good scrubbing and washing and the girls clean the washing machine. After the cows, pigs, and other animals are taken care of I can change for supper.

I count thirteen around the table. Later at the birthday party we are with twenty-six. Brother Gerrit has made a poem about my bare spot on top and hands me a *calotte* to keep my head warm.

It is a nice evening with lots of fun. Mina has made *poffertjes, oliebollen* and nice cookies. With the coffee we get a scoop of real cream.

No letter yet from home. Bedtime comes too early at 10:30 and Gerrit W. has to sleep with Johan and me tonight. At *Neerhof* three letters arrive from Henk Walchien.

Tuesday, January 16
7:30 a.m. Henny, Lien and Mien are leaving. While I am busy looking after the animals the mailman brings a letter for me from Bep and Wim in Castricum and for Gerrit he brings a letter from his fiancée Dick in Apeldoorn. My letter was still for Christmas. It takes long these days for the mail to get through. Sister Nen got a letter from her fiancé Berend Gerrits who is in Berlin forced labour. He is doing very well.

The lights are not working and Frans and I are going to check out the wires. Something is wrong; the copper wire is not properly connected to the Hydro line. We give it a few tries and manage, mostly by luck, to get it in good position. Back at the farm we see that some lights are burning. Early in the evening the lights go out again. Just when I start biking they come on again, slowly at first then brighter and brighter.

This afternoon fighter planes were busy again over the district Barlo.

NEWS: At Sittard (Province Limburg) a new offensive.

Wednesday, January 17

Oom Herman wants to kill a pig and he sends me to get the necessary permit at Hoens, the P.B.H. office that issues permits. The roads are very slippery with ice but I manage to stay on my bike.

We were supposed to help Houwers at *Neerhof* with threshing but again there is no hydro. I prepare the *mantelpot* for making pig slop, crank the handle of the washing machine and feed all the animals. By then it is time to milk the cows.

Frans has a good day; he received a letter from home, the first one in six weeks. Everything is okay in Boskoop, but there are the occasional *razzias*.

At five o'clock the lights go on suddenly. We might not have to bike tonight.

Thursday, January 18

Frans and I are peeling potatoes this morning.

Houwers from *Neerhof* comes to get us. There is power and we can start the threshing. I am to bind up the straw that has been through the machine. At coffee time we get half a pancake and another half at tea time. We had a real good meal at lunch time.

Work is finished at five o'clock. I am hungry, we worked hard today. The table has been set for us and I manage to eat three good sized pancakes and a plate of barley porridge.

Back at the farm I take a good bath and change into some clean clothes. I write a letter to Johan Wouters in Amsterdam and to my sister Jannie and brother-in-law Adriaan in Twello. February 4 is their special wedding anniversary.

NEWS: Island of Walcheren (Zeeland) in Allied hands.

Friday, January 19

Frans and I peel potatoes in the morning. Letter writing to Bep and Wim in Castricum. Cut wood with Johan, Frans and David who came here this morning. David is in hiding at Oom Derk the carpenter. Oom Derk has been forced to do some work for the German army. David does not want to help with it and has to disappear for a while. Here we are, cutting wood. One from Aalten, one from Boskoop, another from Veere and myself from Apeldoorn.

When we are having our noon warm meal, *de Guste* is at the door. She is Fanny's wife, the *Landwachter* farmer living behind us. Frans, Gerrit, David and I disappear out of the door to the cow stable, plates with food and all. You cannot leave these on the table. We huddle together and quietly finish this part of our dinner. It takes more than an hour before the old woman leaves again. She was telling everyone all about her husband who was transported to Brabant to guard railroads against sabotage by the Resistance movement.

In Aalten this afternoon a meeting is held to discuss the terrible hunger in Utrecht.

NEWS: Susteren and Echt liberated. Russian army seems to be doing very well in her march against German army.

David is sleeping here tonight.

Saturday, January 20

I am glad David gets up at 5 a.m. He took all the blankets from me, tossing and turning. Johan and David are leaving for Vragender at 5:30.

It is Saturday and after my breakfast I milk the cows and feed them. The barn must be cleaned and we fire up the *mantelpot*.

First I polish all the available shoes, and then I gather all wooden shoes that I see in and around the house. Mina's fiancé Dirk has dropped in for a short visit. Ready to leave, he looks for his wooden shoes. They are nowhere in sight. Then, to his horror, he discovers his *klompen* floating in the big tank with all the other ones. I fear the worst! But again a woman comes to my rescue: Mina. She is so happy. Dirk cannot leave but has to wait till his wooden shoes are cleaned and dry again.

Frans, who helped me with the shoes, is busy cleaning the little kitchen and together we scrub the floor.

We take baths, and then care for all the animals. After supper: the milking, and some more cleaning up.

Brother Gerrit was in charge of supper and we expected it to be super. Of all things, supper burned. We had to eat burned kale.

For tomorrow we have to peel potatoes, Frans and I.

Sebe comes for a shave by brother Gerrit. On Tuesday, he is going to visit his brother in Apeldoorn and will take along any letters that we might want to write for home.

Gerrit picked up a radio with short wave that somebody promised him. We take it to the pig barn and listen to the latest news.

NEWS: Tilsit and Soldau and Lotz recaptured. Army 15 kilometres from Oppelen.

A gain of 200 kilometres in five days. In province Gelderland, St. Stevensweerd and Zetten liberated.

Johan comes back from the hamlet Vragender where he visited Ome Jan, and brings a real cigar for Oom Herman. The cigar is called The Real American.

Sunday, January 21

A warning that the *Zwarten* are in Aalten. The *Landwacht* came back yesterday.

Church at our farm. Dirk reads the sermon from dominee N. Buffinga, Rotterdam. Attendance 20 young men, collection 6 guilders and 36 cents.

It is 11:45 a.m. and we listen to the BBC for news. NEWS: Russian Army 350 kilometres from Berlin. Railroad Danzig/Siberia cut off by Polo. French army makes some gains.

We had a good lunch. Cleaned up and finish my letter for home. When I feed the animals, Johan comes to tell me he is going to Aalten to see Lien. For some reason she has to stay inside. Johan thinks that Henny cannot come to the farm either. Just when I start feeding the pigs Henny walks into the barn. What a surprise!

For supper we have homemade bread. Delicious, but it makes you think about the people in the big cities who are so hungry!

Dirk says that I don't have to milk tonight; he will do it for me. How nice of him, maybe he is paying me back for cleaning his wooden shoes which made him stay longer with his girl yesterday.

Henny and I can go for a walk now and we drop in at Opa Eppink, one of our neighbours. From there we go for our long Sunday evening walk along the Slinge. It starts to snow and on our way home I put her in the snow to give her a little face wash. She had said I would not dare to do this. She pretends that she is upset, but she cannot even look angry. We come home and warm up by the stove.

Monday, January 22
My nephew Leen Weeda is 6 years old today.

Pigs seem to be hungry animals. We have to make more of the slop again and fire up the big *mantelpot*.

We have enough time on our hands to go for another hunt after rabbits or hares. Four of us, Oom Herman, Heideman, Frans and I. At the *Scholteboer* we spot a hare. This is a really fast one and we cannot keep up. We finally decide to go home. It is time to eat anyway.

At lunch time we take a little break to go outside and look at all the airplanes. About 100 are passing over on their way to Germany.

The letters for Jo Wouters in Amsterdam and for Dad in Apeldoorn will be delivered by Mrs. Wiersinga who will bike to her home again today or tomorrow. We wonder how she will get there as we heard that nobody is allowed to cross the bridge over the IJssel River. We fill some bags with rye for Mrs. Wiersinga to take home with her. I help as much as possible for supper and shortly after our evening meal and some talk around the table we get ready for the news.

NEWS: Russian army 25 kilometres from Bromberg, 290 kilometres from Berlin.

The medical profession has sent a letter of protest to Seyss-Inquart, the Nazi-appointed ruler in Holland. A very sharp letter, condemning the situation resulting from Hitler's Hunger Plan, especially in the western part of Holland.

Dominee Gerritsma, who came for a haircut this morning, will come this Sunday morning to preach at our farm and two weeks from now dominee Kuiper will be here.

Tuesday, January 23
Peeling potatoes with Frans. *Waskamer* cleaned up.

Peter Van Essen

Since we have our own radio we can listen anytime to the news of BBC at 11:45 a.m. NEWS: Russians 25 kilometres from Koningsbergen. They have cut off the railroad Breslau/Upper Silesia. Allied troops captured Haguenau. Duisburg received a heavy bombardment yesterday on a factory that makes synthetic *benzine*. Insterburg and Allenstein captured.

Frans and I are busy scrubbing and mopping the *waskamer* when our work is interrupted by the arrival of two NSB men, Dutch men collaborating with Germany. They have to check all identification papers and ration papers. Herman, Frans and I are already in the *hol*. Oom Herman and Tante have to show only the legitimate papers and not the ones for the *onderduikers*. For this reason these papers are always stored in a separate place. The *onderduikers'* papers are not obtained legally. They come to us illegally through the Resistance organization that cracks safes in German controlled offices throughout our country. When all is safe we reappear and get back to work. After feeding and watering animals we can eat at 5:45 p.m.

Milking is done at seven. Frans has to turn the washing machine but manages, secretly, to connect it with the hydro. Pretty smart!

Johan attended the meeting *Hulpverlening Westen* this afternoon. They are trying to organize a big continual drive for food to help the hungry and the dying people in Western Holland. Eventually it becomes very successful. Many food shipments are made by train and this train will become known as the *Roggebrood trein* named for a specialty black rye bread from this area. Leave it to the people from Aalten, they will find a way to help!

NEWS: Russians 16 kilometres from Koningsbergen, 40 kilometres from Posen.

Gerrit wants to learn how to play the organ.

Wednesday, January 24
Before breakfast we feed the animals and milk the cows. Frans and I are peeling potatoes. We don't have to peel as many as usual because we will have *snert* for lunch.

Papenborg needs some firewood; Frans and I look after it. Papenborg mentions that Dr. de Weduwen, a physician from Aalten who is a member of the

Resistance group, has been killed near Apeldoorn. The car he was driving was hit by bullets from an Allied plane. He was on his way to Den Hague to discuss improvements for Dutch forced labourers in Germany.

Today sees a lot of activity in the air.

Yesterday several young men arrested in Barlo; three boys from Rhebergen; one of them is free again.

Janny takes home the collection money, 36 guilders.

Oom Herman needs my help. We have to bring loads of sugar beets inside onto the threshing floor. When the cows are fed, we eat, and then do the milking. In evening I have a little time to update the diary and darn some socks.

Thursday January 25

Clean sprouts and also the threshing floor with help from Gerrit. Our hand brooms are always hard to find when needed. The three of us plan and make a broom hanger, a wooden board with hooks. The others like it.

We are told that the tobacco is used up too quickly. Maybe it is better that I quit using our tobacco and see if any is available in the store.

Lunch, scrubbing the *waskamer*. Herman and I take bags with rye to neighbour Houwers at *Neerhof*. This is to go to Western Holland, via the committee for help.

Jan ter Horst brings a letter from Berend Gerrits who is working in Berlin. He is doing very well and very optimistic. Letter dated January 16, 1945. I write my sister Nen to let her know he is doing okay.

NEWS: Gleiwitz taken by Russia. Street fights in Breslau, Posen practically surrounded. First tribunal in Den Bosch (Province Brabant).

Friday, January 26

I have answered the letter from Berend in Berlin, and the mailman takes it along. After fixing one of my socks I head out to *Neerhof* farm where they need more help threshing grain.

After one hour of work we stop to go for lunch. A letter came for me from Teun and Stien in Twello. Big surprise, I have another nephew, born January 15 on my birthday. He is named Hendrik Peter. I am now a godfather.

Back to *Neerhof* to finish our work. We drink a cup of tea with a delicious slice of homemade bread covered with *schinke*.

In between regular chores I write a letter to Dad and Nen which will be taken by someone from Amersfoort who is staying here for the night. Diary updated.

Saturday, January 27

Frans and I take care of Saturday's work, scrubbing, mopping, washing chairs etc. Cut some firewood with Johan. Animals fed, we take a bath, then eat and after that milk cows. Got a little snow today.

Letter to Henk Wikkerink in Driebergen. NEWS: Russian army makes good progress.

Sunday, January 28

Church at farm *Neerhof*; dominee Gerritsma preaches. Attendance 21 men.

At 3:45 Johan and I head to Opa and Opoe Wikkerink in town. From there Henny and I will go to *de Haart* to her aunt Gerda and uncle Johan. Henny is excited that I became a godfather.

We hear the sirens in town. There are different ways of sounding the alarm. This one indicates that bombs have fallen. When we get into town later we hear that bombs have fallen near the Roman Catholic Church. Shortly after four o'clock we hear the signal that all is safe again and the people who went to church this afternoon are now allowed to leave and go home.

Henny and I are going to visit Oom Hendrik and Tante Hanna who live just north of town in the district Hollenberg. I am introduced to Oom and Tante and we are invited to eat. I am introduced to all of their 12 children. I count 18 sitting in the room when drinking tea. The tea is very good, made from mostly real tea and mixed with a substitute, probably dried blueberry leaves.

We leave shortly after six and walk to *de Haart*, single file because of the deep snow. Coming to the Walfortlaan there is a bit more room and we can walk beside each other. We reach the farm and have a nice evening with the family. Just before bedtime, there is a terrific noise; a V-2 has come down. Henny and I are allowed to stay up for a few more minutes. We give thanks to the Lord for his protection today and ask Him for a good and restful night.

I sleep with Gerrit, Henny's brother, in the *opkamer*. We talk for an hour before we go to sleep.

Monday, January 29

I had a very good and restful, sleep. No pain in my shoulder as I often have from sleeping in a cold and drafty *hol*.

After breakfast I help with the dishes and peel potatoes, alone. Frans is not here to help me and I suppose he is going it alone too, back at *de Koekoek*. Gerrit and Jan are cutting firewood and I do the splitting. When I get ready to go back to *de Koekoek* they ask, "Why not wait until this afternoon?" And so I do, gladly.

Time flies and before we realize it, lunch is ready. Sauerkraut with bacon and for dessert some nice pudding.

After lunch Henny sits behind the spinning wheel busy with the wool I got for my birthday. I keep her company while peeling potatoes for tomorrow so that Jan and Gerrit are free from this chore tonight.

Uncle Johan Hoornenborg, who just came back from Aalten, tells us that the priest, van Rooyen, died yesterday when the parsonage was bombed. Also a German officer, Feltwebel, suffocated due to lack of oxygen caused by exploding bombs.

4 p.m. It is time for me to walk back to the farm *de Koekoek*. They put two slices of bread in front of me, to eat before leaving. Henny walks with me as far as the wooded area, hands me a ball of wool so I can fix the old socks, then she goes back to *de Haart*.

Part of the way home is along the railroad tracks. Suddenly four American planes come diving down, firing away at something. The action is very close, and I follow it with much interest. The planes are so low that I can read the identification marks.

Walking is difficult. In some places the snow is 50 centimetres deep. I arrive home shortly after 5 p.m., change, eat, and then do the milking. Diary updated. NEWS: Russians reporting very little news. Bedtime at 9, but first I have to make the bed.

Tuesday, January 30

Milking, feed and water animals. Clean up kitchen. Light stove. Cut and split firewood. Cut tobacco for drying. At lunch time we eat hash with onions and beets. Dishes and cleaning up.

Johan and I are trying to make a couple of straw mats, one for the bathroom and one for the bedroom. It is to keep your feet warm. The tile floors are sometimes very cold.

Lien shows up to be with Johan. I leave them alone and take care of feeding and watering the animals. Then Frans comes in to help with setting the table. After supper Johan helps me with milking.

Today it is 12 years ago that the National Socialistic Movement started in Germany. Right now the situation in Germany is chaotic.

The Berliner Zeitung writes, "Where will we find a defence line that is not destroyed in 24 hours?" City of Berlin is evacuated. NEWS: Allied troops have reached the German border near the Ardennes. Airplanes attacked German vehicle movements. Of approximately 2,000 vehicles, 690 are destroyed and 570 rendered useless.

Wednesday, January 31

It is raining.

Regular chores. When the kitchen is clean I start fixing one of my socks. It has a good size hole. Gerrit, who has been in Lintelo cutting hair since yesterday, comes back and helps me set the table. We have two extra guests again, two young girls, one from Rotterdam and one from Gouda. They are desperate for food and buy whatever is available to take back home and save the lives of family members. Frans is warned and we will bring him some food in the kitchen. If he would sit with us his accent would immediately tell the girls that he comes from their area of the country. He cannot speak the dialect from the *Achterhoek*.

The rain is causing problems in the small bedroom upstairs. I clean off the roof tile and put down some hay on the wet spots.

Frans helps to bring some sugar beets from the *koele* to the threshing floor. At five o'clock we water the cows. At six we eat and seven o'clock finds us under the cows pulling four strings. Now we have some quiet time and I get busy updating the diary.

The quiet evening is suddenly interrupted. A terrific noise! One of the windows blows out of its frame and falls in pieces to the ground. A V-2 has fallen in Aalten between the police station on the Ringweg and the water tower. The result is a huge hole and about half of all the windows in town are broken or blown out.

NEWS: Last German stronghold by Biesbosch (Holland) cleaned out. According to news from Germany, the Russian army is now 90 kilometres from Berlin. The Führer, Hitler, has spoken yesterday for about 17 minutes but really did not say anything. Russians captured five more towns.

FEBRUARY 1945

Thursday, February 1

After milking, preparation is made to butcher a pig. This one is killed without a permit. It weighs 230 pounds. A good chunk is going to Willem Rhebergen. He works for a printing company and Mina has asked him for writing paper, printed with Henny's name, so I have a present for her birthday coming up soon.

I get a haircut. Clean the *schoppe*. Make our beds. Feed and take care of the animals. The hydro has gone out again and we have to postpone the milking. The bike is made ready so we can pedal for light. Suddenly the lights go on and we race to get the milking done. Just finished and out it goes. Frans,

Johan, Gerrit and I take turns pedalling and awaiting the return of light. It is still not back on at quarter to nine and we all go to bed.

In town nine hostages are picked up. Tomorrow people have to report for front line duty, digging.

Friday, February 2

Up at 7 a.m. Normal chores and this time it is not Frans but Johan who helps with peeling potatoes. I darn some more socks. Our neighbour gets a visit from *Moffen*; he has to transport men tomorrow to the work site. "Come with your horse and wagon."

Gerrit, who is not doing anything, helps with cleaning wooden shoes. Oom Herman needs my help sharpening some knives. He has to leave shortly for a special council meeting of the church. The church cannot be used anymore since all windows have been destroyed by the V-2 on January 31st. The meeting will be at another place. Last Sunday they had four services in the *Westerkerk*. I help Johan who is making some sausages.

All day long we have been hearing a noise like heavy thunder in the distance, direction Emmerick and Nijmegen. Windows and doors rattled. The fighting must be severe.

The hydro does not go on tonight. The bike, which is hidden in the loft during daytime, cannot be used because of a broken stand. Johan remarks that a heavy bag with rye fell on it but it can be fixed. I jokingly say that it is too bad that a bag of grain fell on it. "It should have been two bags of grain." Gerrit ter Horst gets really mad that I say this. It shows he too is under a fair bit of stress. But it was only meant as a joke.

I take the first turn when Gerrit says, "It is fixed." I mount the bike, start pedalling and it breaks again. We now have to sit beside it and pedal with our hands.

Brother Gerrit writes a letter to our brother Teun and Stien in Twello. They sent us 6 sheets of paper so we can write again. We decide to make it a long letter and fill all 6 sheets. It should make up for not having heard from us in a long time.

NEWS: Russian army about 80 kilometres from Berlin.

Saturday, February 3

Bright weather. A lot of activity by Allies in the air. We worked hard all day; everything has been cleaned. At 8 p.m. I finally find time to wash up by a small oil lamp in front of the cow stable. Suddenly the hydro comes on. What a nice surprise.

Across the border in Germany searchlights are working overtime. We are amazed about the number of bombers coming over.

Sunday, February 4

My sister Jannie and her husband Adriaan were married 12 and 1/2 years ago today. In Holland this is the first important anniversary, halfway to 25 years, and worth celebrating.

I write a few letters, one to Teun and Stien, another to Henk Wolf. Church at our farm. Brother Gerrit is in charge. The sermon is from dominee J. Knap, title "On the Threshing Floor", very appropriate.

At 5 p.m. Henny arrives. She is soaking wet. She has visited her dad in Vragender and biked from there to our farm. Tomorrow morning she is going back to Oom Johan and Tante Gerda at *de Haart*.

Mother Wikkerink would like to have Henk, one of the twin boys, back at home. He is at his uncle's place in Driebergen, Oom Ap and Tante Riek Klein Ikkink. Henny is going to pick him up this week. This is not without danger. Everything that moves is liable to be shot at and Henk is of hiding age. He cannot freely walk the street. He will have to change into women's clothing and hope it is not discovered by a German road check. Henny and I take time out for prayer and ask for the Lord's protection on this venture. Bedtime at 10 p.m.

Monday, February 5

Did not sleep too well. Got up at 5:15 am. I lit the stove and set the table. At six o'clock I start feeding the cows and call the other fellows so they can listen to the BBC. Henny is up early too. Could not sleep much either. She leaves at nine o'clock and I accompany her as far as Welink Herman.

Henny mentions that she will drop in at my Dad's place in Apeldoorn on her way back from Driebergen. Stay there for one or two days and back to Aalten on the 12th or 13th. She will also try to talk Dick, Gerrit's fiancée, into coming back with her.

Oom Herman is replacing a few broken roof tiles over the kitchen and I give him a hand. Gerrit is back from Aalten. He comes back with my socks, from Henny, and mentions that she is leaving Wednesday, for Driebergen.

Today is the last day to report for digging.

Mina's bike has a flat. I manage to fix it. You really have to improvise. Start a letter to Bep and Wim. Henny will take it along. At 8 p.m. I go to bed as I don't feel too good and I have a sore throat.

NEWS: Allies break through Siegfried defence line.

Tuesday, February 6

Had a bad night. I am very hot and have a terrible headache. Glad it is morning. Gerrit brings my breakfast into the *hol*. I will move to the small bedroom upstairs later. I still have to finish the letter for Bep and Wim and I write a little note for Henny. Janny, Henny's sister, dropped in and she takes both letters to give them to her.

The Tommies are very active. You can really sense and often hear that a real war is raging close by.

I stay in bed for lunch. Almost asleep, I hear some excitement downstairs. Somebody came but I do not recognize the voice. Then Gerrit comes upstairs with his girl Dick from Apeldoorn. What a surprise. She is not alone, her aunt came along and also Gini and Jan Gerrits who travelled on to Varsseveld. They are all desperate for food. On Friday they return home, hopefully with their bikes loaded with food.

At five o'clock somebody else comes up the stairs. Another big surprise, it is Henny. When she got my note she decided to pay me a short visit before going to Driebergen. She reads to me the two letters she received, one from her father and one from her mother. Both urge her to be very careful on her way to Driebergen and back, and they will keep her and Henk in their prayers. Tomorrow at 8 a.m. she is going to leave, very calm and trusting that all things will work out. I get a box of matches from her, very hard to come by, and a letter from Lien for safekeeping until she returns.

Dick, who just arrived, brings photos that were taken of Henny and Mina and Nen. They turned out very nice. I have supper downstairs and go back to bed at eight o'clock.

Wednesday, February 7, 1945

Slept fairly well. My sore throat is getting worse. Sky is overcast and we get some rain. We don't hear any airplanes.

Gerrit brings me breakfast and Johan comes with coffee. For lunch I go downstairs. After a nice shave I go back to bed until supper time. After supper I work on my diary and at 8:30 back to bed in the *hol*.

Direction Nijmegen, just south of Arnhem, the fighting seems to be much more intense. Heavy continuous rumbling, almost scary. During the night two bombs fall, probably in town.

Thursday February 8

I eat my breakfast in bed and stay there. I am in the *hol*. It is now 11:30 am. What happens next is hard to describe and I will never forget.

I hear airplanes overhead. The noise is terrible, so low, could not be more than about 100 feet. Then it really starts… Bombs rain down… the farmhouse moans and cracks and shakes like a leaf. I have to get out of this *hol*; I never heard such a noise… awful, terrible. I cry, "Oh, Lord, help us." Throwing open the little trap door I let myself down in a hurry. I don't realize that I am standing bare feet in the manure ditch behind the cows. I cannot even see a cow because of the dust that comes down from the hayloft. Tante Gerri who was using the indoor outhouse comes flying out and screams, "Where am I going? What are we going to do?"

"I don't know," I say and walk to the *enden deur* but then back again to the wall by the cow stable. Everybody is desperate, not knowing what to do. We stand against the wall expecting the house to come crashing down on us.

Later we realize how good it is that we stayed inside. All around the farm the ground is littered with shrapnel. By *Neerhof* a bomb fell in a large tree by the chicken coop. Houwers Sr. had just gathered some eggs and was on his way back to the house. He was standing under this tree when the bomb came tumbling down. These are called splinter bombs, used to destroy troops and equipment. As soon as they touch a hard surface they explode. This one fell on a big branch high up in the tree, exploded, spreading its destructive steel horizontally knocking out nearly all the windows in the farm and making big holes in the roof tiles. The old farmer walked away without a scratch.

It is not so good at his neighbour across the laneway at farmer Eppink, Henny's grandfather. He is working in the field next to the house with his horse and wagon. Eppink is standing beside the old horse and on the other side stands Mink van der Horst, an *onderduiker*. When the bombs fall, the horse is killed and so is Mink.

Eppink, who is senile, walks away to the house. He comes inside and says to his son, "I don't know what happened to Mink and the horse, but we have a bad thunderstorm."

Beside our farm is a pasture of Houwers, farm *Neerhof*. About 10 sheep were grazing there. Most of them are killed or maimed and have to be killed off. The pasture is not green anymore but black. The bombs have ploughed the whole field. Beside this field lives Heideman. Outside sitting against the woodshed are a group of little children, playing school because schools are closed; it is too dangerous and there is no heat. When bombs fall they run inside the house. One of them, Lenie Groen, wants to jump up but cannot. "Oh," she cries, "I have lost my leg." Dead are: Mink van der Horst, Joop from 't Willemke, farmer Brusse, two children from te Grootenhuis farmer, two young men from Stronks who were hiding at te Grootenhuis, three children from farmer Hoogenkamp, Piet van Roon, an *onderduiker* from farmer Neerhof, farm *Nooitgedacht*.

Wounded: farmer Hoopman, Henny's aunt Tante Daatje, who lost her arm while peeling potatoes, Henny's uncle Hendrik Eppink, Lenie Groen, Mrs. Nijenhuis, farmer Nijenhuis, girl from Heideman (Kemena), Mrs. Brusse, a farmer's wife.

A direct hit on the farm of Brusse - threshing floor; te Grootenhuis - kitchen; Hoogenkamp and *Neerhof* farm - bedroom; Houwers farm *de Bleeke* - pig barn. Many animals have been killed too. Our farm has damage to the windows and many roof tiles.

Piet van Roon lost an arm while working in the field. The farmer did not know where he was and Piet bled to death. Immediately people jumped into action to assist where possible. Even *onderduikers* and nobody asked any questions, not even the Germans. My brother Gerrit was carrying stretchers with wounded together with a German soldier, a member of the hated *Landwacht* and a despised NSB.

I write a letter for Henny, and Dick ten Have will take it along tomorrow as she leaves for home again. It is good to let them know how things are here. Back in the *hol* at 9 p.m. I still have a sore throat.

Friday, February 9
Up at seven to set the table and to finish the letters, then back to bed. When Dick and Tante Gerri leave I give Dick ten guilders to buy something for Henny for her birthday. I cannot get the correspondence paper and envelopes from the printers as they were ordered to dig trenches.

I do not feel very good yet and crawl in bed again until 3:30. Time to shave and wash, then update the diary. Veldwijk who is here to pick up the boys Wim Walchien and Cor Man-in't-Veld, helps me with the dishes. Shortly after, I go back to bed.

Saturday, February 10

I did not sleep well. Get a letter from sister Bep in Castricum.

Mr. Tilburscher, from the Department of Public Works, comes to check for any unexploded bombs. If he finds any they will be immediately cleaned up.

After the potatoes are peeled, back to bed. At noon Wim, Cor and Veldwijk leave again. Bartje drops in at mid-afternoon. I am anxious to know how Henny and Henk are doing.

Sunday, February 11

Church at farm *Neerhof*. There are no more church services held in town. It is thought to be irresponsible to have so many people in one building. There are too many air raids and also too many *razzias* by S.S. and *Groenen*. It is decided to arrange church services at different farms. Today there are 25 such services held. Today's text Isaiah 53:10.

After lunch I pick some *snotterbellen;* they look good in a vase. If all things are well, Henny and Henk will be at my father's place in Apeldoorn now.

NEWS: Kleef in Germany in Allied hands. Fighting is heavy and we hear the rumbling all day long.

Monday, February 12

Today is the funeral of the victims who died last Thursday. In the afternoon I go to bed again, this time with a warm water bottle. It feels good.

Tuesday, February 13

I have breakfast downstairs then back to bed. At 9:30 Gerrit calls, "Henny is here." Everything went well. Henk is okay and is at his mother's place.

Gerrit and I get a letter from home, a nice Notaris apple, and a small box of matches. What a luxury. Dick bought a nice text from the money I gave her for Henny. Tomorrow is her birthday and she will come back here to *de Koekoek* for a little while. It is too dangerous for me to go to *de Haart*; the *Zwarten* are hunting for more men.

Henny leaves at 11 a.m. Just then we get a warning that the *Zwarten* are close by, in 't Grevink. We disappear into the *hol* where we get our meal, *snert*. While holed up, I fix my pants. When we get a safe signal we reappear. I pedal for half an hour before going to bed at eight o'clock.

Wednesday, February 14

Henny's birthday, she turns 18 today. She was going to come this morning but did not make it. Jo comes for milk and says that Henny will try to make it on Sunday. Jo takes the collection money, 17 guilders.

Guess who peels the potatoes again this morning?

We see six *Zwarten* on the road behind the farm. Going direction *Peerdeboer* then back into 't Grevink towards town. Allied planes overhead are firing like crazy and we quickly drop to the ground. It is too close for comfort. By the railroad station a long train with ammunition has been put on a side track. People are getting very scared and many are moving out of the area. It is expected that any time planes will fire at it.

6 p.m. supper and then milking and everything that goes along with it. Pedal for half an hour before I go to bed at 8:30.

Thursday February 15

Up at 7:30 a.m. Frans and I are peeling potatoes. Cutting down the *wennenbos;* the branches are used to make hampers and baskets.

"Good morning," I hear behind me. When I turn around I see to my surprise Mother Wikkerink and Dikkie. She is going to stay until this afternoon. "And Henny is coming Sunday after church," she says. By *den Eume* a big pig is being butchered. Dikkie wants to have the bladder filled with air, but it seems to have a small leak. Outside he blows air into it and plans to release the air into Frans' face. Frans sees him standing there waiting for him to come out so Frans stays in the barn and looks through the window. He does not realize that the glass is missing and Dikkie uses the opportunity with a well-aimed shot. The bladder hits Frans squarely in the face, where it loses its last foul air. Dikkie and I have a real good laugh.

After lunch Gerrit cuts my hair. Frans helps me with work on the *wennenbos*. We feed the animals, have supper and do the milking. The sky is cloudy; it is calm in the air and quiet at the front.

Friday, February 16
Polish shoes, clean wooden shoes. Peel potatoes with Frans and again in the evening, for tomorrow.

Saturday, February 17
After milking, Frans and I are… you guessed it: peeling potatoes. Cut firewood with Johan and clean around the farm and barn. We bring fresh straw in for bedding in the cow stable.

Three men with a handcart arrive from the city Amersfoort searching for food. At supper time 12 people around the table.

Lien's birthday today.

Sunday, February 18
Church service again at *Neerhof* at 10 a.m. When we arrive there all the seats are taken, no more room.

Back to our farm; I play on the old organ and update the diary.

At 11:30 Henny and Lien arrive. I had not seen either one of them since before their birthdays on the 14th and the 17th of February. Dinner with 14 people.

We make it to the afternoon church. Henny and I go for a nice walk. We eat late and go for another walk. Home in time for coffee with a Berliner *bol*. Henny tells me all about the trip home from Driebergen.

The winter of 1944/45 is later called Hunger Winter. Three times that winter I biked 150 kilometres one way, bike loaded with food, to my aunt and uncle Klein Ikkink and their four children in Driebergen. My brother Henk, age 16, was also staying there and attending school.

In late January, I travelled with another girl, Bertha. I don't remember much about the trip except one thing: the V–1. V–1s were an early missile launched from Germany destined for England, but hardly any actually made it that far. We heard one coming and jumped off our bikes into the ditch. A little ways ahead we saw it come down and slam into a house. There were so many things to watch out for. We made it to Driebergen, and my aunt and uncle were very happy with the food.

This time I have come to pick up my brother Henk and bring him home, there is not enough food for him to stay with our aunt and uncle in Driebergen.

We leave Driebergen early in the morning. Mr. Kaspers, a retired school teacher, comes along to take us past the usual checkpoints. However, there is no one at the checkpoints and he returns home. Before he heads back, we stand together at the side of the road and pray for a safe journey. While he prays, I feel a calm come over me, giving me new courage for the trip home.

Henk is dressed as a girl. If we are caught at any checkpoint, it will mean concentration camp for him. All men age 16 to 65 are not safe anymore.

Henk is weak from lack of decent food, and sits on the back of my bike, suitcase on his knees.

About an hour down the road, at 8:30 a.m. we reach a long straight stretch of road. Ditches and barbed wire on both sides and green pasture as far as you can see. Up ahead we see something that scares us. Henk says, "We can't go on. We should turn back."

"We can't, Henk. They will see us and shoot."

The roadblock is manned with German S.S., the most feared of all soldiers. Checkpoint!

"Don't be afraid. We prayed, didn't we?" I say to my brother. My heart hammered within me, but we went on. We are stopped by one of the soldiers, none too friendly. I put the bike in Henk's hands, suitcase on the back, and whisper, "Go on, just move and I will catch up."

"Identification please!"

I take the billfold out of my pocket. Henk and I had exchanged clothes, so I was wearing his pants. In the billfold is a picture of a German soldier in dress uniform. One of my aunts gave me this picture of her brother-in-law in Germany and told me to use it if I ever needed it. I had met this 18 year-old young man several times. The S.S. soldier saw the picture, smiled and said something. I nodded. He became very friendly, even picked up my gloves which I had dropped in my nervousness, handed them to me and told me to go on...*Guten tag*!

My brother was faint with relief, but we could have shouted with joy and thankfulness. Again, in a dark moment, God took care of us. His promise in Matthew 28:20 "Lo, I am with you always" was true for us. Our hearts were sad for the ones that got caught.

Overnight we stayed with friends here and there, and after 6 days of travel I delivered my brother to the farm near Aalten, where my parents were in hiding.

Back to Peter's diary.

Monday, February 19

It is washday and I have to fire up the *mantelpot*. It is good for washing clothes, holds a good load and clothes don't get burned. In the meantime I cut some more firewood.

In evening I write a letter home. Sanders, who goes home tomorrow to Apeldoorn with a load of food, will take it for delivery to my father. Bedtime at 9:30 p.m.

Tuesday, February 20

Before our guests leave for Amersfoort, they butcher three geese, one chicken and two rabbits. Johan takes a picture of this activity. They are ready to go on their way at 10 a.m. The handcart is loaded. We help to get it on the laneway, but that is as far as the three men can pull and push it. Gerrit Driessen has a solution. He gets his horse and will pull the cart to the main road. We wonder if they ever will get to Apeldoorn and Amersfoort. Apeldoorn is good 60 kilometres and Amersfoort at least 100 kilometres.

Mr. Haalboom from Driebergen comes to *de Koekoek*. People come and go these days. They are desperate for food.

When we are busy peeling potatoes, Mr. Haalboom goes outside where he falls to the ground… he fainted. Just at that moment two German soldiers come around the corner, raise him up and wash his face with water. It takes a little before he comes to himself again. He has to vomit and we suggest he settles down in a reclining lawn chair where he sleeps for an hour.

Frans and I cut some more wood.

The wash water has been warmed up and it is ready when Grada Bussink arrives after lunch to finish this chore. I help crank the washing machine and clean up afterward.

4:30 feed animals. Supper at 6 p.m. At 7:15 we start to bike for light. Diary updated and we all are in a good mood and sing around the organ. Bedtime at 9:30. It rained all day.

Wednesday, February 21

Normal chores. Gerrit comes back from a two-day visit to Lintelo where he was busy cutting hair. I darn three pair of socks. With this kind of work I take my time. Nobody else darns socks here and they don't dare to say anything about me taking my sweet time to do it. The socks are done just before lunch and the *snert* tastes good.

Mr. Haalboom leaves again. Hope he makes it back home, he is undernourished.

It is beautiful spring weather and the Tommies are very active. Hundreds of planes fly overhead. All bombers accompanied by fighter planes. They come in droves – groups of ten, twenty, or thirty. The German fighters come to meet them, but they do not seem so plentiful any more. The Germans are occasionally successful in shooting one down and we see one tumbling out of the sky, direction Schaarsheide. Three men bail out with parachutes. We see also a fuel barrel falling; it lands in 't Goor by Prinsendiek. Another barrel falls in Barlo. These barrels are attached to planes to give them more long distance. When the fuel is used up they can be disposed of.

Oom Herman asks me to sort out seed potatoes for planting later. When I have enough crates filled up, I put these in the pig barn. I look after the bees, and then the pigs and cows are fed and watered.

I want to look at the Tommies. They are circling overhead again. As I step outside to have a good look, there is a Dutch Policeman standing by the house. I talk to him and ask what he is coming for. He is looking for anything edible. Jo says he is the fiancé of the daughter of ter Haar from the *Mölle*. A very nice person and he does not leave empty handed.

6:00 p.m. *balkenbrij* and *snert* for supper. 6:30 p.m. milking and cleaning up. 7:00 p.m. diary updated.

9:20 p.m. We see three Tommies burning and coming down near the border. They are caught in the searchlights and hit by anti-aircraft fire. It is very clear weather.

Thursday February 22

While we are feeding the cows this morning, we get some visitors, Hendrik Vaags, Johan Heideman and Henk from Boskoop, all from the town of Vragender, a little north of here. The plane that came down near Schaarsheide yesterday crashed in Vaags' field. An English bomber with a crew of 10 or 11. Some died; one has broken limbs and some are without any injuries. All are picked up by S.S. and *Zwarten*. For the three men who came here, farmer Vaags and the *onderduikers*, it is too dangerous to stay at their place as long as the S.S. men are moving about and around their place. Ome Jan who was also hiding at Vaags' place has moved as well.

Brother Gerrit is asked to cut their hair please. While waiting their turn the others help me peel the potatoes and this is done in no time. When Gerrit has his job finished the three move on to safer territory.

Farmer te Grootenhuis, whose farm was bombed the other day, comes back for one of his calves that was kept in our barn.

Making a hotbed this afternoon. We will try to grow some early vegetables.

4:30 p.m. Feed the animals. Clean out the *gruppe*. After the milking we bring in the sheep. Johan and Gerrit are going to Scholten for wheat or barley. They will take it to Aalten tomorrow when Gerrit has to cut Ome Jan's hair at the new place where he is hiding now.

Mail to and from Germany had been stopped for some time, but it seems to be moving again. My sister Nen had sent us a letter for her fiancé Berend in Berlin asking us to get it on its' way the first possible opportunity. Gerrit takes it to Houwers at farm *Neerhof* who will have it taken to post office.

Friday, February 23

When Frans and I are peeling potatoes we have to stop three times to help all the people who come to buy food. The mailman brings a letter from Jo

Wouters in Amsterdam. Frans and I find some time to shell some big beans before lunch time. Lunch at 12:30. Sauerkraut with cooked fresh bacon.

Clean and scrub wooden shoes. Oom Herman goes to Sparanto in Doetinchem with parcels for delivery in Amsterdam. Flour for Wouters and 25 pounds of rye for my brother. I bought the rye from Tony next door for 2 guilders and 50 cents.

Gerrit helps me to cut wood. After this I feed the animals and clean out the *gruppe*. Supper at 6 p.m., then milking.

Oom Herman back from Doetinchem with both parcels. The truck is out of order. I am very sorry. These people in Amsterdam are craving for a little food.

Gerrit ter Horst, son of Oom Herman, pedals for light. Oom Herman has to eat yet and wants to say grace before his supper. Because of the noise it makes, Gerrit stops pedalling the bike until Oom Herman is finished praying. It is now pitch dark. Deep silence in the room. I am wondering how long this is going to take. Don't worry… As proof that Oom Herman is finished he makes a coughing sound and Tante adds a few of her own. She does the same thing at normal mealtimes when Oom Herman is not home. At such times we have silent prayer. Her coughing is a strange but efficient custom that makes me smile every time again. It is as if she wants to say, "You can open your eyes, I'm finished praying."

Today we had a fair bit of rain with a dry spell this afternoon. Not much activity in the air, but at the front so much more.

Saturday, February 24
Today a year ago we celebrated Mother Wikkerink's birthday here at the farm.

I am alone to do the work as Oom Herman and Johan are spreading manure in de Es. Airplanes are very, very, active. Suddenly they turn around and dive down, letting go of their bombs. It is above Aalten close to the *Oosterkerk*. I see three huge smoke columns rising into the air. Opa and Opoe Wikkerink live very close to the church. Shortly after, we get word that the bombs have fallen in the Kruisstraat. Six dead and wounded. By smith Heinen, the 200 pound anvil was blown over the house and landed in the garden. Elsewhere the road from Aalten to Varsseveld is bombed and unsuitable for any traffic. Also the railroad by Lintelo. Four times the airplane dove and let its' destructive power go at this target.

Sunday, February 25
My brother Teun and twin sister Bep are 31 years old today, born in 1914.

9:30 am. Church at our farm *de Koekoek*. Gerrit is reading the sermon from dominee Veenhuizen titled "The only comfort in life and death". Very appropriate as many people are dying from hunger and the ravaging conflict of the war all around us. We are surrounded by fighting armies both on the ground and in the air. Collection 4 guilders and 87 cents. After church Frans and I visit neighbour Hoopman and we get *koffie* with sugar. A special treat. After lunch I write a letter to Henny.

At 3 p.m. a church service with Johan reading the sermon written by dominee Kuypers "What is your gain or profit". When the service is finished at 4 p.m. the stove is out, no fire left.

When I go to get some firewood I hear somebody outside. "That would not be Henny," is my thought, "she has house duties today." But when I step outside I get a big surprise, it is her all right.

Tante Gerda gave her the afternoon off and she can stay until seven o'clock. It makes my day again. I give Henny the letter from Jo Wouters to read, while I take care of the animals. Mina's fiancé Dirk will do the milking tonight. Riekie has come for company of Frans and the two of them do the dishes.

Around 6:30 Henny leaves and I walk up with her as far as de Hanekam. I go back via *Klein Zwitserland*. Johan and I have an invitation to come to Mother's birthday party this coming Wednesday.

Monday, February 26
Today I stay in bed because my throat is acting up again.

Three V-l's fall out of the sky. These are the unpredictable flying bombs meant for England. Brother Gerrit gets a letter from Dick in Apeldoorn who writes that in Beekbergen nine V-l's came down, some of which did not explode yet.

Two ladies from Utrecht are asking for overnight lodging which is given of course. What to do about all the guys here in the house? Gerrit and Frans are promoted to sons of Oom Herman and I am a nephew. The ladies are discussing the look-alikes. Gerrit looks like Mina, the daughter, and Johan and Frans are a spitting image of Oom Herman the farmer. Wow, what an imagination. But I don't look like anyone. That upsets me.

Bep Jamoel from Amersfoort drops in for some food stuff to take home with her. She is a courier for the Resistance. Gerrit hands her the letters for home in Apeldoorn.

Tuesday, February 27

Most of the day in bed. Oom Herman goes to the drugstore to see if he can get something for me to gargle with.

Two V-1's come down in the area.

Roel Beumer's sister is here for food. River IJssel will be closed March 1. Everyone tries to get across the bridge back into their own territory. A friend of Mink van der Horst comes to visit him, but he does not know that Mink has died during the bombardment on Thursday February 8th. Very tragic. Bram Pastoor, Sebe's brother, comes from Apeldoorn in police uniform with someone from The Hague, also for food. Sebe has to take NSB men to Barchem with horse and wagon.

We receive word that the *Zwarten* are raiding again in our area.

Wednesday, February 28

I get up at eight o'clock and I feel a lot better. Good enough to do the dishes and peel potatoes.

Since I did not shave for three days, Gerrit will do it for me and it feels good. I feel like taking a good bath and a pail with hot water is soon available.

My diary is next; nothing done since last Friday. It is noticeable that no city people have shown up today. They must be all heading for the river to get across.

Gerrit, Frans and I cut some more firewood. My throat feels better by the minute. I look after the animals to give them food and water and after supper do the milking.

At 7 p.m. Johan and I are going to the Bredevoortsestraat. We should have been there before supper, but this did not work as we had to look after cows and milking.

Henny is pleased to see me too. She did not expect me because of my sore throat. A nice evening and we get a nice cigar, Horma, 8 cents, and chocolate milk and fruit cocktail.

11:15 bed time. I sleep with Gerrit in the hiding place at Oom Dirk. For cover we get a warm wool blanket and a *gestikte deken*. The quilt is a real treat, but during the night I wake up; the heavy blanket is missing and I am cold. When things are back to normal and we want to go back to sleep Ome Jan calls us to get up. It is quarter to six.

Last night many army trucks came by. NEWS: We hear that the Allies are across the river Maas, Ruhr and Urft. 15 kilometres from Keulen (Cologne). By the town Varsseveld, there was an accident last week. A car with four S.S. officers; all died.

Henny has ordered a cigarette lighter for me. It is made from a machine gun shell.

MARCH 1945

Thursday, March 1

Today is Tante's birthday. Johan and I head back to the farm accompanied by the twins, Henk and Gerrit Wikkerink. Gerrit needs a haircut and Henk comes along for the fun. That's what he thinks! I put him to work peeling potatoes and cutting wood. Gerrit will buy me cigarette paper, 100 meters for 12 guilders.

Since brother Gerrit is not doing much he will help me cut and saw more wood.

At 6 p.m. we get a visit from Mother Wikkerink and Lien. They leave at seven to make it home before curfew. My throat starts to hurt again and the night is not very good. I have a fever again.

Friday, March 2
Henk Wikkerink stays here for a while. Safer than in town. First we peel potatoes, which makes Frans happy, and then cut and saw wood. Papenborg needs to have some more tree stumps removed. We go home when it is time to feed and water the animals. Henk goes home until Monday when he is planning to come back to the farm.

NEWS: Allies have taken some more cities in Germany; Munchen, Kladbach, and Krefield. The Province of Limburg (the Netherlands) liberated.

Saturday, March 3
Frans is again stuck with the chore of peeling potatoes. We bring some *mangels* from the *koele* to the threshing floor. Clean out the pigsties. Load a wagon with wood. I straighten out the manure on the dung hill, behind the cow stable. Now I can clean out the *gruppe* in cow stable. Time to feed animals, then a bath and supper.

46 people are killed by the Kruisberg, likely a reprisal for an anti-German action.

After I have taken my turn biking for light, I go over the printed sermon which I have to read tomorrow.

We eat our supper and as usual Oom Herman will read a selection from the Bible. However it is fairly dark already and he just does not have enough light. Moving closer to the window does not help much either. Looking around, he takes the *tuugbenne*, opens the door and puts the *tuugbenne* upside down in the door opening. "*Noe geet ut wel,*" he says. "This will work."

Since we ate a little early tonight, milking has to be done yet. I have to milk both cows and the one always gives me trouble. Normally Johan milks that one. It will be the third time that I have to milk her. The previous times I nearly lost the milk as she kicked against the pail. I wonder what will happen tonight. About half way through she gives a really hard kick, this is the third one, and her leg hits the handle of the pail spilling most of the precious liquid. She then lets me finish without any more trouble. Most of this milk is for her calf, her first one. We don't have much milk lately as the White cow is completely dry and the Red one is well over halfway. Both are with calf.

Sunday, March 4

Today is my friend Reijndert's birthday. Lien arrives at 9 a.m. and helps with setting up for church which is held here. The sermon is from dominee Veenhuizen, titled "Gethsemane". Text Matthew 26: 36-39. Reading is from Matthew 20: 20-35. Attendance 14 young men. It is raining, but it gets dry later on.

At 11:30 who comes to the farm? Henny! I thought she wanted to eat at her home with Opa and Opoe today. Shortly after noon we are ready for lunch and I count 14 around the table. Henny shows me a letter from Nen that says the children of Jannie and Adriaan and Teun and Stien are being baptized today. Brother Gerrit and I are very happy with this news.

Henny is going to attend the church service that is held at neighbour Houwers, farm *Neerhof*. The service at *de Koekoek*, our farm, starts at 2:50 p.m. Dirk reads the sermon. Attendance 10.

We seem to develop problems at our services. Last week and also today the stove went out while reading the sermon. It got really cold. Gerrit Hoopman says, "We will ask the Reverend to shorten his sermons, because it is not nice that the stove goes out every time."

4:30 p.m. Feed the animals. 5:30 p.m. Feed ourselves. We are now with 15 around the table. Riekie, Frans' friend, has joined us. We eat *krentewigge*, a real treat. After supper Dirk and I take care of milking the two cows. I take the Red one and Dirk the *sterker*, the one who kicked the pail down last time.

Henny and I take a stroll through the garden. Later Jan and Anneke Houwers of farm *Neerhof* come to visit. We have a coffee with two *oliebollen*, then "something in a glass" and a homemade cookie.

At about 9 p.m. Henny and I go to the *opkamertje* and as usual have our prayer time. Precious moments!

When we come downstairs in the *waskamer*, Johan and Lien join us. Finally at about eleven o'clock we decide to go to bed. Normally we go for a long walk but tonight the weather is bad and we have to spend our time inside.

Brother Gerrit is going to Hoornenborg at *de Haart* this coming Wednesday to cut hair. I was able to convince Oom Herman that I should go there too so I can show Gerrit the inside roads and he does not have to travel the dangerous main road. We will go in the evening and come back on Thursday morning. Henny, who stays with the Hoornenborg's, will ask if they can put the two of us up for the night. I'll do anything to see Henny an extra time during the week.

Henny will take along my second and third diary books when she goes back to *de Haart* tomorrow.

Monday, March 5

Up at 7 a.m. Milking is already done by Oom Herman. We feed the animals and then Henny comes walking back from the pump outside where she has washed up. Shortly after, she has to leave. I walk with her around the barn until we reach the cherry tree. A kiss under the cherry tree is a marvelous good bye. Sister Lien is staying at our farm today to help out.

Henk is back at nine o'clock and hands me some *superol* for my sore throat. Henny bought it for me. "She must like you," he says.

Henk and I can get along very well. We cut wood all morning and do a lot of talking. The afternoon finds us busy again with the wood until 4:30 when it is time to look after the animals. Gerrit has to visit *Tante Betje* which is in front of the cow stable. Henk locks him in with the dead bolt on the outside. Gerrit makes an awful lot of noise to draw attention and Tante feels sorry for him.

Frans and I go for a walk and we spend the rest of the evening in the *waskamer*. Lien is busy fixing my jacket. Bedtime at 9 p.m.

Tuesday, March 6

Henk helps me peel potatoes and Oom Herman does the milking. Lien heads for home again. After the potatoes are peeled, Henk and I continue sawing wood. We keep at it until lunch time. The menu shows we have *snert* and nothing but *snert*. It is really good food.

Grada Bussink, sister of Dirk, is here to do the wash and I do the cranking, with Henk taking the odd turn at the handle. The other three fellows, Johan, Gerrit and Frans, are busy in the field. When the wash had its turn, so to speak, Henk and I go to Papenborg where more stumps have to be cleared out. Henk, who is working his heart out, breaks the axe handle. We go home and work on the woodpile. Gerrit ter Horst fixes the axe.

It is about four o'clock and all of a sudden someone is standing behind me in the woodshed. It is Henny. She shows up at the most unexpected times. She has been at catechism class and came to tell us not to go to *de Haart* tomorrow, then leaves again. Stopping and turning around, she asks if I will write her on Sunday, but not half a letter like the last one. I promise if she will write me. And so we agree.

At 4:30 Henk and I take care of the livestock. Six o'clock time to milk. Johan milks the *sterker;* she is the kicker.

Frans de Vries comes here; he needs an address to place a young man. Since it is time to eat, he stays to fill his stomach and plays the organ for half an hour to pay for the food. It is again a normal evening doing the normal things like biking for light, updating the diary and writing letters, smoking, playing checkers and chess, knitting, darning, and sewing.

Moas Johannes Westerveld is picked up by the *Zwarten* and locked up in a cell.

Wednesday, March 7

Today the butcher is coming to slaughter a calf and a pig. Before we help him, we peel potatoes and clean carrots. The pig is killed with a large kind of a pistol. It has a pin instead of a bullet. The pistol is put against the pig's forehead and pulling the trigger releases the pin. I am not sure if it kills the pig, but it is stunned and unconscious at which time the butcher cuts its throat to let the blood flow out. Kind of a bloody mess! Don't like it too well. But I do like the meat, sausages, and ham which is the end product.

Rest of the morning spent sawing wood. I start a letter to brother Henk in Amsterdam. The weather is very nice but there are no Tommies in the sky.

NEWS: Keulen (Germany) in Allied hands, also the ramp of bridge by Homburg (Germany).

In the afternoon I go back to the woodpile while Henk and Frans work in the field. Johan helps Tante Grada who came to make sausages and he cleans the intestines of the pig, a smelly job. A customary visit will be made tonight and visitors do not miss such an opportunity to assess and praise the quality of the pig's meat and bacon. Our neighbour Tony Driessen, his son Gerrit and housekeeper Grada are the visitors.

When *den Eume* comes in he sees me writing again. "*Iej bunt altied an 't schrieven an,*" he says. "*Hoe ne langen brief he'j noe al?*" "You are always writing; how long is your letter by now?"

I tell him that I have come a long way already.

"What are you going to do with it?" he asks.

"Oh, I will read it later to my grandchildren."

"*Huh, Huh, dat zal wel mooi wezzen, wisse we*". "Hoh, Hoh, I am sure it will be a nice long story."

Johan and Henk play chess, Gerrit Driessen and Frans play checkers.

Thursday, March 8

After we have taken care of the animals this morning, Henk and I help to process all the meat from pig and calf. We get the odd taste of the meat and sausage mixture and it is again very tasty. The intestines have to be cleaned once more. They are in a large pot. Henk and I take it to the pump outside to give them a real good rinse.

Are they ever slippery; it is very hard to hang on to them and it gives us a lot of fun and laughs. We borrow a sausage machine from farm *Neerhof* but it does not work properly. Brother Gerrit goes to Scholten to borrow theirs. This one works very well and we make good headway. Even so, it takes us all afternoon and a good part of the evening to finish the job of grinding and cutting the meat. Tomorrow we continue.

This afternoon a woman came to the farm looking for food in exchange for articles of clothing and linen. Lien and Mina both buy something. Lien mentions to me that the woman has a pair of rain protectors, covers for legs when biking. I want to buy these for Henny, but the woman is not supposed to see me. Mina will talk to her about the price, but she forgets. Oom Herman will ask her and the price is ten pounds of rye. I say okay and Oom Herman buys them. When he shows them to us, Mina says that she wants to have them. I don't think this is fair, but I am out of luck.

Many planes in the air and bombs falling. A German plane flies low over Aalten and it drops two bombs.

Friday, March 9

Last night's bombs fell near the Dinxperloseweg. One dead and some injured.

Lunch is very greasy soup and mashed potatoes.

Bernard from *Neerhof* is ploughing a field. Suddenly Tommies come low overhead and turn around him. Wisely he leaves the horses and runs for cover. Luckily the fighter planes move on.

NEWS: Allied over the Rhine between Bonn and Keulen. Russian troops have started attack on Berlin.

Yesterday a letter from Teun and Stien which confirmed the baptism of Henk and Hetty. At Easter they both will do profession of faith. Today a letter from home via farmer Jansen at *te Hennepe*. They included a letter for Berend in Berlin which will be mailed by someone who goes to Germany, just across the border. That way it is quite certain he will get it.

Brother Gerrit helps me scrub and clean wooden shoes. Gerrit and I finish off the soup leftover from lunch. The others don't dare to touch it, it is very greasy.

Saturday, March 10

After working up the compost heap I start cleaning up around the house and barn. Two girls who are looking for food come by with a flat on their bike. It did not take long to fix it and by then lunch is ready.

Peter Van Essen

Continue cleaning outside and I have just enough time to feed animals before supper. After that I take a nice bath and it feels so good to put on clean clothes. Finish letter for Henny and read over sermon for tomorrow.

Gerrit Driessen received a notice to report today for digging trenches. Since he did not report, we may expect some trouble. We live under the same roof, two families in the same farm building.

Sunday, March 11

We had planned the afternoon church service here at our farm, but since we may get trouble, we now will have the service at Hoopman. The sermon is from dominee Kuyper titled "Paradise", Genesis 3: 1-15. Attendance 11.

Lien, who is here, says that she will share a little secret with me, but not until tonight. I wonder what this will be. While I'm talking to Henk and Gerrit Driessen in the afternoon, standing on the threshing floor, who walks into the kitchen? Henny! She was not coming today; she had house duties at her uncle's farm. Another nice surprise which puts me on cloud nine.

When we go to Hoopman church at 2:45, she goes to *Neerhof* church with Oom Herman and Tante. I get a box of matches from her and these are the best you can get: Zwaluw. I should say the best you can not get. You need to search and hunt all over for some matches.

At four o'clock home from church and Henny is already back at *de Koekoek*. Oom and Tante are still visiting at *Neerhof*.

After feeding the animals and then ourselves we find time for our usual walk, via *de Bleeke* and the dam, Slatdiek and Papenborg back home. It takes a good hour for us, but it could be done in half the time. Frans who has been at Riekie's place is just arriving home too. We have a *gezellige* evening and all go to bed at 10 p.m.

Another day is past. It was a good one.

Monday, March 12

Before breakfast Henny and Lien leave. We wonder what this day will bring. Yesterday every home received a notice to report. We decide to disappear for the day. Frans and I leave shortly after 8 a.m. for the marsh at 't Goor. The neighbour's *onderduiker* Sebe has left already with horse and wagon and took our equipment along.

Without trouble we arrive at the Goorsteggendiek where Sebe is busy camouflaging the wagon. We pick up our equipment, load it on the wheelbarrow and walk to the Hagendiek where we will do some work today. We are going to take it easy. It is really dumb work but it gives us something to do. Fill in the lower spots with the higher ground so everything is even and smooth. Wonder if they will want to make a golf course here?

Johan is coming to bring us lunch and he shows up at 12:30. A good size pan with potatoes mixed with *gris*. We keep working until six o'clock, and then walk to Sebe to get a ride home. We did make a very primitive bridge over the large ditch and can reach Sebe in a short time. Otherwise we would have to walk all around the fields taking at least twice as long. When we made this bridge we started with a long beam and let it fall across. It came down with a noise that sounded like it broke in two. Another one beside it and then some old boards to cover it. The bridge is ready!

"Okay Frans, go ahead," I say.

"You want me to go first. Why me?"

"You are not as heavy as I."

Here he goes, slowly he moves half way down, and he comes back. I enjoy this and in my mind, I already see him down in the ditch that is more than half filled with water.

He is going to try again but this time on hands and knees and he makes it safely to the other side. Now it is my turn and the bridge holds again.

Sebe is waiting for us and we start rolling. Just before we reach the Selmseweg, we noticed two vehicles passing. Johan Stronks comes to meet us and is relieved to see us. Because this area has been raided, fears grew that we might be in trouble and Johan volunteered to go and look for us. We reach home at 7:45 p.m. where brother Gerrit and Tante are anxiously waiting for us. Arrangements are made for us to go with Sebe again tomorrow and Oom Herman will wake us at 6 a.m.

Peter Van Essen

Tuesday, March 13

They wake us at seven instead of 6 a.m. Sebe has already left when we finish breakfast so Frans and I start walking. When we get to the Boterdiek Frans says, "I have to do a big one."

"Well then, do it."

"I cannot sit here; what if someone comes along?"

"Go a little ways into that laneway and you will be okay. I will warn you if someone's coming."

He is just sitting when around the corner in the distance there comes a farmer on his bike and, a little behind him, his wife.

"Frans, some folks are coming this way. You better hurry up."

"I am finished!" he yells back. He gets up and instead of dressing himself he just pulls up his pants and coverall holding the works under his armpits. Then he walks to the road and stands there like a puppet with his elbows against his side, his hands clasped together in front of him. The bikers are passing us and he greets them with the customary *moin,* and again *moin,* one for each. I stand there laughing my heart out and it does not get any better. The farmer couple has just passed us and Frans stretches his arms wide out so his coverall and pants drop to the ground. With his coverall hanging down around his ankles, he steps around in a big circle and starts singing. "*Al loop ik in de tachtig, Mijn ouwe hart blijft jong!*" "Although I am in my eighties, my old heart is still young."

It takes a while but he gets everything back to normal and we continue our way to Sebe, pick up our equipment and go on to our field, crossing the bridge.

At 12:30 p.m. Johan comes again with our meal. Potatoes and green beans with a large piece of meat and, for dessert, porridge. The porridge is in a bottle and we are wondering why there are blue lines running through it. We find out it was an ink bottle and apparently did not get cleaned properly. The porridge in the bottom is a little too blue and we leave this in.

Johan spots an owl and suggests we catch it. It flies away and settles in a small tree. We go after it; Johan with a big stick, Frans carries a pitch fork and

I take the *aalenschepper*. The owl is smarter than we are and he is still flying around when we have to leave for home.

Riding with Sebe we turn around a corner in 't Villekesderp and there come two vehicles with Germans. Frans and I jump off the wagon and run for cover. When we reach the farmer Rietman, I hide in the wood shed. Frans is not to be seen anywhere. A little later I find he is hiding in the horse stable.

The vehicles stop right here at Rietman. In the distance we hear loud shouting. Frans and I communicate with our hands and arms, indicating that we should get away from here. Out the back, behind some bushes and then through the field towards Jansen at *te Hennepe*. When we come home it is almost 8 p.m. and Sebe tells us that there are about 80 vehicles in 't Villekesderp that will stay there with all the troops.

Supper finished at 8:15. We do a bit of biking and off to bed.

Wednesday, March 14 Prayer Day.
One of *den Eume*'s cows is expected to deliver a calf today. I stay home to help with this delivery. All the others are going to church which will be held at farm *de Bleeke*; Gerrit is to read the sermon.

I write a letter to brother Teun in Twello. At ten o'clock I have to come into action and all I have to do is pull gently and a calf is born, a bull calf. Shortly after everybody comes home again; the service was short because they had a sermon written by dominee Gerritsma.

Henny comes to visit and tells us that in Vragender the Germans have been hunting like mad men last Friday. They were looking for an American or a terrorist. Ome Jan, her Dad, is hiding in this district, but everything went okay and they did not find what they were looking for.

Oom Johan Hoornenborg, the uncle with whom Henny is staying, is now also digging trenches in Varsseveld. Many more are reporting for this work. Varsseveld is the next town and it seems the Germans are continuing to retreat.

Henny and I go for a walk, but I notice that she has difficulty walking. Her knee is bothering her and we return to the farm. We meet Frans and Riekie and also Gerrit and Herman; all are out for a walk.

Henny darns a pair of socks for me and will take the other 3 pairs with her. She will fix those in her spare time. The collection money, total 32 Guilders, she will hand over for the cause.

I get three packages of cigarette paper and after we have spent a few minutes in the small room she leaves. I accompany her as far as de Hanekam.

Gerrit goes to Aalten to cut hair for some *onderduikers*. When we are in *Klein Zwitserland* we meet Adolf Melitz. It scares us, but he does not say anything. Adolf is a foster child of Koskamp, the *Landwachter*. He is a very fanatic pro-German, and German born. Has a bad name around here and people say, "Watch out for Adolf."

German troops are racing in the direction of Varsseveld with trucks, cars, tanks and horse and wagon.

Home at 8.15 p.m. and at nine o'clock to bed.

Thursday, March 15

Frans and I are leaving for 't Goor. It is beautiful weather and we don't mind the walk. We come to the Hagendiek and we see that the nice young horse from Maos Westerveld is back in his pasture. A few days ago it was there and Frans was so taken in by its beauty that he gave him some of his bread. When we are close to this field the horse comes walking up to the fence gate.

"Oh, look Frans, he is waiting for you."

"Why is he waiting for me?"

"You gave him some food the other day."

"You must be kidding."

"No, I am not kidding, I bet he wants some more."

So Frans starts to unpack some of his bread and sure enough the horse knows what to do with it.

"You could ride it Frans, he likes you." Frans is not so sure, but would like to try it.

"Okay, let us go through the gate and try," I say. This horse has never had anybody riding it; it was too young.

"I don't know how to get on."

"No problem Frans, I'll help you." I had seen this done before. Standing beside the horse I fold my hands in front of me and tell Frans to put his knee in there. "Now hang on to his mane, I count one, two and push you up. You swing your leg over the horse and away you go."

Poor Frans. I push way too hard and he lands on the other side of the horse in the grass.

"That did not work too well," is his remark.

"No, let us try again."

With a carefully measured push he lands on the horse, hanging on to the mane. The horse is surprised, stands still for about three counts then takes a big leap forward straight for the fence. Along the fence there are wild bramble bushes, many of them. They have big thorns. Frans screams when he sees what is going to happen. Either the horse will jump over it or will swing left or right in front of the fence. The fence itself is made of barbed wire. I get a little concerned about the whole thing, but there is nothing I can do now, just watch! It is only a matter of a few seconds. Just before the fence the horse makes a sudden move left. Frans comes down with a crash and lands in the bramble bushes. I have to pull him out and hope he is still in one piece. Nothing broken, only some pretty good scratches from the thorns. When he fell off the horse he yelled, "Ouch, that hurts."

Now we both start laughing and can hardly stop.

The weather is fantastic and our work makes us thirsty. We did not bring any water so I try some out of the ditch. It tastes awful. A short distance away a farmer has put a pump in his field and this water tastes very good.

Johan brings food for lunch at 12:30 p.m. The work ends at 6 p.m. and we walk to where Sebe and Herman are. A ride home and we arrive there at 7.30 p.m.

We eat *balkenbrij* for supper. This is delicious stuff.

Friday, March 16
We eat *balkenbrij* with our bread. Yummy!

Again to 't Goor with Sebe and Herman. It is foggy and we might get some rain. We take a big container with water along. I have also taken my diary along for updating. Several days have to be caught up yet.

Frans helps me recall the events of the last days and when we have reached today we get back to work. When Johan brings lunch at 12:30 we have done a lot of work. We eat sauerkraut with fresh bacon. At four o'clock it starts to rain. We make a makeshift shelter from branches and old boards and have our break. 3:30 or 4 p.m. is called *veeruren*. Always a welcome event.

It is not going to get dry so we start cleaning up. When we get to Sebe and Herman we find that they have also stopped working. In a nearby field Sebe and I discover a small straw shelter made by the *Moffen*. It can hold two people and Sebe and I stretch out for a while. Eventually it dries and we head for home.

Saturday, March 17

Frans and I are peeling potatoes. Clean around the house, in the barn, and cut some wood. Hans, grandson of *den Eume,* has been picked up by the Germans. Most likely will be sent digging trenches.

We eat *snert* for lunch. In the evening I go for a short walk via Papenborg, Slatdiek back to the farm. Papenborg's farmhouse is old, drafty and damp. Spend some time to read the sermon for tomorrow and at 9:30 to bed.

For tonight they expect *razzias* and likely also tomorrow.

Sunday, March 18

We cannot have our church service for the *onderduikers*, it is too dangerous. Dirk, Johan and I are going to attend the service at *Neerhof* this morning. Gerrit and Frans may go this afternoon. The sermon is from dominee Veenhuizen entitled "'God Is Love".

The *onderduikers* are sitting in the bedroom. Sebe and Johan have watch duty and move from window to window to spot any surprises. From our vantage point we see on one side the preacher and the congregation, and on the other side the cows in the stable at the end of threshing floor. When they move their heads the chains rattle and clink and occasionally we are treated with a loud moo, moo...

After lunch Henny and Lien show up. They go with the others to the church at *Neerhof* which is at three o'clock. Dirk and I stay home; Gerrit and Frans go to church as promised. We cannot all go, that would cause problems in case we have to hide suddenly.

I use the time at home to write a letter to Dad and sister Nen. Eventually I have three pages filled with news, and cannot think of anything else. Luckily by then the service is over and Henny comes home. She writes on the last page and fills the sheet nicely.

Two of the three pair of socks she took along have been darned and it feels good to put your feet into socks where your toes are not sticking out. So far the day passes fairly quietly. No rumours of raids.

Riekie drops in after church to see her Frans. It makes him happy.

5:30 p.m. supper. Everybody tries to get a place at the table. It is a happy bunch; Mina and Dirk, Lien and Johan, Henny and me, Gerrit, Riekie and Frans, Oom Herman and Tante. A good evening together and we go to bed not too late because tomorrow we are off to 't Goor again.

Monday, March 19

Early breakfast and the four of us go back to 't Goor. We arrive there at nine o'clock. Jan from farm *de Fukker* comes over for a little talk. He has a piece of land close by and has to do some work there. The Tommies are very active this morning. At eight this morning the castle in Terborg was bombed. It was occupied by German officers. I am sure they left in a hurry.

I take time to write a letter to my sister Bep and brother-in-law Wim Weeda in Castricum. I have taken everything along and since we have to look for work here I make this my work for part of the morning and finish it in the afternoon. We eat at 12:30 p.m., do some work in the afternoon and get ready to leave for home at 6:30 p.m.

When we get back to the farm it is past 7:30. The others have not had their supper yet. You might have noticed that often we *onderduikers* have taken care of making breakfast and/or supper. Tante cannot get all the work done, it takes a long time, and we would be late for almost everything if we don't help by speeding things up. When supper is finished and the dishes are done, it is time to go to bed.

NEWS: Bochholt, just across border, raided with bombs.

Tuesday, March 20

Sebe and Herman have left already, so we walk to 't Goor. It is past 9:30 when we arrive. Farmer Hakstegge who is working on his land close by receives word that the *Zwarten* and *Groenen* are at his farm and have ordered the men from Scheveningen to report for duty tomorrow morning.

At nine o'clock this morning the *Groenen* were chasing two boys who were working in the field across from Sebe. That was very, very close. At noon I go to the Boterdiek and hide in the bushes waiting for Johan who brings us food as usual. We decide to go through the fields and lanes with more cover from bushes and arrive back at our field. Henk and Theo, two boys from farm *de Fukker*, are there too. They will share our food. Then someone from their farm drops off food for them and we share that as well.

Johan mentions that three *Landwachters* came to the farm asking if there were any bikes available. Of course not! At farm *Neerhof* they took an old girl's bike. A little later they are at farmer Neerhof. They are looking for men. "There are no men, everybody is digging trenches," is the reply. "Would you have some water and boil our eggs?" Water is available but no heat.

The Allied airplanes are very busy again. We get home at 8 p.m.

Wednesday, March 21, first day of spring

Back to 't Goor. Frans and I spend a few hours looking for duck eggs but we don't find any.

It is chaos in the town of Aalten. The Germans are raiding the town like never before. Everybody, men and young boys, is being picked up. The Germans are getting more desperate, the war is getting closer to home. So far they have always been fighting in someone else's country, now it is on their home turf and they are losing, and losing badly. We don't feel like working. Uncertainty and excitement is in the air. It probably will not be long now before we are liberated. But how is it going to be? What is going to happen to give us this victory and freedom again? Fighting is severe and not far away either. From 12:30 until 3:30 p.m. we talk about these things, Frans, Henk, Theo, Jan van Houwer, Johan, Herman and I.

On the way home we hear the sad news that the Allied have bombed the trenches and the men who were working there in the neighbouring town Varsseveld. It happened at ten o'clock this morning. Oom Johannes Wikkerink and Mr. Huitink have died.

When we come home we hear that many more men have died, one of them Oom Johan Hoornenborg. He is Henny's uncle from the farm *de Haart* where she is staying with Tante Gerda. It is terrible; the whole town is in mourning!

All day hundreds of airplanes fly over the area. About 30 kilometres away the city centre of Doetinchem is burning. Varsseveld and Zelhem, about 10 to 15 kilometres from here, are also bombed. Bochholt, just across the border in Germany, has been bombed as well.

The German troops want to dig in just east of us and many young men are being picked up. A close neighbour George Vervelde and Henk Deunk from farm *Wulpshof* are some of them. They are now digging near Beek.

A day of mourning for Aalten!

Thursday, March 22
We stay home and stay in the *hol* until 10 a.m. when dominee Gerritsma comes to tell us that in Aalten everything is quiet. What a relief. We cannot wait to get out.

I write a letter to Tante Gerda to express my sympathy and also a letter to Henny who shares in this great loss. Brethouwer, who was wounded, has died. He worked for Ome Jan in the construction business. Lien comes in the evening until tomorrow morning and will take my letters to *de Haart*.

Fighting is very heavy at the front. All day we hear many planes. Bochtolt is bombed three times and Anholt once. It thunders and shakes all day long, not a moment of quiet.

Peter Van Essen

Friday, March 23

We are going to 't Goor again to keep busy doing something. We don't know yet what it will be. Maybe just sit there and talk. After we finish our pancake breakfast we leave, Johan, Herman, Frans and I. Sebe has already left with horse and wagon.

Many German *Jabos* in air this morning. In the afternoon the Allied bombers arrive. They are all around, and the sound, a steady drone, gives you a headache. The sound of anti-aircraft guns is awful. The air is full of smoke and is very hazy. At the horizon, thick clouds of smoke fill the sky on every side, north, west, south and east.

But then shortly before 5 p.m. it really starts. Direction Emmerick (Germany). Bombs rain out of the sky for about an hour long. Then artillery fire and an offensive attack must have been started.

When we come home that evening, we hear that Montgomery has spoken and said, "While I speak, the Allied troops are crossing the river Rhine."

During the last few days we knew something was going to happen. Now we have heard and still hear that something is happening. And this is a fierce battle that is fought about 25 kilomtetres from here.

In Aalten there is a nervous atmosphere. Many people want to leave their homes and go to the surrounding farms. Two sons of dominee Veenhuizen arrive at our farm.

At the consistory meeting this afternoon it was decided not to have any church services this Sunday at any farm.

We go to bed at 9:30, but the air is still filled with the sound of war on land and in the air. Fighter planes are very busy yet. Even during the night we wake up several times from the sound of terrible shooting noises.

NEWS: Queen Wilhelmina has visited Den Bosch in province Noord Brabant and arrived safely back in England.

Saturday, March 24

Our morning walk is back to 't Goor. Many *Jabos* in the air. Some of them drop bombs in Lintelo, a district just south of here.

In the afternoon Allied bombers arrive. A group of 15 are right overhead. Two of them swing to the left and it rains bombs. It is Barlo, the area just north of us. But then it gets even worse. The remaining bombers are now over Aalten and drop their bombs. It is 3:20 p.m. We look at each other with horror in our eyes, and a very uneasy almost defeated feeling. A farmer warns us that the *Moffen* are close by raiding farms. We start moving further away trying to find a decent place to hide.

I panic when I notice that I have lost my tobacco container in which I have carried some diary notes. Only one thing to do; I go back to the field. I find it again after searching most of the field. I do not see any sign that the *Moffen* are close by. I am just about back at the field where the others are, when overhead three Tommies dive straight down to where the other eight fellows are laying down. I see them flying in all directions and luckily the Tommies do not fire at them. They pull up and move on.

It is past five o'clock and we head for home. We come to where Sebe is and really get a taste of war. Behind us is the heavy thunder of cannons.

Looking ahead of us we see bombers dropping loads of phosphorous bombs which fall on farms and homes. To our right Aalten is burning and to our left, the *Jabos* are diving left and right, up and down, shooting like mad. When we get closer to home we meet Houwers, who says that at the funeral of Oom Johann, who was buried last, bombs were dropped.

I cry when I hear this. Nothing is safe; any movement is suspicious and will be attacked. This is why the funerals of today are held separately and no funeral processions are allowed. Everyone has to go on their own, sometimes from tree to tree to reach the cemetery safely.

The Germans are busy going from farm to farm recruiting all the horses they can possibly get their hands on.

We arrive at the farm close to eight o'clock and hear that the factory of Visser has been bombed. 15 dead. Many people are leaving town to find a place in the country. Mr. and Mrs. Boven, Ms. de Jel and two girls from Scheveningen have come to our farm to stay. At Houwers farm *de Bleeke*, are four Italians and three men from Amsterdam. These people fled across the German border into Holland. It is terrible, they say, and anything is better than staying there to risk your life. It is reported that the roads are busy with people escaping from Germany; Russians, Italians, Belgians, French, Dutch.

We go to bed at 10 p.m., but not for long. It thunders through the air, Tommies flying low overhead. They are attacked by guns positioned in the field next door at farm *Nonhof*. I get up and dress. At 11:00 p.m. it gets a bit quieter and I go back to bed, fully dressed, just in case.

NEWS: 40,000 paratroops dropped by Bocholt. Wesel, Rees and two other towns taken by Allied troops.

Sunday, March 25

More townspeople arrive. Family Toop, Tilly, and Lo and Johan Kruithof. Then the Huinink family with 10 strong. They go to *den Eume's*.

At farm *Neerhof* next door there are 20 townspeople and also four German soldiers who stay for one night. It is all so strange, you don't know what to do and so you just walk around in circles.

It is a blessing that the weather is nice. The guests are sitting all around the bomb shelter talking or just staring around. Lo Kruithof puts her younger brother Johan on the pee pot. He sits in a nice grassy spot looking up at all these people, while the war goes on.

We dig some more manholes to jump into if necessary. The *Jabos* are flying off and on, shooting with their onboard guns.

We get very little news these last days. Also no news from the family Wikkerink in Aalten. I write a letter for home in Apeldoorn but twice I have to stop and take cover as *Jabos* shoot overhead. It is a long and unpleasant day. Everybody is nervous and expects the Allied troops to show up anytime. I had hoped to get a letter from Henny, but this is impossible under the circumstances.

We are told that Zus Eppink, daughter of Oom Johan on the Dijkstraat, has died in the air raid yesterday.

Nobody of the Eppink family has been seen and the authorities want to get in touch with them to identify the body of the girl thought to be their daughter. Some people say it is Zus, others say it is not.

Three French refugees who fled Duisburg come by and tell us that almost every meter a bomb has been dropped in Germany. Around Bochholt there are many, many paratroops. Factory belonging to Gussinklo in Bredevoort bombed.

10 p.m. to bed. It is a bit quieter than yesterday.

Monday, March 26

To 't Goor, leaving at 8 a.m. On our way there we stop four times to talk to people. Everybody wants to talk about the situation we are in. Finally we arrive but it is now ten o'clock instead of nine o'clock. Johan, who left a little late and via another route, had also been talking to people.

He said to himself, "I better hurry up, the boys might worry that something happened to me." When he comes to the field where we are supposed to be, he sees no one yet. Now he is worried. After we have discussed this thoroughly we finally get to work. It is now eleven o'clock. Who cares?

It does not take long and there come, and go, the *Jabos*. They dive over Aalten. We get nervous; they dropped bombs.

Oom Herman brings lunch and news that bombs fell at the garage of Veerbeek and the *stelling*. We don't eat much for lunch as there is not too much left. The visitors from Amsterdam ate most of the food.

More bombs on Aalten. This time it was the Farmers Co-op. Four Germans died, also six horses. Two machine guns and anti-aircraft guns destroyed.

Toop, Tilly, and Johan are going back home because their grandfather is very ill and dying.

The family Eppink is okay and Zus is alive and well.

Tuesday, March 27

The news for today is quite good. It is already Wednesday now and I still have to fill in my diary for this day, Tuesday. So much is happening that it is difficult to remember what happened yesterday. It was cloudy in the sky and quiet. Not many airplanes operating. It is different at the front where there is heavy fighting.

We met two Russians from the Ukraine walking on the Boterdiek. We talked to them and asked how things were in Germany. "*Boem, boem, boem, boem, Americano. Weg. Weg.*" was all they could say. "Bang, bang, bang, bang. Americans. Run. Run." We give them some tobacco and they seem overjoyed.

Wednesday, March 28

It is not yet eight o'clock and there come the Tommies. They drop bombs by the water tower. This tower stands out way above the trees and can be seen about one kilometre away. Two German tanks are hit and destroyed. In the late afternoon there is another raid on the tower and more bombs fall. A travelling vehicle with ammunition is destroyed on the Varsseveldseweg by Bent. In the Woldboom just west of here another German vehicle is destroyed. It happened in front of farmer te Kloeze. His wife, daughter and an *evacuee* from Scheveningen are wounded.

The little garden in front of the house needs some work and I spend some time fixing it up. It looks better now. We want to spruce up things a bit for Easter.

Mr. Boven says that he expects the Allied troops to show up this night. He might be right. The shooting is getting closer.

We make another bomb shelter to have enough cover for everybody. Finally at 2 a.m. we go to bed. After a very good rest we get up at 6:30 a.m.

Thursday, March 29

Overcast. Only a few *Jabos*. At the front fairly quiet. We finish work on the shelter.

Two Germans request billeting for four soldiers who will arrive tomorrow. Everything indicates that we are in the middle of the frontal activities these last few days.

Oom Herman and I go to 't Sledevoort to hoe the rye field. Home at five o'clock. Farmer Ebbers has 31 cows in his field, put there by the Germans. How and where did they get them? Don't ask. They take anything to feed the troops. People from town are busy milking these cows. It is a free-for-all. We decide to go milking tonight, but it is not allowed anymore. The soldiers need the milk.

This morning te Brake and his wife came here for safety; they go home again in the evening.

Many German soldiers roam around in our district Dale. The Coen bridge is blown up. Not much news tonight. By Emmerick in Germany the German resistance is much less.

We decide to sleep on the floor in front of the cows tonight. Seems to be safer than in the *hol* which is directly under the roof. Flying shrapnel can easily penetrate the roof tiles. At the front there is a tremendous thunder from cannon fire. We put straw down on the cement floor to soften it up a bit. Now we need a few old blankets. By the time we come back with the blankets, the cows have eaten most of the straw. So much for that idea. We either have to go sleep in the *hol* or stay up for the night.

A young German soldier comes in unannounced and demands coffee. He is very nervous and scared. We don't have any coffee and that makes him mad.

"You can have some water."

He will take that, but does not dare to step outside in the dark. The water has to come from the pump in front of the farm. I take a cup, go for water and give it to him. Oom Herman invites him to sit down. He does, but nervously looks around, hanging on to his rifle. Apparently still angry about the water, he says that he will shoot anybody he will meet. He then leaves.

I have an idea that this is maybe one of the last times I update my diary in hiding. Freedom is closer than ever.

Once I am in bed I am asleep in no time, notwithstanding a very shaky bed, or maybe thanks to it.

Friday, March 30, Good Friday

I slept very well during the night. All the others did not sleep too well, except Johan who also had a good and restful sleep. They cannot understand that we did not hear the terrible infernal noise from the fighting.

We eat at 8:30 a.m. while the war continues full staccato. At farm *de Bleeke*, the dam and the wooden bridge are blown up. In one of our fields, Boesveldsland, the Germans installed three cannons in the winter rye that is sprouting up. *Jabos* are in the air.

Yesterday afternoon the Germans confiscated the reins of *den Eume's* horse and last night the horse. This morning they came and picked up the wagon.

Just now we hear that the horse is standing at the Selmseweg near farm *te Hennepe* and it does not want to move another step. This is where the horse always turns onto the lane towards its home farm and stable.

We hear all kinds of stories. The Tommies are spotted by Dinxperlo and close to Aalten and Bredevoort. German troops have left in direction Lichtenvoorde.

Lien, who came last night, brings us up-to-date about the situation in Aalten. Opa and Opoe Wikkerink are at Oom Herman Luymes; the others stayed home. She had a letter from Henny for me, but forgot to bring it with her. Too bad!

Dirk's sister drops in and tells us that her little brother is very sick. Tante worries that Dirk's sister might not be able to get back home. She will have to bike straight through the battle line.

I want to write a short letter to Henny but cannot even start as the mortars start to fly. You hear them coming; a whistling sound that reaches a certain pitch, then BOOM! I don't want to stay inside the house and run to the barn for cover. An occasional short lull in the firing, and then a new round approaches. Also the machine guns are firing steadily. I stop writing after only two lines and go out to stand by the bomb shelter. I see that everyone except Gerrit is in the shelter.

We see eight German soldiers crawling through the field by farm *Nonhof*. Two are wading and crawling through the ditch along our chicken coop. They are soaking wet. They are falling, rising, running, falling, rising, running. We have fun watching them and call the others. Some join us, others stay in the shelter. And the *Jabos* are flying back and forth trying to destroy everything that moves.

On the Slatdiek behind us is a German vehicle but they don't bother with it. Suddenly the house of Fanny and *de Guste* is attacked and starts burning, also a German vehicle that is stuck and left behind. Some *Jabos* dive like lightning and attack a vehicle in front of neighbour Houwers at farm *Neerhof*. It burns out in no time. Now they are over Jansen's farm, *te Hennepe*. It too starts to burn. Johan, Gerrit, Frans and I run towards it. Not much we can do. Two calves are burned, and the house is a total loss, in ruins. Also the barn and grain stack.

We walk to the *Zondagschool* building to see if there are still NSB men lodging in it. We hope it will be empty; the Jansen's may want to move in temporarily. No luck, a group of NSB is still living in it, but Jansen can move in with Welink Herman, a neighbour from 't Villekesderp.

The NSB group had vacated the *Zondagschool* building, taking all possessions on a cart, and started to run for their lives to escape the advancing Allied troops. When they came to the Selmseweg they got so scared of the flying mortars and machine gun bullets they hurried back into the building, leaving their possessions behind. We were wondering why all this stuff was just left on the road.

Gerrit and I want to look at *de Guste*'s house. Not much left of their place either. Then suddenly the mortars are flying again. Gerrit says, "We better try to get home." Looking toward *Nonhof* we see that this is now under fire. And so is the water tower. A big black cloud bursts out of the top section. If there are still Germans in there they won't know how to get out fast enough.

We are going into the bomb shelter for it is getting somewhat nerve-wracking outside. We start to sing in order not to hear the noise from outside. It helps a little! Every so often there is a short pause. We talk about going into the house to eat but every time we try and come out the shooting starts again. We better stay in and eat a little later.

It is now 7:00 p.m.

Stronks and Rhebergen come by the farm and tell us that they have shaken hands with some Allied soldiers. I hear the people shouting and laughing and I wonder what is going on. I am sitting under the cows milking for we had a little pause in the firing. Just enough time to quickly feed the cows and start milking. But when I hear the word Tommies I jump up and leave the cow. I want to hear the good news from these two men and when they tell me I jump and jump and jump in the air. Then I walk over to Lien who stands by the gate in the garden fence and we start to cry. The pressure is being released and the misery of occupation is past, at least for us.

At *Neerhof* farm, five Allied soldiers shake hands with everybody, and then walk on. Their sten guns ready, they sneak along the ditches firing a new round every so often, cleaning out each and every bush and ditch. Very interesting to see, as they use some ammo that lights up, called tracers. You can see exactly where the bullets go.

On the Varsseveldseweg is the heavy sound of army vehicles; tanks, combat trucks, and cars. At 2:30 a.m. the first tank is seen on the Kemena, a street on the outskirts of Aalten.

While still in the bomb shelter we give thanks to the Lord in prayer and with our songs. The relief that the pressure is gone and we are FREE again is overwhelming. It is as if your heart is bursting. It cannot take it all in. We also realize that north of us people are not yet liberated. I am wondering how Henny is making out at *de Haart*.

A strategy nobody was aware of is that the Allied troops stopped every night and then continued the next morning. When Aalten was liberated, a farmer from just north of here was in town. Excitedly he went home on his bike with the great news that we are FREE! But he was not liberated yet. When the troops resume their fighting next day, one of the first things they do is fire at his farm and it burns down. Apparently there had been German soldiers staying at his place. Our neighbour Jansen's farm *te Hennepe* that burned down had a German Red Cross flag hanging outside on a pole. But, as with so many things, it was just camouflage. And the advancing troops knew. They picked them off one by one. It took a little while, but we learned shortly after our liberation that it was mainly the Canadians who gave us our precious freedom. We never had such a Good Friday.

At 10:30 p.m. we go to bed, trying to get some sleep. At 1:30 I am up again. I cannot sleep in this thundering noise. Although they seem to stay put at night, they keep firing.

Mr. Boven is also up and we talk until 4 a.m. We then go back to bed and I manage to get a little sleep.

Although we are liberated, the noise of the war lingers on for several days.

LIBERATION 1945

MARCH 1945

Saturday, March 31

Ome Jan comes to *de Koekoek* at seven in the morning. He is able to walk around freely and does not have to be afraid that he will be arrested. He gives each of us a special treat, a Chief-Whip cigarette, and says that he can use a few men. Johan and I go along to report for duty. Frans is nowhere to be seen. It would not be surprising if he is already in Aalten.

I have to run some errands for Ome Jan who takes on the function of deputy mayor of Aalten. From now on he can be called Father Wikkerink again.

We found four vehicles with 2,500 loaves of German bread outside Prinsen grocery store in the Hogestraat. People on the street are already taking the bread from the vehicles. One person has a child's wagon full of bread. We pack everything up and move it into the grocery store. Once in a while we receive an English cigarette, which we enjoy very much.

I eat at the Wikkerink home. No church service tonight. Tomorrow from 1 to 6 p.m. there will be a special service. Now I can go to *de Haart* tonight, right after I finish my supper. The road seems awfully long. Tante Gerda is just walking behind the shed. I follow her as Henny comes out of the kitchen. In the dark, she doesn't see me, so when I say hello she is surprised. She had not expected me today.

As of today our curfew is 9 p.m. It is a nice evening and we go to bed at 10 p.m. Henny and I first go upstairs to pray together. I share a bed with Henk

Luimers, the farm hand for Hoornenborg. For a moment a thought enters my head; now the *Zwarten* might come.

APRIL 1945

Sunday, April 1

Slept very well. We go to church where dominee Kuiper preaches. The church is very full. It feels very good to be able to attend church so freely and not to be afraid of a *razzia*.

The sow is expected to deliver tonight. Henk will stay up, and I ask him to wake me at midnight, so I can take a few hours watch by the sow. When I wake up it is already morning and there are seven new piglets. At first the sow does not want to suckle the piglets, but a bit later everything works out.

Monday, April 2

Father Wikkerink goes with the police to the home of the Allied commander who is staying in the house of Vissers. A bit later he comes home with four sausages and two coupons from Vissers, given to him by the commander.

Alex can soon go home to Russia via Eindhoven and France.

Tuesday, April 3

Before breakfast, I walk Henny to *de Haart*. In Aalten, I register at the City Hall, together with Henk and Alex. From there we are sent to Janssen in the Dijkstraat, who sends eight of us to the bridge in the Landsbulten to clean up. Under the water we don't have to do anything; that is work for the NSB men. At 1:30 we go to the Slatdiek bridge. Some litter close to the bridge draws my attention. It is covered with a few smaller branches. "A nice start," I think. As I reach out, my arm is pulled back by Alex!

He indicates with his arms in the air, "BOOM, maybe?" We see a land-mine under the bundled branches that we regularly walk over. Along the road there are also some landmines. Henk goes to warn the leader, and we are not allowed to work along that one side. Our report to head office: please check for landmines. I thank Alex for his sharp observation. My Russian life saver.

Oom Herman says he is very busy, so I plan to stay home tomorrow to help him. On the way home I stop at the Jansen farm to help bury two burned calves. Get a letter from home. This morning, a letter from Miep. I bought my first package of cigarettes today from Gerrit.

Wednesday, April 4
The church is very full again, and we sing two stanzas of the National Anthem. But first we sang, "*Nu dankt zij allen God.*" "Now Thank We All Our God."

Thursday, April 5
Herman comes home to help cut rye and now we are with the four of us. The Bovens want to see our hiding holes, so we show them. Tonight I will sleep in the *hol* for the last time. Listened to the news at Wisselink. NEWS: West of Aalten, Allies over the Rhine.

Friday April 6
While we cut rye, a bullet whistles past our ears. We look for it but cannot find it. Stormy weather.

Saturday, April 7
Beautiful weather, not like yesterday. After supper, peel potatoes.

Sunday, April 8
At nine to *Oosterkerk*. Henny is also at church. It is very cold in the open windowless church. Dominee Gerritsma preaches.

Yesterday was the 24th wedding anniversary of Father and Mother Wikkerink Mother has asked us to come to the family celebration tonight. However, Henny has already promised Tante Gerda that she will stay with her this evening, as Tante really would like the company. Her husband, Oom Johan, was killed digging trenches a few weeks ago.

NEWS: Zutphen–Coevoerden liberated.

Monday, April 9

To Houwers in 't Goor to get the name of the *onderduiker* there. He is the only one who did not put his name on the list last September for the monument. I assumed then that he was a Resistance worker. Meeting of the committee to organize a reunion of *onderduikers*. Gift for Aalten: Fountain. 1,670 guilders collected.

Tuesday April 10

By the three cannons of the *Moffen*, we see a hand grenade. By Stronks, we meet some soldiers, and we warn them about this. There is much traffic on the Lichtenvoordseweg, in both directions. Hundreds of *bommenwerpers* to and from northwest Germany.

Lies van der Male will go home to Zeeland on Monday with Zandee.

Wednesday, April 11

An English car picks up the munitions on the Boterdiek. Sudden loud racket. This sounds like more munitions found somewhere.

Beautiful warm weather. Wonderful to sit quietly with your own thoughts. You can think of anything, like this. I often think about when and how I will be able to go to my real home in Apeldoorn. Perhaps I will be going home alone. Gerrit is busy at the barbershop, and maybe will not be able to get away. Henny might be able to go with me, except for the current situation at *de Haart*. We had often imagined how this home-coming would be. The first time that I can go home to Apeldoorn, she would go with me; that would be a nice experience. But I find it admirable that she can put this aside in order to fulfill her duties at *de Haart*, and stay here. NEWS: by Zutphen 2,200 people were killed.

Thursday, April 12

Many *Jabos* come over. *Onderduiker* van Rensink from *Walforthof* tells us the Allied are over the IJssel. At 6:30 we are home and Johan tells us that the Allied are pushing towards Apeldoorn, but from which direction he does not know. Today the weather was soft with a few rain showers. NEWS: Between

Zutphen and Deventer over the IJssel, a 1.5 kilometre by 3 kilometre front. Hooray, now they are heading to Apeldoorn.

Friday, April 13

Clean rye in Boesveldland. At the same time we fill the holes left by the *Moffen*. Oom Herman sticks the straw on fire. We warn him there might be munitions in there. It does not take long before things start to pop. We keep our distance until the fire burns itself out. Gerrit ter Horst found a bag with revolver bullets today.

NEWS: Front at Deventer–Zutphen is 3 kilometres wide and 7 kilometres deep. President Roosevelt died yesterday, of a stroke.

In the local paper today is an article about the reunion of *onderduikers*.

Saturday, April 14

Frans and I listen to the news broadcast in town. NEWS: Allied heading for Apeldoorn. Twello and Wilp liberated.

Sunday, April 15

Father Wikkerink has been offered a choice of homes to live in, all from former NSB families, but he does not want to live in any of them. The family will stay in the emergency shelter. NEWS: In Apeldoorn, street fighting.

Monday, April 16

NEWS: In Apeldoorn, heavy fighting.

After supper Gerrit and I go to listen to the radio by ten Have. NEWS: In and around Apeldoorn, fighting for 10 kilometres along the canal. From Arnhem to Otterlo the Allies are passing towards Amersfoort and Apeldoorn.

Tuesday, April 17

The whole day here at the farm cranking the washing machine. I think often of home today (Apeldoorn). NEWS: Troops from Otterlo 10 kilometres from Harderwijk. *Moffen* (parts of 4 divisions) partially retreat into Harderwijk.

Monday morning the Royal Dutch Brigade Princess Irene will leave Aalten.

Father Wikkerink was requested to report to the Market Square today. Here is what happened:

War's frontline with all its activity has barely passed and is slowly moving on in a northwestern direction. People start to wake up to being liberated, being FREE again. They want to celebrate, to show their exuberance of what the Allies and in particular the Canadian troops have given back to them.

The Market Square is full with town people mixed with Canadian troops and their commanders.

People are calling for speeches.

A strong voice yells, "WHERE IS OME JAN?"

Answer? "At his job, of course!"

One Canadian officer says, "Go and get him. Get him as he is."

Somebody jumps into a jeep to pick up Ome Jan from his work site. On the way to Market Square, Ome Jan wants to go home for a decent change of clothes.

The driver says, "Our commander said to get you as you are, and that we will."

When Ome Jan gets on the podium the people give him a thundering ovation. Because he is WHO he is: wooden shoes, work clothes and all.

Wednesday, April 18

Mother Wikkerink has read in the paper that Apeldoorn is liberated. If only I can find out now whether everything is okay back home. Father Wikkerink gives me two coupons for bike tires, so that I can ride my bike again.

Monday, April 23

50 to 60 NSB men from Drente are paraded from the barracks through the Market Square to Irene. Irene is a community hall recently converted to a temporary prison for NSB members. Dominee Gerritsma goes to Apeldoorn tomorrow. Quickly write some letters for him to take along.

Tuesday, April 24

Another parade of NSB men.

Wednesday, April 25

An advertisement in the paper for police helpers in the big cities.

Thursday, April 26

I apply to be a police helper; so do Johan and J. Wikker. Brother Gerrit gets a letter. All is well in Driebergen, and also in Wilp and Twello.

Sunday, April 29

NEWS: Mussolini executed with 17 others. Raining hard today.

Monday, April 30

Tomorrow Father Wikkerink goes to Apeldoorn and will take a letter from us. The *Blauwen* left today. We hear that food for the larger cities is arriving by planes in what is called Operation Manna.

MAY 1945

Tuesday, May 1

Canadian picture in the paper of the *Westerkerk* with an article about the 48 young men picked up in January 1944. Aalten is known to have sheltered Allied pilots. Father Wikkerink, Willem Wikkerink, Onnink, among others. Pilots were not always as quiet as the *onderduikers* when they were in hiding. Neighbours sometimes had to warn the family when there were German soldiers nearby.

Wednesday, May 2

Opa and Opoe Wikkerink have been married 50 years.

Opa Wikkerink continued to work every day in his masonry business.

Thursday, May 3

NEWS: Hitler and Göebbels commit suicide. Dönith takes over. Church service this evening, a prayer vigil especially for Western Holland where there is great need; many are dying of hunger in accordance with Hitler's Hunger Plan.

Friday, May 4

9:00 p.m. Gerrit from *den Eume* tells us that Germany has capitulated at all fronts. We don't believe it, although we hear many sounds of shots being fired in the town of Aalten. If we had been in town we would have known for sure something special had happened. Everybody is up and in town, but the family Wikkerink is asleep in bed. The people want them to come out; the whole family. The party lasts until well after midnight. Father Wikkerink speaks to the crowd referring to 5-5-45 (today) which is, except for five days, five years from the start of the war on 10-5-40.

Saturday, May 5

Nobody does much work today. At 3:30 p.m. memorial parade for Dr. der Weduwen. At 7:00 p.m. all churches have a thanksgiving service. Emotional service. Psalm 46: 9-12.

Sunday, May 6

I feel somewhat down because I still have no permit to travel to my home in Apeldoorn. At lunch time Father Wikkerink has an idea to get a permit. "You issue a work order to trace important information and need to cross the river IJssel."

Singing by the organ with Lien and Henny; Johan plays the organ. "*Heerlijk is dat, echt huiselijk.*" "This feels wonderful, just like normal." It is not necessary for men to be silent in the home anymore; we may sing as loud as we can.

Thursday, May 10

Five years ago was the onset of the terrible oppression by the German army. The last two years especially heavy to endure.

Friday, May 11

Sister Nen's birthday.

Saturday, May 12

Henk Wikkerink comes to the farm to get some buttermilk. He says his father is back from Amsterdam. Traveling was a problem, with many delays.

Sunday, May 13

Brother Gerrit comes and we talk about the possibility of crossing the river IJssel. I will type a letter in the name of Mr. Viset asking Gerrit to come back to Apeldoorn as soon as possible to resume his employment with his previous boss, Viset.

Monday, May 14

I type a detailed note for Gerrit to get across the IJssel. We have a good impression that it will succeed. And we laugh about it. Rumour: Father Wikkerink nominated as city councillor.

Wednesday, May 16

Success: Smit has travel pass all ready. I have to pick it up in Winterswijk soon.

Saturday, May 19

Pentecost Weekend. The trip home.

Finally, after 21 months away from home, Gerrit and I go back to Apeldoorn for a few days. At 3:00 p.m. we step on our bikes at *de Koekoek* to begin our journey with loaded bikes. Tante gives us all kinds of things and the suitcase is stuffed full.

The weather is beautiful. Only a fairly strong wind is against us. This does not help as my bike is very heavily loaded.

In Lichtenvoorde we have to stop at a grocery store with a ration coupon to pick up butter. After this brief stop, we are on our way again. Lichtenvoorde is quickly behind us and we reach Zieuwent. After a while, we trade bikes, which is a big relief for me.

When we reach the main road in Ruurlo, Gerrit looks in shock at his rear tire, which appears to be almost out of air. We do not think of patching right away. First we check, and then pump air in. After three minutes the tire is flat again. We really need to patch the tire. Once I have the tire loose, it occurs to me that the valve could also be leaking. And yes, it is, so all work is in vain. On we go, but the result is not good. Already the tire is empty, and now we start to patch. We will do this in a *stelling* by the side of the road, made by the *Moffen*. Gerrit finds the hole, and in 10 minutes the tire is patched and in working order. It holds until we reach Apeldoorn. We each enjoy a beautiful English cigarette before we go further.

Brothers Peter and Gerrit.

In Vorden, we start to feel hungry. We have nothing else with us except rye bread, but that tastes good. We settle into a spot in the woods beside the road, right beside the grave of four German soldiers. With my *zakmes,* I cut some thick slices of bread, put a bit of butter on top, and our meal is ready.

Our stomachs are happy now, and after another cigarette, we step back on the bikes.

At 7 p.m. we reach the IJssel, after passing the heavily damaged city of Zutphen.

Checkpoint. "Sirs, everything is in order; continue." Our home-made paperwork passed inspection!

Now we are in more familiar territory. Everything we see now is of great interest to us, especially as we come closer to Apeldoorn.

We arrive at 8:30 p.m. By the skating rink, we see three people walking. One crosses the road, and suddenly I see that it is Sjaak from den Haag. He had seen me coming. Naturally we are both astonished to meet like this. He has just arrived from Lubeck (Germany). We want to know how they have come this far with all the obstacles in travelling. After talking a while, we complete the last few hundred metres of our journey. Everything looks quite normal in our neighbourhood, and it seems as if our town is smiling at us and welcoming us home.

The closer we get to our home, the more excited I feel. It is a warm feeling of thankfulness that washes over me, as we turn off the road into the driveway of Wieselseweg 54. Our home. The gate is closed which means that no one is expecting us yet.

As soon as we reach the back door, Nen comes flying out of the house to hug us both. Father is overjoyed that we are both home. Tante Dina from Oom Henk is also just here for a short visit. Henk and Janna are in Apeldoorn. All is well with them, and also in Castricum.

The first thing we get now is a few sandwiches which taste wonderful after our long trip, especially as I am eating them in our very own living room. Naturally there are lots of questions, and lots of discussion. Dick has not arrived yet, so Gerrit goes to get her.

We realize that one of the suitcases is ripped. That will cost us a new one, and a frown from Joop, its owner. But we won't think about that now; the time is too precious for that.

Henk and Janna have come to see how things are with us, and we are also thankful that they are healthy. They leave at 10:30 because there is still a curfew here. Nen plays the organ and we sing a few songs, then read Psalm 116 and end with a prayer of thanksgiving.

It is now midnight, and we head off to find our own beds. It is as if my bed has not forgotten me, because it welcomes me, and I am asleep in a few minutes. Miep has placed a nice sachet between the sheets.

Sunday, May 20 First Pentecost Day

In the early morning of this Pentecost day I awake refreshed. I go to the church service which starts at nine; dominee Goris preaches. Father, Miep, Gerrit and Dick go to the *Groote Kerk*. After church I meet Sebe. He has been appointed to be a police helper in one of the cities.

On the way home from church, I bike past Koldenhof where only son Johan is home. At eleven I am home; the others are not back from church yet. Suddenly I feel very alone, very lonely. I start the stove and put the potatoes on. Not long, and the others come home and set the table.

Father and I go out to inspect the garden and the bees. When we come back in, it is time for lunch. The table is set festively with vases filled with cut flowers and clippings from a beautiful azalea bush. By each plate is a small glass of red wine. We spend the afternoon surrounded by family and have supper at 5 p.m. I get my own special plate, cup and saucer, which have been carefully saved for my return.

At 6 p.m. to church with Miep, Gerrit and Dick. After church Miep goes to Beekbergen and I stop by Hajee and Wolf. Wolf is not home.

We spend a pleasant evening together as family; Henk and Janna are also here. At ten we get quite a thunderstorm and heavy rain. At eleven we go to bed.

Monday, May 21 Second Pentecost Day

7:30 up, breakfast and to church. There is an interfaith Pentecost service in the *Hervormde kerk*. It is raining heavily. I am now wearing a raincoat from father and carry his umbrella above my head so I will keep dry. Someone says, "Henny should see you like this!" Yes, Henny, I think you would have laughed if you had seen me dressed this way. Dominee de Bruyn and dominee Karres preach today. Family from Twello has arrived, and there are 14 people around the table for lunch. Very *gezellig*. Too bad Berend and Henny are not here.

In the afternoon we are together with about 20 people. Henk and Janna come over, and Oom Teun and Tante Dina also drop in.

After supper the Twello family goes back by *karretje*. Gerrit and Dick go to Groeneweg, so father, Nen and I are left. Father tells us some things that happened at the palace during the war; how the bosses had behaved during the occupation of the palace.

> After the German army invaded Holland in May 1940, the Queen and her family went to England for their safety. Soon after, the Germans moved into the palace and transformed it into a recovery centre for wounded army officers. It was also used as a temporary prison for important members of the underground movement recently caught and awaiting speedy shipment to, and punishment in, Germany.
>
> Father was now the head gardener of the gardens surrounding the palace. This included the upkeep of the ivy which covered the outside palace walls from bottom to top. One day after trimming ivy, he did not take the ladder down and lock it in the toolshed. The next day Dad had to report to a German interrogator.
>
> "It was not funny," Dad said. "They even threatened me with the death penalty."
>
> "For what?" Dad had asked.
>
> "Someone escaped through the window of the prison room using your ladder," he was told.

Dad told us what happened a year or so earlier while working outside the palace. He was working behind a closed gate close to the main road when someone called out to him. A gentleman stood there on the other side of the fence. He asked my dad if he was the head gardener, and, if so, could he talk to him. Dad unlocked the gate and led the man toward a maze that was located some distance away. Although it was not a simple maze, Dad led him straight to the centre. Dad trimmed the hedges of the maze, so he knew his way. Here they sat down to talk.

The stranger said he was sorry that he was not allowed to identify himself and my father was not allowed to ask any questions. The stranger asked a lot of questions about the goings-on at the palace. When he unbuttoned his jacket, Dad saw a small box hanging around his neck and wondered what that might be. After a lengthy conversation, Dad let him out through the gate again. The man said he hoped that he or someone else would be able to speak to dad again after the war to explain what this was all about.

The staff members of Prins Bernhard are also at the palace. Prins Bernhard has spoken with the workers, but not with the bosses yet; that is still to come.

When Gerrit and Dick come home, we read from the Bible and have a prayer of thanksgiving. Then to bed. A very good rest and I wake up refreshed again.

Tuesday, May 22
A quick visit to Henk Wolf after supper. Lots of visitors tonight: Henk and Janna, Oom Hendrik and Tante Dina, Mrs. Koldenhof with Johan, Jo Nijdeken and Grada, and later in the evening dominee Slump. This afternoon Miep was home for an hour.

Wednesday, May 23

When father goes back to work after lunch, it is very difficult for him to say goodbye to us. He does not want to show it, but I can feel it. This parting seems to be difficult for me too; I would have given anything to remain at home here.

At 2 p.m. we step on the bikes. It is raining lightly, which is not so nice to bike in. However, when we come to Zutphen it dries up. By the bridge checkpoint I show my recently updated identity card and everything is in order. I would like to know if this card is also good enough to get me over the Ijssel, then I am covered if I cannot get a travel pass. Yes. Now I know.

The rest of the journey is uneventful, except that I have to pump air into my tire at least five times.

Wednesday, May 30

Aalten. Two co-workers of Father Wikkerink, Gerrit and Bob, are here to tell the good news that they have been released from Dachau concentration camp. Margo comes for a short visit.

Thursday, May 31

I take a bag of rye to Geert Lammers for my brother in Amsterdam. He will take care of the shipment; they are still dying of hunger in the west.

Since mid-April I have been entrusted with the responsible task of administrator of the Bureau *Roerende Goederen* of Enemies and Traitors. A farmer from the neighbourhood Barlo came in with 2,982 guilders, a part of it half burned, left behind by retreating German soldiers. Right now we are questioning a group of prisoners at Irene about their *vermogen*. Some of them have hidden their belongings in five different places.

JUNE 1945

Monday, June 4

Tomorrow we get our salary, at last. I surely can use it for I have only two cents left in my pocket. Yesterday I had to borrow some money for the church collection.

Tuesday, June 5

News: Henk Walchien is back in Valkenburg (the Netherlands).

Alex arrived this morning at the Patrimoniumstraat accompanied by three Russian officers. It was suspected that he has been a spy. His papers showed he was a Russian pilot. Apparently he was only a labourer in Germany. Father Wikkerink has severely reprimanded Alex about this deception.

As remuneration for expenses, the officers handed Father Wikkerink five Mark of 50 and some cigarettes. They also told him, "The name Wikkerink is well known by the partisans in Poland."

Wednesday, June 6

Dickie Beskers and a guard from Irene went to the restaurant Schiller-Prins with a request to transfer their beer inventory to Irene. And to know that Irene is housing prisoners incarcerated for sympathizing with the German Nazis! The request is flatly refused.

Fanny, our neighbour near *de Koekoek*, is arrested for his activities as a *Landwachter*. Rumour: NSB Vossers arrested. Confirmed: Is in prison Leeuwarden.

Thursday, June 14

I buy a pair of wooden shoes for my Dad because I am going to Apeldoorn this coming Saturday with Lammers, the wholesaler. Also a pair for sister Nen and potatoes for brother Henk in Amsterdam.

Saturday, June 16

Father and Mother Wikkerink go with a busload of *onderduikers* to Rotterdam to bring them home again. Roads and bridges seem to be passable along the main routes.

Sunday, 17 June

Apeldoorn. On my way home from church I see Berend Gerrits' father on the bike to tell us the great news that his son is on the way home from Berlin in Germany. A little later the rest of the family comes home, including Nen. When she sees Mr. Gerrits sitting in the chair she fears the worst. Berend is her fiancé; Berlin was the most bombed city in Germany. Seconds later she hears the great news. He is almost home.

Another visitor is at the door, Mr. Koldenhof, my friend Reijndert's father. Reijndert arrived home yesterday evening.

"And," says my sister, "Henk Walchien also came home last evening." What blessings: You can read it on the face of every person.

Monday, 18 June

First thing this morning is to make a visit to my friend Reijndert who came home from Germany on Saturday. On my way home I catch up with my sister Jannie and her daughter Hetty. When I tell Jannie that Berend is on his way home, she breaks out in tears.

Thursday June 21

Aalten. We have discovered that among the prisoners at Irene is one who served in Germany as a member of the fearsome S.S.

Monday, June 25

Today two years ago I came to Aalten and met the family Wikkerink.

Tuesday, June 26

Two years ago I met the family ter Horst at *de Koekoek*.

Thursday, June 28

Henny got a letter from my sister Nen. In it she says that the Queen had asked Dad how his children were doing. He told her that two sons (Gerrit and I) had been hiding in the town of Aalten and survived the war. She is also aware of the behavior of some of her employees with regard to the German injured officers living in her home, the palace *Het Loo*.

Saturday June 30

The citizen band brings a serenade to Father Wikkerink on his birthday. Ex-mayor de Monnik is also present. When she serves the coffee, Lien has put salt instead of sugar in the mayor's coffee by mistake.

When the band plays the national anthem Dikkie, sitting on my shoulder, starts to cry. I take him into the bedroom and ask why he had to cry.

"It is so sad that uncle Johan had to die so recently, because of the German war." The sensitivity of this young boy strikes me.

JULY 1945

Thursday, July 5

Evening: Pick up 4 rye bread loaves at Brunsveld in IJzerlo for shipment to brother Henk in Amsterdam.

Wednesday, July 11

The NSB prisoners from Irene surprise us. They come with 7,900 guilders in bank notes. These notes are now declared invalid by the Government.

Friday July 13

To the office. Write a letter to Mr. Doeleman with an explanation of the necessary work to determine the rental value of homes or parts of homes, available to people who lost their homes by war activities.

Thursday, July 19

7:00 am. A long conversation with Father Wikkerink The result is that I will quit working at Aalten City Hall. I am homesick for Apeldoorn.

Friday, July 20

A letter from Wim Weeda. He might have found work for me at firma Reighmann in Huizen.

Sunday, July22

The first time in Apeldoorn Henny and I can go to church together.

Monday, July 23

Application written for work in Apeldoorn.

Wednesday, July 25

I have asked for approval to be dismissed at Aalten City Hall as of Saturday August 4, 1945.

Thursday, July 26

At *de Koekoek*, we get a visit from my brother Henk from Amsterdam and his wife Janna. Also a Mrs. Biesbos, looking for food.

Tuesday, July 31

Oom Herman's birthday; 57 years old.

AUGUST 1945

Saturday, August 4

Back to Apeldoorn. I have been longing for this day. Arrive at home shortly after eleven o'clock.

Tuesday, August 7

To town with four of us to enjoy the bagpipes playing in the *Oranje Park,* Apeldoorn. It is a group of military from Canada who liberated us in Aalten on March 30. They perform in the park several times a week and it draws crowds of people every time.

Wednesday, August 8

NEWS: The *Atoombomb,* small but big in its effect, is dropped on Japan. A terrible way to create destruction. One very small bomb wipes out more than 60 percent of a city of 300,000 people.

Wednesday, August 15

NEWS: Japan surrendered (Official). Tomorrow, August 16, will be an official holiday in the Netherlands, and August 19 will be a nationally established Thanksgiving.

Thursday, August 16

Today we have a big parade at the Palace *Het Loo*; we don't want to miss this. At four o'clock we are there and find a very good spot close to the big gate facing the main steps of the palace. Now we hear that the parade is not starting until 5:30. It is worth the wait. Resistance workers will be recognized and honoured with a medal.

Wednesday, August 29

In Aalten. Speeches tonight at the Market Square by dominee Gerritsma, dominee Klijn, and the priest Kerkhofs. The flag is stuck almost three quarters up the pole. Father Wikkerink asks for a volunteer to untie it and Visser is up in no time to fix the problem. He gets a loud applause.

Thursday, August 30

To the Open Air Theatre to see and enjoy *Nederlandse Vlag.*

Friday, August 31
Queen Wilhelmina's birthday today.

SEPTEMBER 1945

Tuesday, September 4
8:30 am. Back to Apeldoorn by truck with the Postal service. It is a time con-
suming trip; first to Winterswijk, Groenlo, Zuurlo; from there via Borculo and
Vorden to Zutphen where they drop me off at the train station to Apeldoorn.
I arrive at 1:15 p.m.

Wednesday, September 5
A letter written to Mr. Reighmann to ask if I still may count on some answer
with regard to my application.

Monday, September 10
Father was able to catch five young rabbits; he slaughtered them so we are
going to have a feast this week.

Wednesday, September 12
Minister Lieftink announces that all our money will be confiscated and be
replaced with newly printed bills.

Friday, September 21
Wimke Herfstink's birthday. He is two today.

Saturday, September 22
The twins Gerrit and Henk Wikkerink's birthday.

Monday, September 24
The train connection between Aalten and Apeldoorn is finally restored. Gerrit
and Dick have made use of it.

Tuesday, September 25
An old friend, Aart Brouwer comes to visit. He has been in hiding too and we both share our mutual experiences.

Saturday, September 29
A letter from Mr. Reighmann. He cannot hire me for the vacant position. I will look for other possibilities.

OCTOBER 1945

Wednesday, October 3
I am looking for work in Apeldoorn.

Monday, October 8
Visiting Henny in Aalten. Making brooms from tree branches at *de Haart*.

Tuesday, October 16
To the employment office in Apeldoorn for information. They send me to two addresses; Combinatie Growers (no openings) and Rijkskolen Bureau (come back later). A resume to No. 656 national newspaper Trouw is my last and final attempt for this day.

Wednesday, October 17
This morning I tried a few more places. First to Wepa (phone back this afternoon). To daily newspaper *Trouw* with a letter and also to place an ad seeking work. Wepa no result.

Evening: I contact a newly started institute called *Handels Avondschool*, a school for learning anything and everything pertaining to business. Business Law, Business Correspondence, Bookkeeping, Accounting, Applications. Just what I need and am looking for.

Thursday, October 18
I send an application to *Raad van Arbeid*.

Monday, October 22
I see an ad in the paper; firm Koldewijn looking for personnel. I decide to go there tomorrow with my resume.

Tuesday, October 23
Visit Koldewijn. They are looking for someone 18 to 20 years old. They advise me to go to the *Apeldoornse Glashandel* where they are in need of someone for the bookkeeping. Immediately I head for this company and have a pleasant conversation with the director.

"You know what? Bring me, this afternoon, a short letter about our conversation of what we discussed this morning. As soon as possible I will let you know what I plan to do."

Wednesday, October 24
I am working at home on another application for work when the doorbell rings. Nen opens the door and here is the director of the *Glashandel*. He tells me that I can begin as of November 1.

I gladly accept this offer. Salary starts at 125 guilders a month and after three months up to 130 guilders. My work will be bookkeeping and all other financial affairs. A welcome job. Suits me perfectly!

Friday, October 26
Johan ter Horst sent me the newspaper *Graafschapper* which shows a picture of Queen Wilhelmina paying a visit to the Wikkerink family at their temporary shelter *Nooitgedacht* on October 24. The Queen said to Opa Wikkerink, *"U hebt een dappere zoon."* "You have a brave son."

Queen Wilhelmina honored Hendrik Jan Wikkerink with the *Ridder in de orde van Oranje Nassau.*

Queen Wilhelmina leaves the emergency shelter of the Wikkerink family in October 1945. Dikkie stands beside the door. From the newspaper Graafschapper, 1945.

Wednesday, October 31
Mr. Veldhuis from *Apeldoornse Glashandel* comes to our house and asks me to come to their office this afternoon so he can introduce me to the other personnel and to give me instructions about work for tomorrow.

NOVEMBER 1945

Thursday, November 1
I start today to work at the *Glashandel*.

Thursday, November 29
To Maaskant to buy a necklace for Henny to cover two occasions: *St. Nicolaas* and her birthday.

DECEMBER 1945

Saturday, December 1
This is a special day. I receive my first salary in a long time.

Sunday, December 9
I write a letter to Henny. Our contact is mostly by mail. We don't have a telephone yet at our house.

Thursday, December 20
After office hours, to the home of Mr. W. to pick up some papers. He was recently released from Germany and tells me he has only one pair of shoes. His shirts have been repaired from the bottom cut off of these shirts and he only has two underpants; one is way too small.

JANUARY 1946

Wednesday, January 2
The glass business is doing very well. We are busy replacing wind shields in all kind of vehicles. We also get two rail cars of glass for homes, stores, and factories. The glass business is going to boom! I have talked to the boss about a great opportunity to help the town of Aalten. Situated four kilometres from the German border, Aalten has suffered great destruction on homes, warehouses, factories, and churches. Many, many housing units are without windows; unsuitable to live in. A great need, waiting to be filled. We talked also to Father Wikkerink, now deputy mayor of Aalten. It worked perfectly.

Week after week we go to Aalten with truckloads of glass; all kinds of glass. For homes, store windows, factories and businesses. We are well organized. And it pays off with an extra bonus for me. I often go along with the work group to deliver invoices and other information to painters and installers about the next load of windows such as the date and time of day. The bonus is extra time to see my girl, Henny.

Peter Van Essen

Monday, January 7
We get another permit for a wagonload of glass.

Friday, January 18
This afternoon we got a notice at the office that a new load of glass from America has arrived by train. This is real good news. Top quality material; very good for store windows and mirrors. It will make Mr. Engels happy. He is the grinder who makes fancy edges around pieces of glass; a fine artist.

FEBRUARY 1946

Monday, February 4
As usual glass is one of the articles that are rationed. You need coupons to obtain it; quite a procedure and a fair amount of administration. It is worth a lot of money and since I am responsible for the bookkeeping it is one of my duties to keep the coupon administration up to date.

Notice: Two railroad cars with glass arrived and are waiting for us in Zutphen about 20 kilometres from here.

Our message: Urgent. Send to Apeldoorn.

Tuesday, February 5
9:30 a.m. Rail cars arrive in Apeldoorn. 2:00 p.m. unloading starts; total 21 tons of glass.

Wednesday, February 6
We unload the second railroad car.

Saturday, February 9
I receive a letter from G.A.C. *Groote Advies-Commissie der Illegaliteit*. They would like to receive my diaries.

Monday, February 18

Aalten. At 7:00 a.m. with Tjerk Molenaar back to Apeldoorn by train. I left my gloves at the station in Aalten. These were special, as they were knit by Queen Wilhelmina. This reminds me of something my sisters told me about knitting during the war.

During the war there was a shortage of supplies, including yarn for knitting. That is when my sisters got an idea. They went to the textile box in the attic, and pulled out the long 6-ply scarf that the Queen had made and given to our Opoe. They completely unraveled the scarf and made it into balls of 2-ply wool. The resulting 32 pairs of mitts and socks were donated to the war efforts.

Monday, February 25

The twins Bep and Teun's birthday.

MARCH 1946

Monday, March 4

Letter from Gerrit; he and Dick are getting engaged May 5, 1946.

Thursday, March 7

Father has applied for other work. At his age it is becoming difficult to continue with the same work such as carrying long ladders and trimming the ivy.

Thursday, March 21 Spring

A year ago today Varsseveld was bombed. The weather is not as sunny but the birds are singing and at their best.

Friday, March 22

A letter from G.A.C. *Groote Advies-commissie der Illegaliteit*. Diaries received.

APRIL 1946

Wednesday, April 3

Gorgeous weather, like summer. Start work at 7:30 a.m. again. On May first I will get 156 guilders a month.

Sunday, April 7

The Big Day. I am in Aalten for the 25th wedding anniversary of Father and Mother Wikkerink.

Wednesday, April 10

Back to Apeldoorn. I phone Henny to tell her I arrived. She says, "What a strange voice you have." This is the first time she heard my voice on the phone.

Saturday, April 13

My sister-in-law Janna is over. I ask her approximately how much would a ring cost? About 95 guilders.

Saturday, April 20

Ineke's birthday. I go to Aalten. Father Wikkerink asks me, "When are you two getting engaged?" As if he can read our thoughts! Henny and I decide to get engaged on July 20th.

MAY 1946

Friday, May 3

Stille Omgang, a memorial service in Apeldoorn.

Sunday, May 5

Bevrijdingsdag. Liberation day. One year of freedom.

Friday, May 17

Voting today. The first time since 1940. We did not have to vote, or rather were not allowed to vote, during the Nazi occupation. When I leave after voting I am told that the Anti-Revolutionary Party already had a big celebration last evening for having a great majority of the total votes. *Hoera*, a solid government!

Saturday May 18.

I take the morning train to Aalten. I meet Gerrit Hoopman stepping onto the train in Zutphen. He is one of the men who got away from the *Westerkerk* in Aalten with the help of the ladies from Scheveningen.

Sunday, May 19

A quick visit to *de Koekoek* while I am in Aalten for the weekend.

JUNE 1946

Saturday, June 8

Apeldoorn. Henny and I go to the photo studio to get our engagement picture taken. I try to buy a shirt but this is not available without coupons. To shoemaker Oxener for a pair of shoes and to Maaskant to try on a pair of rings; 160 guilders. Today is the first time Henny and I do shopping together.

Henny and Peter engagement photo, June 1946.

Tuesday, June 11
Brother Gerrit is here until tomorrow morning. He has to go to Arnhem for his barber diploma and wants me to come along as his model. He likes my hairstyle and is used to it.

Wednesday, June 12
It is almost three years ago that I arrived in Aalten. Gerrit got his diploma.

Sunday, June 23
Talk with Father and Mother Wikkerink about our planned wedding. We get their approval to marry next year April or May. Nen and Berend are getting married this summer.

Wednesday, June 26

In Apeldoorn the season for picking *bosbessen* started. An estimated 1,000 persons are now in the Wieselse *bossen* picking.

Friday, June 28

Jannie here with the children to pick blueberries. The pay is now 75 cents a Dutch *pond*. When we picked as kids we got just 4 or 5 cents a Dutch *pond*.

JULY 1946

Wednesday, July 3

Sister Nen in *ondertrouw*. Mina ter Horst and Dirk Bussink are married today. Father and I take the train to Aalten for the wedding.

Saturday, July 6

I recall the parlour game one year ago, *Love, Friendship and Hate,* when I was rewarded with a kiss. To Mr. Boon, the tailor in Apeldoorn, to Maaskant the jeweler to have our rings engraved and to Oxener the shoemaker.

Monday, July 8

Letter from Henny; she is afraid that I will forget to pick up the photos and rings. Swimming in the pond at park *Het Loo* after supper.

Friday, July 12

Many letters received from Henny related to our upcoming engagement on July 20, 1946.

Saturday, July 20

Today two years ago I looked and longed for closer contact with Henny and today we are engaged. At 10:00 a.m. we go to the burned out home next door to the temporary shelter to exchange our rings and to ask the Lord to bless this engagement. Awesome moments. What a lovely girl I have in my life.

It is nice to be able to celebrate openly with both of our families together.

Patrimoniumstraat 12 was burned out on October 17, 1944. This is where I first met Henny in June 1943. The home was eventually repaired and still stands today.

EMIGRATION

Some people have asked us, "Why did you emigrate?" A good question! It is not so easy to give a good answer. You have to think about the events that preceded it and that led us to make that decision.

Growing up in the depression years, 1920 to 1940, was not easy. Many people were unemployed and the near future looked even bleaker. You started to believe that nowhere was as bad as it was in your own country. The Netherlands is a small country, with a large population, and so much controlled by the government. Personal initiative was nipped in the bud. The war and occupation from 1940 to 1945 killed the most precious thing left, namely freedom. Many young people had to abandon their studies and their jobs and were forced to work in Germany, or they disappeared into hiding, hoping to survive.

After the war, the Queen said in her throne speech, "Emigration is a must; it is important for our country. There is not enough work for our workforce." This sounded reasonable, considering our experience of the past ten, twenty and even 30 years.

Henny's father, Jan Wikkerink had a construction company in Aalten, and in 1946 he was asked to build a factory in Australia for a local client. He planned to emigrate with most of his children, but the factory project did not go ahead and the family remained in the Netherlands.

Peter and Henny on May 29, 1947

On May 29, 1947, Henny and I were married in Aalten in a double-wedding ceremony with her sister Lien and Johan ter Horst, from *de Koekoek*. Our honeymoon trip was a short one. At the end of the evening festivities, we got into a taxi and went home to Apeldoorn. The driver was Willem Lammers and beside him sat my Dad, as he had to get home too. Henny and I sat in the backseat.

At about midnight we stopped at our address, Wieselseweg 52, right beside my Dad's place at 54 where I was born. Now we were neighbours! We had rented two small rooms in the home of old Mr. and Mrs. Beer.

I was now employed as bookkeeper in the export department of the Apeldoornse Nettenfabriek von Zeppelin. Indonesia was one of our larger export areas for fishing yarn and nets. The company received approval from the shareholders to start a division in Indonesia. Three people would be sent out to direct and oversee this project: a Company Director, a Technical Director, and a Bookkeeper (me). The three men all accepted the challenge and shortly after we started learning Malay, the Indonesian language.

Due to political unrest, plans for a division in Indonesia were put on hold. The Netherlands sent in troops to Indonesia to control strong communist activities. Under pressure from England and the USA, the Netherlands had to give early independence to this colony.

Our company exported to other countries in Europe, Africa, the Far East, and to America and Canada. We were now in process of starting a division in Nova Scotia. I read many of the magazines and news items that arrived from Canada. Canada had a good name in Holland and especially in Apeldoorn since we were liberated by the Canadian troops in April of 1945.

Then one day Father Wikkerink started to talk about Canada and the opportunities that Canada presented for immigrants. Henny and I had learned a few things about Canada and shared some of our thoughts. Canada is a large country but sparsely populated. We were now beginning to investigate this new possibility more seriously - immigration to Canada.

Notwithstanding warnings to the contrary, the Nettenfabriek continued to purchase large quantities of yarn and other supplies for markets in Indonesia. However no orders were forthcoming. This practice had far reaching consequences and created financial difficulties. Many people from the office and also the factory were laid off. Things became chaotic in several departments; suddenly workers were being called back to work but there was a drastic cut in wages and salaries. You had to accept the cuts; if you did not, you would be laid off six months after the calendar year-end, in June 1953.

It was now February/March 1953. There were terrible floods in many parts of the Netherlands. Hundreds of people died, especially in the province of Zeeland.

Henny and I were more and more convinced that Canada was the country of our future. We were seeking the Lord's will for our lives. The difficulties at work encouraged us to continue with the possibility of emigration. If we decided to emigrate there would be no need to accept a cut in salary. I asked for, and received, a letter from the boss stating that I would keep full salary until I left the company, no later than six months after the fiscal year-end of the company. I now had a job with full salary until the end of December 1953, if I wanted to stay that long.

Henny and I had done a lot of preparation for our upcoming move to Canada. We had already visited the Canadian Embassy in The Hague and had our pre-emigration medical check-up. The extra money from my work at the Nettenfabriek came in handy. We did not qualify for government subsidy as many other emigrants did.

Before we left for Canada, my father wanted to take us for one more walk in the woods at the palace *Het Loo*. We were with the five of us; Dad, Henny and I, and our two children Dela (4) and Gerrit (2). It was nice weather and we took a route that was not too close to the palace. The reason? The flagpole on the roof of the palace had the royal flag on top. This meant that Her Royal Highness Princess Wilhelmina was in residence. If she was out for a little walk in the park, you tried not to disturb her. We did not know that she had ventured out a little further by going for a bike ride.

Our route brought us to the area of Little Switzerland and then to the Willems Temple, a small round building with walls made of tree trunks, and a pointed roof covered with a thick layer of heather. The benches against the inside walls were also made of tree trunks. This was a good spot for a short rest.

We sat down for a while. When Dad got up to look through one of the windows, he saw someone coming.

"We better get up," he said. "The Princess is coming on her bike and I think she wants to take a rest here."

Princess Wilhelmina stood beside her bike. Apparently she heard the children talking and wondered who was in the little building. When we stepped outside, she recognized Dad and continued toward us, then stopped to greet us. Dad introduced Henny and me and the two children.

It was a nice conclusion of our last days living in Holland.

Peter Van Essen

DIRECTION: CANADA

On Thursday November 12, 1953 at 1600 hours we boarded the ship *Groote Beer*, named after the Great Bear constellation, in the Rotterdam harbour. There were five of us: Henny, age 26; Peter, age 31; Dela, age 4; Gerrit, age 2; and Ina, Henny's youngest sister, age 19.

Ina, Gerrit, Henny and Dela on the Groote Beer.

We took along as much as possible. It took two big crates to ship everything. We knew that winters in Canada could be very cold, so we took along our DAVO coal-burner. It was a wedding present from my father, Gerrit van Essen. We also took along an old cupboard, just in case. This cupboard was purchased from a Ms. Rietveld who moved from the city of Deventer to Apeldoorn to work for the Nettenfabriek. She had no room for it in her apartment. It had bullet holes and damage from shrapnel when the Canadian troops liberated her city just north of Apeldoorn in 1945. This cupboard has now a place of honour in a granddaughter's home.

On Friday November 13, we arrived in Le Havre, France, to pick up more passengers and left again at 1300 hours. The crossing started. The first three to four days everything went fine, but then we entered an area where a big storm was brewing. The ship tried to stay out of its way, but it was hard hit by big waves. We were now going at half speed to minimize the force of the waves. Walking was almost impossible. We went up and down and sideways at amazing angles. Ropes were strung on deck to help with walking, but one day we were not even allowed to go on deck. Too dangerous! A crew member fell down a stairs and injured his leg. The barber had hurt his arm and was out of commission. When we were allowed to go on deck again to use our chairs, we slid from one end to another.

The *Groote Beer* was not a luxury liner. Before our departure we were told by our neighbour Mr. Slijkhuis that this type of boat was not built as a passenger ship. It was a so-called liberty ship, built to transport heavy war equipment by the Americans. A heavy transport load gave it a perfect draft but loaded with people the ship sat too high in the water, and was tossed to and fro. We thought of telling the passengers to eat all they could so they would gain weight and give the boat more stability. To judge by the yellow faces and the reaction of some passengers standing by the railing, there was enough evidence that this would not be a welcome suggestion. One person told me his wife was so sick, she refused to come out of bed and she believed the boat was going to sink. In the meantime, we crawled further over the ocean. Direction: Canada.

Peter Van Essen

After eight days, we were told that we would soon see land. It was welcome news. The sea became less boisterous and people who, a few hours before, said they would never eat a biscuit again, started talking about eating some food. We reached Canada at the mouth of the St. Lawrence River. We landed at our destination, Quebec City, on the 20th of November 1953. Six years later, on November 30, 1959, Henny and I became Canadian Citizens.

At the time we first arrived in Canada in 1953, we never expected that we would see our parents or siblings again. In 1959, however, Henny's parents came for a long visit to Canada. By this time five of their eight children lived in Ontario. In the summer of 1960 my father also came for a visit; he was 75.

> Dad told us that a few years after the war a man came to talk to Dad at his home. The man said he was looking for a van Essen who worked at the palace during the war. He had already been at three van Essens so far but had not found the right one.
>
> "Oh, you must have been at my brothers," said Dad. "They all worked for the Queen."
>
> "The one I am looking for was the head gardener," he said.
>
> "In that case you have found the right one."
>
> The visitor explained that, during the war, he came to the palace and talked to the head gardener by the gate. (see May 21, 1946) Then they had talked sitting in the maze. Dad remembered everything in detail.
>
> "I have one question. What was that little box you had hidden under your jacket?"
>
> The man explained that it was a tiny recorder. He was on a mission from England to make a detailed report of everything

going on in and around the palace *Het Loo*. Back in England, the next day, it was directly reported to Queen Wilhelmina.

The Van Essen family in 1962. Back: Gerrit and Dela. Front: Peter Jr., Henny, Peter, Herbert and John.

Henny and I made quite a few visits back to the Netherlands, sometimes together, sometimes alone, depending on the family occasion. We always visited the *Paleis Het Loo* during each visit. One time Henny was resting on a bench in the pavilion while a group of school children were touring the palace garden. One little girl stayed back after the rest of the group moved on and approached Henny. The liitle girl looked at Henny with wide eyes and asked her, "Are you the queen?"

Pavilion in the palace gardens.

From left: Museum director Han Timmer, brother Gerrit,
Henny, sister-in-law Dick, and Peter. December 2004.

In December 2004, Henny and I travelled back to Aalten (our last visit to the Netherlands) to attend the opening of the Onderduikmuseum Markt 12. Together with my brother Gerrit and his wife Dick, we were able to see the exhibits first-hand, some of which are based on entries from my diary. My original four notebooks have been donated to the Museum, along with an oil painting that I made of *de Koekoek*.

I had a chance to speak with Wim Papiermole again and also Gerrit ter Horst, a nephew of Oom Herman. A few weeks later I got a note from Gerrit's sister, Annie, from Eindhoven (see July 16, 1943): *Dear Peter, I sure remember what happened in July 1943. But what you don't know is what I did afterward. Just to be sure you boys were right I snuck out to find what I needed behind the old barn.*

In the summer of 2014, a grandson of Oom Herman from *de Koekoek* came to visit me to ask lots of questions, and encouraged me to consider publishing my book. He brought a nice surprise from the Jansen farm, *te Hennepe*. No, not a letter for Maria Jansen, but a bottle of wine from the grapes on the farm as it is today.

AFTERWORD

In the 1940s I carried a tobacco pouch in my pocket, with a pencil and some scrap paper. I made notes of activities during the day and would update my notebook in the evening or during a quiet time. The book itself was hidden behind the straw in a wall in the barn where I could reach it easily. As each book was full, I would give it to Henny who took it to *de Haart* for safekeeping. By the time we were liberated I had filled four notebooks and was working on a fifth.

In 1946 the Dutch government requested people to submit their diaries to a national database for war documentation (RIOD). Many of the diaries were copied in whole or in part. In 1954 a collection of excerpts from many of these diaries appeared in a document called, *Dagboek Fragmenten 1940-1945*. This was edited by M. Nijhof and published in 1954. *Dagboek Fragmenten* is available from http://www.niod.nl/nl/dagboekfragmenten-1940-1945.

Before emigrating from Holland, I requested that my diaries be returned to me.

After I started translating the diaries into English (1992-1998) I often spoke at schools and read excerpts from the diaries at Remembrance Day events and history classes. In 2002 the diaries were translated from the English back into Dutch by Hans Lichterink of Aalten. The proceeds of the Dutch book were designated to the fundraising efforts of the Onderduikmuseum Markt 12 in Aalten. In 2004 the original four diary notebooks were donated to this museum in Aalten.

http://www.aaltensemusea.nl/onderduikmuseum

In May 2008 the Consul-General of the Kingdom of the Netherlands hosted a WWII conference in Toronto called *Honour our Past, Celebrate the Future*. I read the excerpt from September 21, 1943. In 2009 this story and 99 others were collected into a book entitled *Personal Histories: War memories of a Dutch Canadian generation*.

In October 2014 I started translating the final diary which dates from April 1945 to August 1946. The tone of that diary was very different from the one during the war years, as there was no longer the need for secrecy and hiding.

To this day one question remains unanswered for me: How did Mr. Wolf know to contact me within two hours of me receiving the final warning letter from the Manpower Office in May 1943? Was there an inside system that identified the young men receiving such a letter to those in the Resistance movement? Most of the people involved in this type of activity are no longer here, so I may never learn the answer.

DUTCH WORDS AND ABBREVIATIONS

aalenschepper   a long heavy pole with a pail at the end

Aalten   village in south-east corner of Achterhoek, about 4 kilometers from the German border

Achter in Wiesel   the back of Wiesel, a small village about 4 kilometres from Apeldoorn

Achterhoek   back corner district of the province Gelderland, borders on Germany

Apeldoorn   city in Gelderland, location of *Paleis Het Loo*

appelflappen   a type of apple fritter

Arbeidsbureau   manpower office, employment office

Atoombomb   atom bomb

balkenbrij   a mixture of pork scraps and trimmings combined with flour and spices to form a loaf

beddestee	bed built inside the wall in the living room with doors or curtains in front, and storage space underneath
benzine	gasoline
Bevrijdingsdag	Liberation day in the Netherlands is May 5 to mark the end of the Nazi occupation in 1945
Blauwen	those who wore the blue berets of the Royal Dutch Brigade Princess Irene
de Bleeke	name of the farm owned by Gerrit Houwers
boerderij	farm
boerekool met worst	kale with sausage and mashed potatoes
Boerenleenbank	credit union
bommenwerpers	bomb throwers
bosbessen	blueberries; literally- forest berries
bossen	woods or forest
Brussels lof	Brussels endive, also known as *witlof*
calotte	beret
daag	goodbye
Dale	District of Aalten where *de Koekoek* is located

de	the
De Gekantelde Karos	The Wrinkled Stagecoach
dominee	Reverend, preacher, minister of a church
druufkes bezen	dialect term for red berries
eigen gebakken wigge	homemade bread
Ekster	magpie
elshout	alder wood
enden deur	door at the end of threshing floor
't Engeland	name of a pasture in 't Goor
den Es	name of a piece of farmland
den Eume	a dialect term for the uncle; our adjoining neighbour at *de Koekoek*, Tony Driessen
evacuees	persons displaced from their homes and towns by the activity of war
Fritz de Zwerver	Fritz the Wanderer, alias for Reverend Slomp
G.A.C. Groote Advies-Commissie der Illegaliteit	a committee established by the Queen in July 1944 to coordinate the efforts of various underground groups in the Netherlands; disbanded in July 1946

Gereformeerde kerk	Reformed church; until 2004 when it joined with other Protestant denominations
gestikte deken	a stitched blanket, a quilt
gezellig	cozy
Glashandel	glass manufacturing
't Goor	name of a marsh area developed into pasture
Groenen	Green Police; uniformed military unit of NSB members; green uniforms
gris	meat scraps and trimmings
gruppe	manure ditch in the cow stable
guten tag	good day
haantjes soep	soup with meat from a young rooster
Hagendiek	part of 't Goor
haksel	finely cut straw made in a contraption called hakselmachine
Handels Avondschool	evening business school
hofleverancier	provider of food and supplies to the royal family

hol	hollowed out space in an attic or under a floor; a hiding place for onderduikers with a hidden entrance, either in the farmhouse or in the barn
hooiwagen	literally a haywagon; also a word for a daddy-long-legs spider
Hulpverlening Westen	an organization to lend support for the West
imker	beekeeper
IJzerlo	a district south of the village of Aalten; IJ is equivalent to a Y
Jabos	fighter planes; the word *Jabo* is short for the German Jäger-Bomber
Jeugddienst	youth services training young people in the principles of the National Socialistic movement
Jodenbosch	a Jewish psychiatric hospital in Apeldoorn
Jood	Jew
kabelsteek	cable stitch in knitting
kale kont	bare behind
karnemelk sause	buttermilk sauce used as a gravy
karretje	a two-wheeled cart pulled by a horse

kelder	cellar
Klein Zwitserland	little Switzerland, an area near Aalten
kleine	small, little, also *klein*
klompen	wooden shoes
knollen	food for cows which looks like very small turnips
knollengroen	leaves on the knollen
koek	cake
koekoek	cuckoo
koele	winter storage place for both animal feed and human food; space dug out of the soil, then covered with straw, filled with root vegetables, covered with more straw and a heavy layer of soil
koffie	coffee
Koningsschool	Kings School in Apeldoorn, for sons of the palace employees
kortiezer	short saw; a long saw used to cut things shorter
krentewigge	bread with currants
L.O./Landelijke Organisatie voor hulp aan Onderduikers	National Organization for Assistance to People in Hiding

Landwacht	armed unit of the NSB
liefde	love
lof	chickory
mangels	sugar beets
mantelpot	the food kettle for preparing pig food; a cast-iron double boiler
mattenklopper	a gadget to beat dust out of mats, made from branches
Meibos	May woods
miege	a dialect word used for horse urine; also slang for very wet
mengmolen	large mixer for grain
Moffen	an ethnic slur used during World War II for some German soldiers
Mölle	grain mill
NSB/ Nationaal-Socialistische Beweging in Nederland	National Socialist Movement, a Dutch organization for people sympathetic to the German cause, considered traitors by other Dutch people
Nederlandse vlag	Dutch flag

Nieuwe Kerkhof	new cemetery
oliebollen	yeasty specialty deep fried for New Year's Eve celebration
Ome	dialect for *oom;* uncle
onderduiker	person in hiding; literally under-diver
ondertrouw	no English equivalent word; a civil process in the Netherlands, similar to applying for a marriage license or the reading of banns in church
Oom	uncle
Oosterkerk	East Church
op sap	with juice
opkamer	bedroom over the cellar
Opa	grandfather
Opoe	grandmother
Ortzcommandant	German army officer in charge of an area
P.B.H./Plaatselijk Bureau Houder	German controlled office issuing permits related to farming and/or food
Paleis Het Loo	Palace *Het Loo,* home of Queen Emma and Queen Wilhelmina in Apeldoorn

Peter Van Essen

pap	cereal
Peerdeboer	a farmer's nickname meaning horse farmer
Peerke en zijn kameraden	Peer and his Friends
plankenbrugge	wooden bridge
poffertjes	a type of puffed pastry
pond	a Dutch *pond* was about 494 grams; an English pound is about 454 grams
Raad van Arbeid	unemployment office
razzia	raid
Ridder in de orde van Oranje Nassau	Knight in the Order of Orange-Nassau
rijksdaalders	silver coins, each worth 2 and one-half guilders
roerende goederen	moveable articles such as furniture
Roggebrood trein	Black Bread Train, the train taking food to the western parts of the Netherlands
S.S. / Schutzstaffel	German army unit, especially feared by the Dutch citizens
schinke	dried, pickled or smoked meat

Scholteboer	gentleman farmer who leases out several small farms
schoppe	barn
Sinterklaas	St. Nicholas
slamierus	slimy creature
Slingebeek	winding creek
snert	pea soup
St. Nicolaas	Saint Nicholas; special occasion on December 5
stelling	a German radar station for tracking airplanes
sterker	young cow expecting first calf
stille omgang	quiet procession
stoof	foot warmer, a wooden box with a ceramic or cast iron bowl to hold hot coal or peat embers
straat	street
't	short for *het*, meaning "the"
Tante	aunt
teil	aluminum tub large enough to sit in for a bath

Tommy	English plane
torenvalk	a hawk that nests in a tree or tower
tuugbenne	a big woven basket in which the harness and other supplies for a horse are kept
V-1	German flying bomb; also known as doodlebug, or buzz bomb
V-2	German rocket; a guided ballistic missile; an improvement on the V-1
veeruren	four in the afternoon, when you have coffee and bread
Verboden voor Joden	Forbidden for Jews; Jews not allowed
vermogen	possesions
viemhoop	heap or grain stack
't Villekesderp	a small area in the district Dale
't Vree	pasture across the lane behind the farm *de Koekoek*
waskamer	little kitchen
weg	road
wennenbos	a kind of willow tree

Westerkerk	West Church
wieme	where meat, sausage and bacon hangs to cure on beams between the rafters
Wiesel	village near Apeldoorn, close to *Het Loo* forest and parklands
IJzerlo	a district south of the village of Aalten
Zandhegge	sand dune; a dune at the edge of the forest in the Veluwe near Apeldoorn
zakmes	pocket knife
zes en een kwart	literally, six and a quarter; what we called Seyss-Inquart
Zondagschool	Sunday school
Zwarten	Black Police; uniformed military unit of NSB members; black uniforms
Zwartje	Blackie; nickname for the fish seller because of his white horse
zwerver	wanderer

SLATDIEK

DE KOEKOEK FARM

PATHWAY TO 'T SLAT

RYE STACK

RABBIT HUTCH

BARN (schoppe)

MANTELPOT

CALF STABLE

HIDING PLACE

TRAP DOOR

PIG PENS

N

CHICKEN COOP

KOELE

DITCH

"DEN EUME" DRIESSEN BARN

COWS or PIGS

KITCHEN

TOILET

THRESHING FLOOR

TRAP DOOR

HIDING PLACE

COWS

TOILET

KITCHEN (WAS-KAMER)

DRIESSEN LIVING QUARTERS

TER HORST LIVING QUARTERS

PATHWAY TO NEERHOF

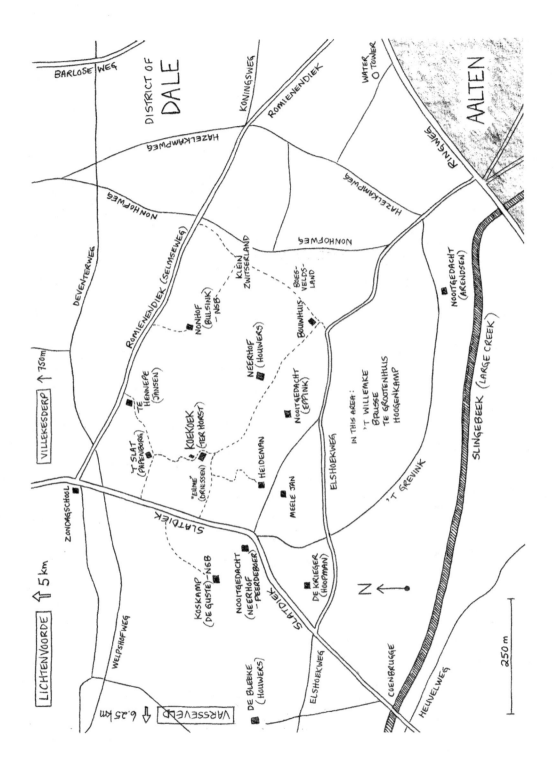

CPSIA information can be obtained at www.ICGtesting.com
Printed in the USA
LVOW03s0907310815

451987LV00012B/114/P

9 781460 267783